Fantastic Fungi

COMMUNITY COOKBOOK

EDITED AND WITH ESSAYS BY **EUGENIA BONE**
RECIPES FROM **THE FANTASTIC FUNGI COMMUNITY**

PHOTOGRAPHY BY **EVAN SUNG**

INSIGHT
EDITIONS

San Rafael • Los Angeles • London

CONTENTS

NOTE TO THE READER: Please refer to additional information on each mushroom group provided at the end of the table of contents wherever indicated with an asterisk (*) below.

Introduction 10

A Note About These Recipes 14

🍸 MUSHROOMS ON THEIR OWN OR WITH VEGETABLES

Dried Porcini Onion Dip by Alison Gardner (Boletus group*) 18

Maitake Mushroom Pâté by Julie Schreiber (*Grifola frondosa*) 21

Morels and Brie en Croûte by Larry Evans (Morel group*) 22

Sherry-Creamed Pleurotes on Toast by Dorothy Carpenter (Oyster group*) 24

Morel Gratin by Eugenia Bone (Morel group*) 25

Agaricus Salad with Blood Oranges and Fennel by Sean Sullivan (*Agaricus bisporus*—white button) 26

Brussels Sprouts with Truffles, Two Ways by Jack Czarnecki (*Tuber oregonense, Leucangium carthusianum*) 28

Spring Porcini Salad by Langdon Cook (Boletus group*) 29

Warm Endive and Oyster Mushroom Salad by Annaliese Bischoff (Oyster group*) 31

BBQ Teriyaki Chicken of the Woods by Paul Stamets (*Laetiporus sulphureus*) 32

Candy Cap Oatmeal with Brandy by Allison Gardner (Candy Cap group*) 33

Champiñones al Ajillo (Mushrooms with Garlic) by Marta Cabrera (*Agaricus bisporus*—cremini or white button) 34

Cauliflower-Shiitake Stir-Fry with Numbing Chile Sauce by Irene Khin Wong (*Lentinula edodes*) 37

Chicken-Fried Chicken of the Woods by David Logsdon (*Laetiporus sulphureus*) 38

Hot Buttered Oyster Mushrooms by Venori Keshy Liyanage (Oyster group*) 41

Potato Mushroom Tortilla by Marta Cabrera (*Agaricus bisporus*—cremini or white button) 42

Shiitake Fennel Latkes by Annaliese Bischoff (*Lentinula edodes*) 45

Huitlacoche Crepes by Charles Luce (*Ustilago maydis*) 46

Black Trumpet and Fig Pizza by Mary Smiley (*Craterellus cornucopioides, Cr. fallax*) 48

Huitlacoche Mushroom Tacos by Rick Bayless (*Ustilago maydis*) 51

Oaxacan Wild Mushroom Quesadillas by Jane B. Mason (mixed cultivated and/or wild) 53

Mushroom Tempura by Don Pintabona (*Pholiota microspora, Flammulina velutipes, Pleurotus ostreatus, Hypsizygus tessellatus*) 54

Woodland Wild Mushroom Strudel by Sebastian Carosi (mixed cultivated and/or wild) 56

Lake Prespa Baked Mushrooms by Neni Panourgia (*Agaricus bisporus*—cremini or white button) 59

Squash and Mushroom Pie by Neni Panourgia (*Agaricus bisporus*—white button; Oyster group*, Boletus group*) 60

Mongetes amb Bolets (Beans with Mushrooms) by Chad Hyatt (Boletus group*; mixed wild mushrooms) 65

Ultimate Mushroom Halloumi Burger by Sarah Jones (*Agaricus bisporus*—portobello caps) 67

THE KITCHEN MYCOLOGIST, AN ESSAY 68

🍸 MUSHROOMS WITH EGGS

Black Trumpet Deviled Eggs by Jill Weiss (*Craterellus cornucopioides, Cr. fallax*) 75

Porcini and Sweet Corn Custard by Charles Luce (Boletus group*) 76

Baked Eggs with Porcini and Peas by Annaliese Bischoff (Boletus group*) 78

Cheesy Baked Eggs with Mushrooms by Charlotte Greene (mixed cultivated and/or wild) 80

Creamed Eggs with Mushrooms by Eugenia Bone (mixed cultivated and/or wild) 83

Mushroom and Prosciutto Frittata by Chambliss Giobbi (mixed cultivated and/or wild) 84

Mushroom and Wild Onion Quiche by Gary Lincoff and Irene Liberman (mixed wild mushrooms) 87

Duck Eggs with Morels by Olga Katic (Morel group*) 89

Poached Eggs with Chanterelle and Ham Cream Sauce by Jack Czarnecki (Chanterelle group*) 91

THEY ARE WHAT THEY EAT, AN ESSAY 92

🍸 MUSHROOM SOUPS, PASTA, AND RICE

SOUPS

Enoki Mushroom Soup by Dipa Chauhan (*Flammulina velutipes*) 99

Spargelsuppe with Morels by Eugenia Bone (Morel group*) 100

Dryad's Saddle Soup with Stuffed Matzo Meal Dumplings by Elinoar Shavit (*Cerioporus squamosus*) 103

Lobster Mushroom Chowdah by Graham Steinruck (*Russula brevipes* parasitized with *Hypomyces lactifluorum*) 106

Smoky Black Bean and Huitlacoche Soup by Sebastian Carosi (*Ustilago maydis*) 109

Matsutake Dobin Mushi by Langdon Cook (*Tricholoma matsutake*) 110

Crab and Cordyceps Bisque by Sebastian Carosi (*Cordyceps militaris*) 113

Cream of Porcini Soup with Chicken by Thomas Jelen (Boletus group*) 114

Chanterelle Vichyssoise by Jean O. Fahey (Chanterelle group*) 116

PASTA AND RICE

Spaghettini al Louie by Eugenia Bone (mixed cultivated and/or wild) 117

Porcini Lasagna by Langdon Cook (Boletus group*) 118

Chanterelle Ravioli in Saffron Corn Broth by Mary Smiley (Chanterelle group*) 121

Farfalle with Black Trumpets and Gorgonzola Sauce by Michael Wood (*Craterellus cornucopioides*, *Cr. fallax*) 124

Porcini and Pumpkin Pappardelle by Sean Sullivan (Boletus group*) 127

Hen of the Woods Spaetzle by Catherine Gavin (*Grifola frondosa*) 128

Linguine with Lion's Mane White Clam Sauce by Jean O. Fahey (*Hericium erinaceus*, *H. coralloides*) 131

Tagliatelle with Morels and Duck Confit by Pam Krauss (Morel group*) 132

Rigatoni with Mushroom Bolognese by Spike Mendelsohn (mixed cultivated and/or wild) 133

Miso Kabocha Risotto with Roasted Maitake by Adam Berkelmans (*Grifola frondosa*) 134

Polenta on the Board with Honey Mushroom Sauce by Edward Giobbi (*Armillaria mellea* or Boletus group*) 137

Chanterelle Risotto by Kelly Demartini (Chanterelle group*) 139

Matsutake Gohan by Dr. Gordon Walker (*Tricholoma matsutake*) 140

THE WILD ONES, AN ESSAY 142

🍸 MUSHROOMS WITH FISH

Chanterelle and Crab Salad by Sandy Ingber
(Chanterelle group*) 148

Mussels, Porcini, and Potatoes by Graham Steinruck
(Boletus group*) 151

Setas con Almejas (Mushrooms with Clams)
by Chad Hyatt (mixed cultivated and/or wild) 152

Morel-Encrusted Tuna by Tim Leavitt (Morel group*) 155

Rice Pilaf with Mushrooms and Shrimp
by Neni Panourgia (*Agaricus bisporus*—cremini) 156

Scallops with Black Trumpets by Gary Gilbert
(*Craterellus cornucopioides, Cr. fallax*) 159

Scallops with Truffles by Mary Smiley
(*Leucangium carthusianum*, or *Tuber
melansporum, T. aestivum, T. brumale*) 160

Trout with Ramp Pesto and Morels by Jean O. Fahey
(Morel group*) 162

Parmesan Fish with Oyster Mushroom Rockefeller
by Jean O. Fahey (Oyster group*) 163

**Pompano with Black Trumpets and Key Lime
Beurre Blanc Sauce** by Mary Smiley
(*Craterellus cornucopioides, Cr. fallax*) 164

LET FOOD BE THY MEDICINE, AN ESSAY 166

🍸 MUSHROOM WITH POULTRY AND MEAT

POULTRY

Duck and Shiitake Congee by Graham Steinruck
(*Lentinula edodes*) 173

Turkey Breast Roulade with Sous Vide Porcini
by Charles Luce (Boletus group*) 175

Chicken with Morels and Sherry by Britt Bunyard
(Morel group*) 178

Chicken Thighs with Porcini and Leeks
by Gary Gilbert (Boletus group*) 181

Simple Matsutake Chicken by Chris Phillips
(*Tricholoma matsutake*) 182

Cornish Game Hens with Cauliflower Mushroom
by Jane B. Mason (*Sparassis crispa*) 185

Chicken Chanterelle Paprikash by Paul Sadowski
(Chanterelle group*) 187

Pheasant with Leccinum au Vin
by Derek Moore (*Leccinum aurantiacum*,
Boletus group*) 188

**Mom's Red-Cooked Chicken Wings with Wood
Ear Mushrooms** by Cathy Resident
(*Auricularia auricula*) 190

MEAT

Mushroom Vin with Lamb Chops by Harry Koeppel
(*Lentinula edodes*, other dried mushrooms, or a mix) 191

Mushroom Gyoza by Eugenia Bone
(*Agaricus bisporus*—cremini or white button) 195

Garbanzo Beans with Cremini and Uncured Bacon
by Neni Panourgia (*Agaricus biosporus*—cremini) 198

Morels Stuffed with Sausage and Sage
by Sebastian Carosi (Morel group*) 201

Mushroom Sausage Rolls by Eugenia Bone
(*Agaricus bisporus*—white button) 203

Karbonāde by Charlotte Greene (Chanterelle group*,
Armillarea millea, Agaricus bisporus) 205

Pork with Chanterelles and Apricot Jam by Kevin Bone
(Chanterelle group*) 206

Beef Fillet with Chanterelle Marsala Sauce
by Justin Courson (Chanterelle group*) 209

Braised Short Ribs with Porcini by Graham Steinruck
(Boletus group*) 210

Pot Roast with Porcini and Mashed Potatoes
by Eugenia Bone (Boletus group*) 213

WITHOUT YOU I'M NOTHING, AN ESSAY 214

🍸 SWEET MUSHROOMS, DRINKS, AND CONDIMENTS

SWEET MUSHROOMS

Poached Pears with Candy Cap Syrup by Eugenia Bone
(Candy Cap group*) 221

Strawberries Poached in Birch Polypore Syrup
by David Bennett (*Fomitopsis betulina*) 222

Candy Cap Sugar Cookies by Cindy Davis
(Candy Cap group*) **225**

Chaga Chocolate Chip Cookies by David Bennett
(*Inonotus obliquus*) **226**

Chanterelle Shortbread by Jane B. Mason
(Chanterelle group*) **229**

Candy Cap Éclairs with Reishi Chocolate Glaze
by Graham Steinruck (Candy Cap group*,
Ganoderma lucidum) **230**

Candied Wood Ear by David Bennett
(*Auricularia auricula*) **233**

Flan with Brown Sugar Candy Cap Syrup
by Pam Krauss (Candy Cap group*) **234**

Chanterelle Frozen Custard by Marissa Biswabic
(Chanterelle group*) **236**

DRINKS AND CONDIMENTS

Candy Cap Milk Punch by Jane B. Mason
(Candy Cap group*) **239**

Longevity Lassi by Annaliese Bischoff
(*Inonotus obliquus*, *Ganoderma lucidum*) **240**

Spicy Chaga Chai Tea by Kristen Blizzard
(*Inonotus obliquus*) **243**

Chanterelle Shrub by Jane B. Mason
(Chanterelle group*) **244**

Golden Vodka by Kelly Demartini (Chanterelle group*) **247**

Black Trumpet Butter by Charles Luce
(*Craterellus cornucopioides*, *Cr. fallax*) **248**

Pickled Grayling Mushrooms by Charles Luce
(*Cantharellula umbonata*) **251**

Soy-Preserved Shiitake Mushrooms by Don Pintabona
(*Lentinula edodes*) **252**

Sriracha Pickled Chanterelles by Sebastian Carosi
(Chanterelle group*) **254**

Truffle Oil by Rosario Safina
(*Tuber melanosporum*, *T. magnatum pico*) **255**

Mushroom Escabeche by Alan Macgregor
(mixed cultivated and/or wild) **256**

Porcini Powder, Butter, and Salt by Eugenia Bone
(*Boletus rubriceps*, *B. edulis*, *B. aereus*, *B. pinophilus*,
B. reticulatus) **259**

Index of Recipes by Mushroom Type **261**

Acknowledgments **262**

*In some cases, a group of mushrooms may be used in a recipe. The mushrooms included here are the more common species. There are other boletes, for example, that are edible and work in the recipes, but they are not included here for reasons of space, bandwidth, and to generally avoid Latin fatigue. Except where noted, the following applies:

THE BOLETUS GROUP: *Boletus edulis, B. aereus, B. barrowsii, B. rubriceps, B. regineus, B. aestivalis, B. pinophilus, B. reticulatus, B. rex-veris.* The boletes that are eaten raw are *Boletus rubriceps, B. edulis* (with caution and in lesser quantity), *B. aereus, B. pinophilus, B. reticulatus.*

THE CHANTERELLE GROUP: *Cantharellus cibarius, C. formosus, C. cascadensis, C. californicus, C. roseocanus,* *C. phasmatis, C. spectaculus, Craterellus tubaeformis* (the yellowfoot)

THE MOREL GROUP: *Morchella esculenta* clade (the yellow morels) and *M. elata* clade (the black morels) All morels are edible, but only if sufficiently cooked.

THE CANDY CAP GROUP: *Lactarius fragilis, L. rubidus, L. rufulus*

THE OYSTER GROUP: *Pleurotus ostreatus, P. citrinopileatus, P. djamor, P. salmon, P. columbinus, P. populinus.* The king trumpet is *Pleurotus eryngii.* While there is no recipe exclusively calling for this mushroom in these pages, they can be used in the dishes that call for cultivated and/or wild mushrooms.

INTRODUCTION

BY EUGENIA BONE

I've pretty much eaten mushrooms every day during the last year. You'd think that would imply a certain amount of repetition. But, in fact, almost every dish I have eaten has been different. That was a revelation. Even though I have long been enamored of eating mushrooms, until I got involved with the *Fantastic Fungi Community Cookbook*, I never dreamed how many ways they could be prepared, and how different those preparations could taste.

I've been a wild-food enthusiast all my life. When I was young, our family never did any sporty stuff, but we did forage. I grew up seining for whitebait, gathering mussels and blueberries, wild watercress, and morels. I started pond fishing as a child and later took to duck hunting, but it was the silent hunt I loved the most: the search for critters that hide rather than the chase after critters that flee. And of the silent quarry, I love hunting mushrooms the most, especially the moment when I can see past their camouflage and the hidden life of the forest floor is suddenly, miraculously, revealed.

I got into mycology because if you want to find wild mushrooms, it helps to know a little about where they live, and to understand that, it helps to know why they live there. I was by trade a cookbook writer, recipe developer, and food journalist, but I became so captivated with mushrooms that I wrote a book about hunting them called *Mycophilia*. (That's Greek for "fungus lover.")

I met filmmaker Louie Schwartzberg around 2014, when he was in the early stages of developing his movie *Fantastic Fungi*. We talked many times about mycology and the challenges of telling the complicated story of Kingdom Fungi. In 2019, he completed his film, which in my mind illustrates his learning arc about mushrooms, much as *Mycophilia* represents mine.

Louie self-distributed his film, building an audience one theater at a time and a community by word of mouth. He went to premieres all over the country and always introduced the film by thanking the mycelial network for bringing the audience together. To Louie, fungal mycelium is a metaphor for collective action—how we all do better when we help each other. It was a message that resonated for many people.

In the summer of 2020, Louie contacted me, asking if I would be interested in doing a cookbook. I was hesitant: The notion of a mushroom cookbook with recipes by Eugenia Bone just seemed, I dunno, irrelevant. There are many good mushroom cookbooks out there by other forager chefs. Who needs one by me? And then it hit me. Louie had nurtured this wonderful community of mushroom enthusiasts through the film. Why not tap into that cohort to create a community-based cookbook? I love community cookbooks. There is an honesty and unpretentiousness about them, and the recipes tend to be tried-and-true dishes that people actually make for dinner. These cookbooks also reflect something bigger than just a collection of recipes: They represent a community.

With the help of the company Magical Threads, we built a mushroom recipe-sharing platform on the *Fantastic Fungi* movie website. The plan was to build the platform, and, if enough folks participated, we could put together a collection of recipes. There were lots of challenges to building the website, and I was worried about everything, including how to handle recipes that called for borderline-edible mushrooms or preparations that might make some people sick. I had to read every recipe before it was cleared for posting to determine its safety, and I was freaked out by the responsibility. So, I enlisted Emily Schmidt and Ryan Bouchard from the Mushroom Hunting Foundation to help me make those determinations regarding mushrooms east of the Rockies, and David Campbell of Mycoventures

for mushrooms west of Rockies. Turns out there were very few controversial recipes posted—the oddest being a preparation for magics.

I was also worried about getting enough mushrooms to test the recipes. New York City, where I live, is pretty provincial when it comes to wild-mushroom retail, so I went hunting every weekend with my friends Charles Luce and Paul Sadowski of the New York Mycological Society. These outings were not only productive—I froze lots of species for future testing—but for me, there is nothing as grounding as a day with one's companions in the woods. I tried to step up my mushroom-cooking knowledge and got on the phone with folks like Alan Bergo (Foragerchef.com), and the queen of mycophagy, Elinoar Shavit, where I learned all sorts of important stuff, like the fact that mushrooms retain their shape basically no matter how hard you cook them.

The website was up and running by September 2020, and as the recipes at first only trickled in, I started to upload my own with a few of my friends' recipes. I lurked on Instagram and Facebook, looking for good mushroom cooks to invite to submit. I sent an invitation to share recipes to every mycological club I could get an address for.

By December, recipes started coming in every day. Many were absolutely delicious, giving me confidence that we'd be able to do a book. People

wrote recipes using mushrooms in place of meat, like *Hericium* crab cakes and portobello burgers. Others augmented traditional recipes with mushrooms. One author was a master of this, producing a virtual United Nations of recipes from a wide variety of cultures, like English beef pie, Senegalese chicken *yassa*, and Moroccan lamb tagine, all featuring mushrooms as a central ingredient. There were recipes using medicinal mushrooms, and recipes for drinks like shrubs, teas, and infused spirits. The recipes came from all over the United States and Canada, and a few from further afield. You can find them all on the website.

And then the tipping point arrived, and I knew there was enough material to start a book. I shared the good news with Louie, and we contacted Insight Editions, the publisher of the book version of Louie's film. I reached out to many of the authors whose dishes I had tried to see if they were interested in participating. Almost everyone did, and a few responded to the positive feedback by coming up with even more recipes.

With the cookbook now officially underway and a deadline on the horizon, I doubled my efforts. I tested the recipes submitted on the website, as well as recipes shared by home cooks and chefs I knew. My criteria were simple: Did the recipe work pretty much as written—meaning, did the cake rise? And if the cake rose, was it delicious? I also had to find a balance of recipe types and a balance of species. So, as the weeks passed, if a recipe came in with a new species, and it was possible for me to acquire the mushroom, I was gung ho to see it work. All I can say about the recipes that didn't get collected in this book is that I wish I could do a Volume II. Perhaps one day we will be able to.

Testing the recipes came with other challenges as well, such as figuring out what, exactly, a handful of black trumpets means. Because both mushrooms and vegetables (and hand sizes) vary all over the country, we decided to use weights and measures. I went over each recipe with the author to make sure that my conversions matched their intentions, and we chatted about their recipe and how they got into mushrooms, sometimes for hours. These conversations, while time consuming, were the most satisfying aspect of the entire project. To meet so many people from all different walks of life and realize we are all connected by our common interest in mushrooms was, well, uplifting, especially during a very sad and scary year. Indeed, if I didn't hear from an author for a while, I would get nervous about their health and email them incessantly. It turns out a few were laid low by COVID-19.

I wanted this book to be illustrated with beautiful pictures, and we asked Evan Sung to come aboard. Evan is master of the subtle art of food photography and super easygoing, even when it took three friggin' times to get the potato mushroom tortilla right. I used my own frozen and dried wild mushrooms in the dishes, but more significantly, we used absolutely gorgeous, incredibly fresh wild mushrooms sent to us by Far West Fungi and other purveyors. I wanted each photograph to express the fact that these recipes were coming from many authors, so every setup was propped differently, but at the same time, I wanted the book to have an overall vibe, a kind of woodsy gourmand feel that represented the community as a whole. To that end, I borrowed plates and platters from everyone I knew and depended heavily on the goodwill of Pam Krauss and Neni Panourgia, true kitchen goddesses tattooed in burns, who, with about 80 years of experience between them, handled the cooking.

We shot various recipes different ways—whatever made them look most delectable—but there are some recipes where the mushrooms just aren't obvious. I mean, how do you show the mushroom in a black bean and huitlacoche soup? It's not that easy. But we did the best we could, and overall, I think the dishes look as delicious as they are.

I hope the authors are happy. I hope all those who contributed and continue to contribute to the website are pleased, and I hope the community of mushroom enthusiasts feels well represented. This is their book, after all.

But even more, I hope this book makes mycophiles of those of you who aren't already.

A NOTE ABOUT THESE RECIPES

This book calls for an array of wild mushrooms, which are palatable for most people. However, some can cause gastro upset. For example, some people may get a stomachache or other symptoms from eating chicken of the woods. Other people need to be cognizant of potential interactions between a specific fungus and the drugs they are taking. Chaga, for example, may interact with blood thinners or diabetes medication. Wild mushrooms are delicious and interesting foods that you will benefit most from if you take the time to learn a bit about how your body interacts with each species. Take it easy, take it slow, and get to know your mushrooms!

The recipes are all tested at sea level, so readers living at different altitudes need to make the appropriate adjustments. The recipes call for cultivated mushrooms and wild, fresh, and dehydrated. When substituting cultivated mushrooms for wild, try to keep in mind the density of the mushroom you are replacing, because that can affect cooking. So, for example, if a recipe calls for matsutake, you could use king trumpets, or enoki for graylings. Many recipes will work fine substituting dried for fresh mushrooms. To replace fresh mushrooms with dried in a recipe, use about three ounces of dried mushrooms for every pound of fresh mushrooms.

People have all kinds of techniques when it comes to rehydration, but in general, some mushrooms (morels and trumpets) hydrate fast, others (porcini and wood ear) slower, and others (matsutake, lobsters, chanterelles) really slow, and you can rehydrate them in a variety of liquids, not just water. There are more details about preparing mushrooms in the first essay, "The Kitchen Mycologist."

Always wash mushrooms before cooking, and in the case of wild mushrooms with lots of crevices, like hen of the woods or morels, where bugs can hide, wash thoroughly! I once removed a three-inch-long salamander from inside a morel.

Mushrooms constitute a large, exciting food category that we hope you will enjoy exploring. And wild mushrooms are particularly interesting. But you must be smart. Don't eat a wild mushroom you aren't 100 percent certain is safe, and don't pig out on them until you've seen how your body responds. Just as you might learn mushroom species one at a time, think about learning how to cook them one at a time, too. If you are like all the folks who have contributed to this book, you will become a master of what's growing nearby, and then, if you like, maybe you will share your recipes on the website.

I hope so, because there's a whole community of us looking forward to trying them.

MUSHROOMS ON THEIR OWN OR WITH VEGETABLES

DRIED PORCINI ONION DIP

BY ALISON GARDNER, CALIFORNIA | YIELD: ABOUT 2½ CUPS

*This recipe is just a basic French onion dip recipe with added dried porcini (*Boletus *group). It's very simple and quick and not dependent on mushroom season. In 2014, I published* The Wild Mushroom Cookbook: Recipes from Mendocino *with Merry Winslow. I invented a whole slew of recipes for the book, but I didn't print them all. This one was not included, but it is a favorite at mushroom events. The recipe is extra delicious with the addition of dried candy caps (*Lactarius rubidus *or* Lactarius rufulus*).*

2½ tablespoons salted butter, divided

½ cup minced onion

1 teaspoon minced garlic

¼ teaspoon dried thyme

¼ cup ground dried porcini (see note)

½ teaspoon ground dried candy caps
(optional) (see note)

1 pint sour cream

Salt

NOTE: To prepare the porcini and candy caps, break up the mushrooms into small pieces and grind to a powder in a coffee or spice grinder.

Heat 2 tablespoons of butter in a medium skillet over medium-high heat. When the butter has melted, add the onion and cook, stirring frequently, until it turns golden, about 5 minutes. Add garlic, thyme, and dried porcini and sauté for a few more minutes, until the mushroom powder has absorbed the butter and the onion is coated. Add remaining ½ tablespoon of butter if the pan gets dry and the powder starts to stick. Continue cooking until the onions are caramelized and the mushrooms become aromatic and take on a deeper color. If you choose to add ground candy caps, stir them in now and cook for another 30 seconds. Then turn off the heat and allow the mushroom and onion mixture to cool.

In a small bowl, combine the sour cream and mushroom-and-onion mixture. Add salt to taste. The dip can be served immediately with chips or crackers, but it is better if it is chilled for at least 1 hour, which lets the flavors meld.

MAITAKE MUSHROOM PÂTÉ

BY JULIE SCHREIBER, CALIFORNIA | YIELD: ABOUT 1 PINT

I am a winemaker and professional chef, but I cook for various mushroom events in my free time. I have been cooking dinners at the Sonoma County Mycological Association's mushroom camp for years. At those events, I like to serve mushroom pâtés as starters, because they bring people to the table. I found a basic mushroom paté recipe online years ago, and have made countless adaptations over the years. This version is my favorite.

3 tablespoons unsalted butter, divided

12 ounces maitake mushrooms, broken or sliced into chunks

Salt and freshly ground black pepper

½ cup thinly sliced white onions

3 small bay leaves

4 whole juniper berries

⅓ cup dry hard apple cider

Squeeze of lemon juice

⅓ cup heavy cream

Heat 2 tablespoons of butter in a large skillet over medium-high heat. When the butter is melted, add the maitake and cook, for about 5 minutes, until the mushrooms start to brown. Add salt and pepper to taste. Cover and lower the heat to medium-low. Cook gently for 10 to 15 minutes, stirring periodically, until the mushrooms release their liquid, and the liquid begins to evaporate.

Remove the lid and add the remaining 1 tablespoon of butter, the onions, the bay leaves, and the juniper berries. (Count the leaves and berries, because you will remove them later.) Increase the heat to medium and cook until onions are golden, about 5 minutes. There may be brown bits accumulating in the bottom of the pan. This is good! Increase the heat to medium-high and add the cider, stirring to scrape up all the brown bits. Allow the liquid to cook off completely, a few minutes, then add the squeeze of lemon juice and stir.

Lower the heat to medium and add the cream. Cook gently for another 5 minutes, stirring frequently, to reduce the liquid. Taste to see if it needs more salt, then take it off the heat. Let the mushrooms cool, then pick out all the bay leaves and juniper berries. Pour the mushrooms into a food processor and pulse to blend to a rough paste. Pack into a pint jar (or, for individual servings, four quarter-pint jars) and refrigerate. The pâté holds in the refrigerator up to five days.

Serve the pâté at room temperature with marinated olives, cornichons, and bread or crackers, if you like.

MORELS AND BRIE EN CROÛTE

BY LARRY EVANS, MONTANA | YIELD: ONE 6-INCH WHEEL

In the days of Prototaxites, *I developed an interest in edible mushrooms, and I've seen a lot of evolution in the study of mycophagy since the twentieth century, eating and singing my way through mushroom forays and festivals across the continents. After my CDs came out, people called me the Fungal Boogieman, and after my role in Ron Mann's film* Know Your Mushrooms, *I've been leading mushroom expeditions and working to decriminalize* Psilocybe. *My late wife, Kris Love, and I came up with this dish, and the recipe won a national award in 1997. It's a dream recipe for gatherings, because it's easy to prepare ahead of time and comes out of the oven ready to serve in 20 minutes.*

3 tablespoons unsalted butter

6 ounces fresh morels or ⅓ ounce dried (see note)

Salt and freshly ground black pepper

6-inch wheel of brie cheese

¼ teaspoon ground nutmeg

1 pack (two 8-inch sheets) frozen puff pastry dough, thawed

NOTE: Rehydrate dried morels by soaking in 2 cups of water for about 5 minutes until they are plump and soft, then drain.

Preheat the oven to 375°F.

Melt the butter in a medium skillet over medium-high heat. Add the morels and cook until they lose their water and the water evaporates, about 10 minutes. Add salt and pepper to taste.

Slice the brie at the equator as you would a bagel. Cover one exposed half with the prepared morels and sprinkle with nutmeg. Place the other half of the brie on top of the mushrooms.

On a floured board, use a rolling pin to roll out 1 sheet of the puff pastry dough until it is smooth and pliable. Place the brie in the center of the dough. Roll out the second sheet of dough and lay it on top of the brie. Crimp the edges of both dough sheets to create a pastry envelope.

Place on a cookie sheet and bake 17 minutes, until the pastry is golden brown. Serve with a baguette, if you like.

SHERRY-CREAMED PLEUROTES ON TOAST

BY DOROTHY CARPENTER, MISSOURI | YIELD: 4 SERVINGS

I'd always hunted morels in Missouri, but then I met Gary Lincoff of the New York Mycological Society and just fell in love with the whole idea of learning more about mushrooms. Gary was so generous with his knowledge, and I think of him often when walking in the woods, looking for mushrooms like the oysters I use in this dish. Sherry-Creamed Pleurotes is a throwback to times when people weren't afraid to feast on unabashedly rich fare. It's the perfect adornment for a big, old-fashioned roast, but it serves just as well as the single delicate course of a proper ladies' luncheon menu. Main course or side dish, it will always be the star of the show.

8 tablespoons unsalted butter

1 pound oyster mushrooms, coarsely chopped

½ teaspoon freshly ground black pepper

1 tablespoon flour

2 tablespoons olive oil (if needed)

¾ cup medium-dry sherry

½ cup sour cream

½ teaspoon herbes de Provence

½ teaspoon dried tarragon

½ teaspoon Worcestershire sauce

½ teaspoon soy sauce

Dash of cayenne

½ cup heavy cream

4 slices toasted bread

2 tablespoons minced flat-leafed parsley, for garnish

Heat the butter in a large skillet over medium-high heat and add the mushrooms and black pepper. Cook for 8 to 10 minutes, until the mushrooms have released their liquid and the liquid has evaporated. Sprinkle the mushrooms with the flour, and stir to coat. If the pan looks dry, add the olive oil. Add the sherry, sour cream, herbes de Provence, tarragon, Worcestershire sauce, soy sauce, and cayenne. Turn the heat down to medium and cook, stirring, for about 5 minutes, until the flour has dissolved. The sour cream may look curdled at first, but keep stirring. Add the heavy cream and continue to simmer for a few minutes more, until the sauce is smooth and the cream slightly reduced to the consistency of gravy.

To serve, place the mushrooms and sherry-cream sauce over toast and garnish with parsley.

MOREL GRATIN

BY EUGENIA BONE, NEW YORK | YIELD: 4 SERVINGS

Morels are my favorite mushroom to hunt. I collect them on the burns in the Sierras and along roadsides under dying elm in the tri-state area. I even hunt them in my dreams, where I experience the same rush of excitement as when I am in the woods. Fresh morels do not tend to produce as much water as some other wild mushrooms. That said, while cooking them with the onions, if the morels throw off water, you must cook them until the water is mostly evaporated or your gratin will be runny. Be sure to give rehydrated or defrosted morels a squeeze to remove extra water before cooking. This dish is quite rich and is wonderful served with a grilled meat or a nice acidic salad to counter its creamy cheesiness. Wine is nice, too.

1 to 2 tablespoons unsalted butter, divided

4 medium Yukon gold potatoes

4 slices thick cut bacon, cubed

1 cup thinly sliced white or yellow onion, cut in slices no longer than the morels (if necessary to help achieve the right size, cut the onions in halves or quarters before slicing)

24 to 30 small fresh, rehydrated, or defrosted frozen morels (see note)

½ cup heavy cream

¾ cup Gruyère cheese or other melting cheese (like cheddar or Comté, or a combination), grated on the large holes of the grater

Salt and freshly ground black pepper

¼ cup breadcrumbs

NOTE: if using dried mushrooms, soak them in warm water for 15 minutes, until plumped up, and then squeeze out the water. if using frozen mushrooms, drain off liquid before cooking.

Preheat the oven to 400°F.

Use 1 tablespoon of butter to grease a medium (about 10-by-7-by-2-inch) casserole pan. I prefer a wide, low oval-shaped pan.

Place the potatoes in a large pot of salted water and bring to a boil. Boil the potatoes gently until almost al dente (until a fork can penetrate the potato with some effort), about 15 minutes. Drain and let cool.

While the potatoes cool, in a medium skillet, render the bacon over medium to medium-high heat, about 5 minutes. Do not brown. Add the onion and cook until it is translucent, about 4 minutes. Do not brown. Add the fresh morels and continue cooking for 7 to 10 minutes, until the mushrooms give off their water and then the water mostly evaporates. If using rehydrated or defrosted morels, cook until they collapse and are fork-tender. Alternatively, you can forgo the bacon and instead sauté the onions and morels in 1 tablespoon of butter.

Peel and cut the potatoes into slices about ¼ inch thick. In a large bowl, gently combine the potato slices, the morel-and-onion mixture, cream, and cheese. Season to taste with salt and pepper.

Place the potatoes-and-morel mixture in the greased pan. Spread out the mixture so that the morels and potatoes are well distributed. Sprinkle the breadcrumbs on top.

Bake for 10 to 15 minutes, until the potatoes are tender and the top is golden brown and bubbly.

AGARICUS SALAD WITH BLOOD ORANGES AND FENNEL

BY SEAN SULLIVAN, NEW YORK | YIELD: 4 SERVINGS

Shaved fennel is a refreshing addition to practically any type of mixed salad; it's my go-to when something fancy is called for. Ditto with the blood oranges. The mushrooms make a mellow foundation for the big flavors of the other ingredients. There are three types of mushrooms you can use in this dish, and all must be young and very fresh. They are Agaricus bisporus, Amanita caesarea, *and, of the porcini group,* Boletus rubriceps, B. aureus, *and* B. aestivalis.

8 ounces white buttons, Caesar's
    mushrooms, or baby porcini

Juice of ½ lemon

15 springs fresh parsley

2 blood oranges or navel oranges

1 medium (8-ounce) fennel bulb

Salt and freshly ground black pepper

1 tablespoon olive oil

1 teaspoon sherry vinegar

2 ounces Parmesan cheese, shaved,
    for garnish

Slice the mushrooms very thin. Place them in a salad bowl and toss with the lemon juice.

Pull the leaves off the parsley. You should have ½ to 1 cup of leaves, lightly packed. Add them to the mushrooms.

Supreme the oranges: Trim off all the skin and pith. Then, over the bowl containing the mushrooms, hold an orange in one hand and, with the other hand, cut along the segment membranes to release the crescents of pulp and drop them into the bowl. Repeat with the second orange. Make sure all the dripping juices go into the bowl as well.

Cut the fennel bulb in half and trim out the solid core. Slice as thin as possible. (A mandoline works best.) The fennel should be soft and pliant. Add it to the bowl. Add salt and freshly ground black pepper to taste.

Add the olive oil and vinegar directly into the salad and toss well, about 30 seconds, until the mushrooms take on some of the color of the oranges and everything wilts.

Serve garnished with the shaved Parmesan cheese.

BRUSSELS SPROUTS WITH TRUFFLES, TWO WAYS

BY JACK CZARNECKI, OREGON | YIELD: 4 SERVINGS

I published the original version of this dish in my most recent book, Truffle in the Kitchen: A Cook's Guide. *This recipe calls for two different treatments of steamed brussels sprouts—one with truffle butter and one with truffle oil—although you can choose to do the whole batch one way or another.*

1 pound fresh brussels sprouts (about 40 small sprouts)

Salt and freshly ground black pepper

2 tablespoons Oregon white truffle butter (or other truffle butter)

2 tablespoons toasted, chopped hazelnuts

2 tablespoons Oregon white truffle oil (or other truffle oil)

2 tablespoons microgreens (like pea shoots or sunflower)

Remove any brown leaves from the sprouts and cut in half. Fit a large pot with a steamer insert, and fill with water to the bottom of the insert. Bring to a boil over medium-high heat and add the sprouts. Steam, tossing occasionally, until they are fork-tender, 5 to 7 minutes. Divide the sprouts between two serving bowls, then add salt and pepper to taste.

Toss the truffle butter in one bowl of sprouts, making sure the butter is melted, and garnish with the chopped hazelnuts.

Toss the truffle oil in the other bowl of sprouts and garnish with the microgreens.

SPRING PORCINI SALAD

BY LANGDON COOK, WASHINGTON | YIELD: 4 SERVINGS

This simple yet satisfying salad is perfect for enjoying outdoors with a glass of rosé after a day of scouring the woods. The combination of cool, crisp greens and warm, just-off-the-grill porcini can't be beat. A slightly sweet vinaigrette and shaved Romano cheese complete the picture. I'll make it in the fall with Boletus edulis, *but my preference is for the springtime* B. rex-veris, *a West Coast porcini variety that fruits just as the weather turns warm and the morels are calling it quits. Always use fresh rather than dried mushrooms for this preparation, which is a classic Italian way to enjoy the rich, nutty flavor of grilled porcini.*

¼ cup olive oil

2 tablespoons minced fresh thyme leaves

2 tablespoons minced fresh oregano leaves

2 tablespoons minced fresh flat-leafed parsley

1 teaspoon minced garlic (optional)

Salt and freshly ground black pepper

8 to 16 ounces fresh porcini buttons, sliced ¼ inch thick

4 ounces spring greens, rinsed and plated

Pecorino Romano, thinly shaved, for garnish

Vinaigrette or similar salad dressing

Heat the outdoor grill or a grill plate on your stove to a medium-high heat.

In a small bowl, whisk together the olive oil, thyme, oregano, parsley, garlic, salt, and pepper to taste.

Brush the olive oil mixture on the sliced porcini. Using tongs, place the mushrooms on the grill and cook until golden and slightly crispy, 3 to 5 minutes. Flip the mushrooms over and cook a few minutes more.

Remove the porcini from the grill and arrange them over the plated greens. Scatter a few shavings of cheese on top, and drizzle with vinaigrette dressing.

WARM ENDIVE AND OYSTER MUSHROOM SALAD

BY ANNALIESE BISCHOFF, MASSACHUSETTS | YIELD: 4 SERVINGS

I started writing down recipes for the first time in my life in 2010. I happened upon Food52, the recipe-sharing website, and have contributed 320 recipes as Sagegreen. I got to know people all over the world through this site. I love sharing my recipes, so when I found out about the Fantastic Fungi Community Cookbook, *I immediately wanted to contribute. This recipe is inspired by my Food52 cooking friend Gingerroot's wilted kale and shiitake mushroom salad.*

2 tablespoons olive oil

½ cup minced shallots

1 teaspoon sliced garlic

1 to 2 teaspoons grated ginger

Freshly ground black pepper

6 ounces oyster mushrooms

1 tablespoon white or black sesame seeds

2 marinated white anchovy fillets, chopped

2 Belgian endives, leaves separated and cut into 2-inch sections

Juice from ½ Meyer or regular lemon

Pinch of kosher salt

⅓ cup chopped fresh cilantro or flat-leafed parsley for garnish

2 whole scallions, chopped on the diagonal for garnish

Drizzle of high-quality white truffle oil, for garnish (optional)

Grated Parmesan cheese, for garnish (optional)

In a wide skillet, heat the olive oil over medium-high heat. Add the shallots and garlic and sauté until golden, a few minutes. Stir in the ginger and pepper to taste. Tear the oyster mushrooms into bite-sized pieces and add. Cook for about 5 minutes, flipping the mushrooms over, until they release their liquid. Add the sesame seeds and toast them in a bald spot in the pan for 1 minute or so. Turn the heat down to medium, add the anchovy and endive, and cook until the endive wilts, a few more minutes. Take off the heat, add the lemon juice, and season with salt.

Garnish with the cilantro and scallions and, if you like, white truffle oil and a sprinkle of Parmesan cheese.

BBQ TERIYAKI CHICKEN OF THE WOODS

BY PAUL STAMETS, WASHINGTON | YIELD: 4 SERVINGS

I often find chicken of the woods in the Pacific Northwest—sometimes a lot. A great advantage of this recipe is that when you find a large amount of chicken of the woods, you can cook it all up this way and then freeze the strips for future snacks. When preparing the mushrooms for cooking, be sure to use young mushrooms and remove any brown edges or soft spots, as these may be due to the presence of bacteria, which can cause stomach upset.

½ cup olive oil, divided

⅓ cup teriyaki sauce, divided

8 fresh young brackets chicken of the woods mushrooms, cut into ½-inch-wide slices

Combine ¼ cup of the olive oil and 3 tablespoons of the teriyaki sauce in a wide bowl. Add the mushrooms and toss them thoroughly in the mixture, then allow to rest for about 30 minutes. If you like, you can soak the mushrooms in the sauce overnight in the refrigerator.

Heat the grill to high heat. Combine the remaining olive oil and teriyaki sauce in a bowl. Remove the mushrooms from the marinade and place in a basket on the grill. High flames are good: They will help crisp up the mushrooms. Cook until the edges become brown and crispy, around 3 minutes per side, flipping once and basting with the remaining sauce.

The mushrooms can hold in the freezer for up to a month.

CANDY CAP OATMEAL WITH BRANDY

BY ALISON GARDNER, CALIFORNIA | YIELD: 1 SERVING

This is a version of a recipe I published (with Merry Winslow) in my 2014 book The Wild Mushroom Cookbook: Recipes from Mendocino. *The recipe is best with slow-cooked oats rather than instant oats. Brown sugar, honey, butter, and milk or cream all may be served on the side.*

1 serving old-fashioned rolled or
    steel-cut oats

4 dried candy cap mushrooms per serving

1 tablespoon brandy per serving

Cook the single serving of oatmeal as instructed on the package, adding the dried candy caps when the oats are added to the boiling water. When the oatmeal is ready, plate and garnish with 1 tablespoon of brandy.

CHAMPIÑONES AL AJILLO (MUSHROOMS WITH GARLIC)

BY MARTA CABRERA, NEW YORK | YIELD: 4 SERVINGS

This is a typical tapas plate in Spain. It is full of flavor and easy to make. I often make this recipe with very small, whole mushrooms. I brush them clean and plunge them in a bowl of water with a tablespoon of lemon juice to prevent browning, then dry them thoroughly with a kitchen towel. This dish is wonderful served with crusty bread and a glass of wine.

4 tablespoons olive oil

16 ounces cremini and/or white button mushrooms, sliced (about 5 cups)

2 tablespoons minced garlic

Salt

1½ teaspoons Spanish sweet paprika

⅓ cup of dry white wine

2 tablespoons chopped flat-leafed parsley

In a large skillet, heat the oil over medium heat. Add the mushrooms and minced garlic and sauté for about 1 minute, then add salt to taste and the paprika. Continue to cook until the mushrooms release their liquid and the liquid evaporates, another 8 minutes or so, shaking the skillet from time to time. Add the wine and parsley, take off the heat, and let come to room temperature.

CAULIFLOWER-SHIITAKE STIR-FRY WITH NUMBING CHILI SAUCE

BY IRENE KHIN WONG, NEW YORK | YIELD: 4 SERVINGS

I grew up in Burma, which has a vast number of mushroom varieties, so we always had mushrooms on our plate. During my years as a professional chef, I've explored the mushroom cuisines of different cultures, but at home, I tend to cook them in a variety of Asian styles, as in this quick, very spicy recipe. You can use regular cauliflower or flowering cauliflower, which has a longer stem and smaller florets; both work. While I like to use 2 tablespoons of spicy fermented bean paste, it is hot, so if you aren't sure about the spiciness, start with 1 tablespoon and take it from there.

¼ cup vegetable stock or water

2 tablespoons Shaoxing wine or dry sherry

1 tablespoon soy sauce

2 teaspoons cornstarch

2 tablespoons peanut oil or vegetable oil

1 medium head (about 1¼ pounds) flowering cauliflower or regular cauliflower, rinsed and cut into bite-sized florets

1 cup sliced shallots or yellow onions

1 tablespoon minced garlic

1 tablespoon minced ginger

3 dried chili peppers (optional)

2 tablespoons Doubanjiang (spicy fermented bean paste), or less, as desired

1 teaspoon ground Szechuan peppercorns, or 1 tablespoon Szechuan peppercorn oil (optional)

¼ pound shiitake or oyster mushrooms, sliced

1 tablespoon slivered scallions, for garnish

In a small bowl, make the sauce: Whisk together the vegetable stock, Shaoxing wine, soy sauce, and cornstarch.

Heat the oil in a large carbon steel or cast-iron pan over medium-high heat. Add the cauliflower and let it char a bit, about 5 minutes, stirring occasionally. Add the shallots, garlic, and ginger and cook, stirring until lightly browned, a few minutes. Add the dried chili if using, and stir a few times to release the fragrance, then add the Doubanjiang to taste and ground Szechuan peppercorns, if using. Stir-fry for 1 minute or so, until the vegetables are evenly coated. Add the mushrooms and ½ cup of water and lower the heat to medium.

Pour in the sauce. Stir again to mix well, then cover the pan and let the cauliflower steam until tender, 4 to 6 minutes. (Regular cauliflower takes a bit longer than flowering cauliflower.) Every 2 minutes or so, check on the cauliflower's doneness by piercing it with a fork.

When done, the cauliflower and shiitake will be glazed with the spicy sauce. If there's still a lot of liquid in the pan, you can turn up the heat and cook a little longer, uncovered, stirring occasionally to let the liquid evaporate.

Garnish with scallions and serve hot with steamed rice, if you like.

CHICKEN-FRIED CHICKEN OF THE WOODS

BY DAVID LOGSDON, NEW YORK | YIELD: 4 SERVINGS

I live and work in the Catskill Mountains, and about six years ago I bought a little house in the middle of the woods surrounded by a huge variety of plants and mushrooms. I had to learn about these things, so I joined the New York Mycological Society and the Mid-Hudson Mycological Association and bought a lot of mushroom books. I've been mushroom hunting ever since. This recipe is from an old Kentucky backwoods recipe handed down from Daniel Boone. Just kidding! The mushrooms are tenderized by soaking them in buttermilk overnight. That said, some people have a sensitivity to chicken of the woods mushrooms. If you are one of them, then start by boiling the mushrooms until they can be pierced by a fork.

4 cups buttermilk

3 teaspoons Hungarian hot paprika or Old Bay Seasoning (see note), divided

1 teaspoon garlic powder, divided

8 fresh young brackets of chicken of the woods mushrooms, cut to about the size of playing cards

4 cups all-purpose flour

Salt and freshly ground black pepper

Corn oil or other neutral oil, for frying

NOTE: Old Bay Seasoning is high in sodium, so watch the salt!

In a large bowl, combine the buttermilk, 2 teaspoons paprika, and ½ teaspoon garlic powder. Submerge the mushrooms and cover. Refrigerate for at least 4 hours, but overnight is best.

When you are ready to fry, place the flour in a wide, shallow bowl and combine with the remaining paprika and garlic powder. Remove the mushroom pieces from the buttermilk (reserve the liquid), tap off the extra buttermilk, and dredge in the flour. Allow the mushroom pieces to rest for a few minutes, until the batter sets.

Line a plate with paper towels and set aside. Add about 1 inch of oil to a large nonstick skillet and heat over medium heat until the oil pops when a dash of flour is thrown into it.

Re-dip the mushrooms in the buttermilk and re-dredge in the flour, then add to the hot oil, making sure not to crowd in the pan. If necessary, cook in batches. Fry the mushrooms until they are golden brown, about 5 minutes, then flip over and continue frying for another 3 minutes, until both sides are golden brown, about 8 minutes total.

Drain the fried mushrooms on the prepared paper towel–lined plate.

Serve immediately with boiled bitter greens dressed with vinegar, if you like, or in a sandwich, as pictured here. They are also surprisingly good cold, served with salsa, relish, or caviar.

HOT BUTTERED OYSTER MUSHROOMS

BY VENORI KESHY LIYANAGE, NORTH DAKOTA | YIELD: 4 SERVINGS

During the COVID-19 pandemic, my husband and I became vegans. We replaced meat with vegetables and found that mushrooms were a great meat substitute. This recipe is adapted from hot buttered calamari, a dish from Sri Lanka, where my family is from. We love to serve this as a hot appetizer, but it is also great as a main dish served over white or fried rice. I typically use chickpea flour (also known as gram or garbanzo flour) for the batter, because I like its sandy texture, but the recipe can also be made with all-purpose flour. You also can increase the chili pepper if you like it hotter.

1 cup finely ground chickpea flour, or all-purpose flour

1 cup full-fat coconut milk

Canola or other vegetable oil for deep-frying

8 ounces oyster mushrooms, washed, dried, and torn into long, thin strips

Pinch of salt

4 tablespoons vegan or unsalted butter

1 teaspoon minced ginger

1 teaspoon minced garlic

2 medium red bell peppers, thinly sliced (about 12 ounces)

2 teaspoons sugar

1 teaspoon chili flakes

1 teaspoon red chili powder, or smoked paprika

4 scallions, sliced on the diagonal into ½-inch pieces

4 lime wedges, for garnish (optional)

In a small bowl, mix the flour and coconut milk until combined in a smooth batter. The mixture will be thick.

Add 1 inch of oil to a medium or large nonstick skillet. Bring oil to 375°F over medium heat. Then reduce heat to medium-low to stabilize the oil temperature. Dip each mushroom strip into the batter, shake off any excess batter, and add the battered mushrooms to the heated oil. Depending on the size of your pan, add about 3 to 4 pieces of battered mushrooms at a time; do not overcrowd the pan, or the temperature of the oil will drop and the mushrooms will become soggy.

Fry the mushroom strips for 2 to 3 minutes, until they are golden and release easily from the pan, then flip them over and cook the other side. Remove the mushrooms when they are golden all over and drain on paper towels or a rack. Repeat until all the mushroom pieces are fried to crispy perfection. Sprinkle with salt.

Heat the butter in a large nonstick saucepan over medium heat. Add the garlic and ginger and cook for 1 to 2 minutes, stirring frequently, until the mixture becomes golden and aromatic. Add the bell peppers and sauté for a few minutes to soften. Reduce the heat to low, add the sugar and chili flakes, and mix. Add a pinch of salt and red chili powder to the mixture. (If you don't like it spicy, add 1 teaspoon of smoked paprika instead of chili powder.) Add the deep-fried mushrooms and scallions and sauté for about 2 minutes, until everything is well combined.

Serve immediately as is, or with a side of rice and a lime wedge, if you like.

POTATO MUSHROOM TORTILLA

BY MARTA CABRERA, NEW YORK | YIELD: ONE 9-INCH CAKE

The tortilla española is a traditional staple in Spanish cooking and life. It is simple, cheap, nourishing, and very delicious. It can be eaten from morning to night for any meal or occasion. You can hardly spend a day in Spain without being offered or asking for a "¡pincho de tortilla!" The classic tortilla española is made of eggs and potatoes; adding onions is optional. It can also be enhanced with chorizo, peppers, spinach, or whatever is in the pantry. One of my favorite additions is mushrooms! I often make this tortilla with boiled potatoes, which are easier and less messy than frying. Simply slice the potatoes and boil them in salted water for about 8 minutes, until fork-tender.

1 cup olive oil

1 pound whole or yellow potatoes, sliced no thicker than ¼ inch (see note)

1 cup chopped onions

1¼ cup chopped white button mushrooms

1 teaspoon minced garlic

Salt and freshly ground black pepper

4 large eggs

NOTE: For very thin slices, use a mandoline.

Heat the oil in a medium nonstick skillet over medium heat until a slice of potato dropped in sizzles gently, a few minutes. Add the potato slices a few at a time so the oil doesn't drop in temperature too much. This is a gentle oil poach, so no more than tiny bubbles should appear. Add the onions and continue cooking until the potatoes are fork-tender, turning them over gently, about 8 minutes. Remove the potatoes and onions with a slotted spoon and place in a bowl, reserving 4 tablespoons of the oil. You can reuse this pan without washing it to cook the mushrooms. Just pour out the excess oil.

Heat 2 tablespoons of the reserved oil in the skillet over medium-high heat and add the mushrooms and garlic. Cook, stirring frequently, until the mushrooms give up their water and the water evaporates, about 10 minutes. Season with salt and pepper. Add the mushrooms to the reserved potato mixture and combine gently.

Beat the eggs in a small bowl and add them to the potato-mushroom mixture and combine gently. Press the potatoes down so they soak up the egg.

In the same nonstick skillet used for cooking the potatoes and mushrooms, heat the remaining 2 tablespoons of the reserved oil over medium heat. Pour the potato-and-mushroom mixture into the skillet. Try to arrange the potato slices so they lie flat. Cook for a few minutes, until the edges of the tortilla firm up. Turn the heat down to medium-low and continue cooking until the eggs have mostly set, about 10 minutes. If you shake the pan, the tortilla should move as a whole in the skillet. Slide the tortilla onto a plate and flip it over back into the pan. Allow to cook for a few more minutes to set the eggs. Serve warm, room temperature, or cold for breakfast, lunch, or dinner!

SHIITAKE FENNEL LATKES

BY ANNALIESE BISCHOFF, MASSACHUSETTS | YIELD: ABOUT 16 LATKES

I've been an enthusiastic and experimental home cook since kindergarten. My passion for food fuses together a spirit of adventure, a love of travel, and a growing curiosity about mushrooms. When I was of college age, I lived with a German family who took me mushroom hunting in the Bavarian Forest so we could make soup. My evolving curiosity led me to the Sonoma Mycological Association's mushroom camp in 2016. I love learning about the world of fungi and cooking the results. Work once brought me to Belarus, where my hosts took me into birch-beech forests to gather boletes for dinner, which we ate with their national dish, draniki *(Belarusian latkes). The following dish, inspired by those memories, integrates mushrooms right into the latkes.*

5 ounces (about 1½ cups) finely diced fresh shiitake mushrooms

2 cups grated russet potatoes, skin on or off, grated on the big holes of the grater (about 1 pound potatoes)

½ cup grated fresh fennel bulb, grated on the big holes of the grater (about ¼ of a bulb)

½ cup grated yellow onion, grated on the big holes of the grater

1 teaspoon kosher salt

½ teaspoon freshly ground black pepper

½ teaspoon freshly ground fennel seed

1 teaspoon minced fresh ginger

2 eggs, beaten

⅓ cup all-purpose flour

Neutral oil (like peanut or grapeseed oil), for frying

1 cup plain Greek yogurt or sour cream, for garnish

2 tablespoons sliced scallions (green part only) or chives, for garnish

In a large bowl, combine the mushrooms, potatoes, fennel, and onion and stir. Add salt, pepper, fennel seed, and ginger, and stir to combine. Let the mixture rest a few minutes.

Transfer the mushroom-potato mixture into a colander lined with cheesecloth and wring out the excess moisture.

In a small bowl, mix the eggs and flour. Combine with the mushroom-potato mixture.

Generously coat the bottom of a heavy skillet with oil. (The skillet doesn't have to be deeper than ⅛ inch.) Heat over medium-high heat until a drop of liquid sizzles in the pan, 1 minute or so. Using a slotted spoon, scoop up a spoonful of the mushroom-potato mixture, allowing excess liquid to drain off. Drop the spoonful into the hot oil and fry for about 2 minutes on each side, until latkes are just golden. They will not be cooked through. That's okay. Drain them on a rack or paper towels. At this point, you can refrigerate the latkes for a few days or freeze them for up to two months.

To serve, preheat the oven to 350°F.

Place the latkes on a baking tray and cook for about 10 minutes on each side. They will turn a rich golden brown. Before serving, latkes may need to be blotted on a paper towel.

Serve the latkes warm with a generous dollop of thick Greek yogurt or sour cream and sprinkled with scallions or chives.

HUITLACOCHE CREPES

BY CHARLES LUCE, NEW JERSEY | YIELD: 12 CREPES

*This recipe came to me from Mexico City–based graphic designer Anna Ocón Beltrán, who learned it from her grandmother. Anna did the design for my gluten-free bread mix packaging (you can find my recipes in my newsletter at Luces9grains.com) and she's a good friend to boot. We bonded over a mutual love of huitlacoche. I've adapted the recipe to accommodate my celiac disease, making the crepes gluten-free. Using nixtamalized corn flour (*masa seca*) gives them an enchilada flavor, which can be tamped down if desired by diluting the corn flour with oat or brown rice flour. Alternatively, one can make traditional wheat-flour crepes, although in my opinion corn goes better with the fungus than wheat. Use fresh huitlacoche if you have a source, but canned will do.*

FOR THE CREPES

1 cup nixtamalized corn flour (*masa seca*)
2 large eggs
Pinch of salt
¼ cup of milk
Butter, for greasing

FOR THE FILLING

2 tablespoons unsalted butter (not
   necessary if using canned huitlacoche)
1 pound fresh or one 14.8-ounce can
   huitlacoche
Salt and freshly ground black pepper

FOR THE SALSA

2 pounds unhulled tomatillos
½ cup diced white onion
2 tablespoons diced jalapeño or chile
   verde pepper
2 cups chopped fresh cilantro
2 tablespoons olive oil
½ cup full-fat sour cream
Pinch of salt
1 pound shredded Monterey Jack or
   mozzarella cheese

TO MAKE THE CREPES:

Whisk together the corn flour, eggs, salt, and milk in a medium-sized bowl until a smooth batter forms, a few minutes.

Heat a crepe pan or a large, well-seasoned skillet over medium-high heat until a dab of added butter froths immediately. Using a wadded paper towel or a fine heatproof brush, smear the pan with a very thin layer of butter. Using one hand, lift the skillet or pan and with the other hand dip a ladle with ¼ cup of batter into the pan while tilting and swirling. The goal is to create a very thin, circular pool of batter.

Allow the batter to steam off and partially dry, 30 seconds or so, then use a spatula or pancake turner to flip. Remove when cooked through, less than 1 minute. Pile up the finished crepes on a plate and cover loosely with a kitchen towel.

TO PREPARE THE FILLING:

If using fresh huitlacoche, heat the butter in a medium skillet over medium heat and add the huitlacoche. Sauté until black, fragrant, and steamy. Add salt and pepper to taste. If using canned huitlacoche, no cooking is necessary.

TO MAKE THE SALSA:
Preheat the oven to 350°F

Add 8 cups of water to a large saucepan and bring to a boil. Add the tomatillos and boil until soft, about 5 minutes. Strain and place the tomatillos in a bowl to cool.

In a food processor, add the cooled tomatillos, onion, and jalapeño. Pulse to puree to a smooth sauce. (You can also add the ingredients to a bowl and puree with an immersion blender, or puree in a regular blender.) Pour back into the bowl and add the cilantro and mix well by hand.

Place a large skillet over medium-high heat and add the olive oil. When the oil shimmers, in a matter of seconds, add the salsa mixture and boil gently for about 4 minutes to cook the onions and jalapeño. Turn the heat down to low, add the sour cream and salt, and stir to combine. Simmer gently for 1 to 2 minutes, stirring to prevent the cream from breaking. ("*No se corta la crema*," Anna says.)

To assemble the dish, fill the crepes with 2 to 4 tablespoons of huitlacoche filling and roll them up. Place in a large stoneware or Pyrex baking dish. Cover the crepes with the salsa and scatter the cheese over the crepes.

Bake, uncovered, until the cheese melts and bubbles, about 30 minutes. Serve immediately.

BLACK TRUMPET AND FIG PIZZA

BY MARY SMILEY, DELAWARE | YIELD: ONE 12-INCH PIZZA (PLUS ADDITIONAL DOUGH FOR ANOTHER)

I got into mushrooms in 1982 through the wife of a friend, who, in turn, got me interested in fly-fishing. To this day, my fishing vest often comes home full of mushrooms. At first I was only interested in learning about edibles, but then I joined the Mycological Society of San Francisco and began learning mycology. In 2013 I started the Cooking with Wild Mushrooms Facebook page for people who make interesting mushroom dishes. This recipe is from that page. I created it after I began wondering how figs would pair with mushrooms and thought that perhaps black trumpets would be good on a pizza with ricotta and porchetta. It turns out they are! The pizza dough recipe is by Deborah Madison from her book Local Flavors.

FOR THE DOUGH

1¼ cups warm water

1 scant tablespoon active dry yeast

Pinch of sugar

3 cups bread flour, divided, plus more as needed

1 teaspoon sea salt

1 tablespoon olive oil, plus more for greasing the dough bowl

FOR THE TOPPINGS AND PIZZA

¼ ounce dried black trumpet mushrooms

3 tablespoons unsalted butter, divided

2 heaping cups thinly sliced yellow onions

Salt and freshly ground black pepper

¼ cup finely chopped shallot

½ teaspoon chopped fresh thyme

Juice of ¼ lemon

1 cup fresh (preferably not fully ripe) figs, halved if small, quartered if large, or 4 tablespoons fig jam

Coarse ground cornmeal (if using wooden peel and pizza stone)

1 cup ricotta cheese

2 to 3 pieces porchetta or prosciutto, thinly sliced

2 to 3 tablespoons pine nuts

3 ounces burrata (optional)

2 tablespoons balsamic vinegar glaze or reduction (see note), or a drizzle of plain balsamic vinegar

TO MAKE THE DOUGH:

Put the warm water in a medium mixing bowl and stir in the yeast, sugar, and 1 cup flour. Set aside until foamy and puffy, 20 to 30 minutes.

After the mixture is foamy, stir in the salt and oil, then start stirring in the remaining flour until the dough is fairly stiff. When the dough is too stiff to stir, turn it out onto a lightly floured board and knead until the dough is smooth and shiny, about 10 minutes. Add more flour as needed.

Lightly oil a clean bowl and add the dough, turning to coat. Cover with plastic wrap, and set aside to rise until doubled in size, about 1 hour.

Divide the dough into two equal pieces. You will use one piece for this recipe (or you can make 2 pizzas and double the ingredients for the topping). The spare dough can be frozen in a freezer-safe resealable bag for up to 3 months.

TO MAKE THE TOPPINGS AND PIZZA:

Preheat the oven to 500°F.

It is best to use a ceramic pizza stone and a wooden peel to transfer the pizza to the oven. Otherwise, a flat cookie sheet will do. If using a pizza stone, place it in the oven on the middle rack.

Rehydrate the dried mushrooms in about 2 cups of hot water until softened, about 15 minutes.

Continued on page 50 . . .

BLACK TRUMPET AND FIG PIZZA

NOTE: You can buy balsamic glaze or reduction or you can make your own: ½ cup of balsamic vinegar will reduce to 2 tablespoons syrup in about 15 minutes over medium-low heat.

Heat 2 tablespoons butter in a large sauté pan over medium-high heat. Add the sliced onions and cook until they start to soften, then turn down the heat to medium or medium-low and add a pinch of salt and pepper. Allow the onions to cook slowly, stirring occasionally to allow the onions to contact with the pan and gradually caramelize. Cook until the onions are very soft and golden, about 20 minutes. Don't rush it, or you will burn your onions. You should have about 1 cup of caramelized onions when you are done. Remove from the pan and set aside.

In the same pan, add shallots and cook until very soft, about 5 minutes. Add the rehydrated mushrooms and cook over medium heat for a few minutes, then add the fresh thyme and lemon juice and continue cooking until the mushrooms are tender, 5 to 10 minutes. Add salt to taste. Remove from the pan and set aside.

Add 1 tablespoon butter and add the fresh figs to the pan and sauté until slightly browned and softened, a few minutes. If the figs are very soft, just warm them through and don't worry about browning. Add the mushrooms and shallots back into the pan.

Roll out the dough into a 12-inch disc. Transfer the dough onto your peel or cookie sheet. (If using a peel, put some coarse ground cornmeal on it first. The meal will act like ball bearings for the dough and allow you to wiggle it off the peel onto the stone.)

On top of the raw dough, gently smear the ricotta and then cover the ricotta with the caramelized onions. Add the mushrooms and figs and spread out over the dough. Tear the porchetta and arrange it over the mushrooms and figs and sprinkle the pine nuts all over. If using, add small clumps of burrata before putting the pizza in the oven, or a few minutes after (so it doesn't melt as much).

If using a pizza stone, gently transfer the pizza dough onto the hot pizza stone, giving it a little shake to keep it loose on the cornmeal.

Bake the pizza for 10 to 12 minutes, or until the edges are brown and the center bubbles.

Remove the pizza from the oven and drizzle with balsamic glaze or vinegar.

HUITLACOCHE MUSHROOM TACOS

BY RICK BAYLESS, ILLINOIS | YIELD: 4 SERVINGS

In Mexico, huitlacoche, that mysterious-looking fungus that grows right out from the ear of corn, is pure luxury. Here, in the States, it's considered a blemish at best and evil corn smut at worst. So it's true: one man's meat is another man's poison. For the record, you can count me in the camp that considers huitlacoche a delicacy. The flavor is (unsurprisingly) like an earthy, sweet mix of dark mushrooms and corn. In other words, it's a fantastic ingredient to add to your kitchen repertoire—or not. It depends on which side of the meat-and-poison divide you fall. Here, I'm bolstering all of that complex flavor with meaty oyster mushrooms, tomatoes, onion, garlic, herby epazote, and a quick hit of queso añejo. While it's common to buy cobs with the huitlacoche attached in Mexico during the rainy season, it's most commonly sold in stateside Mexican markets in jars or cans. You might also have luck procuring some by asking around your local farmers market.

2 fresh poblano chiles

2 tablespoons olive oil

1 medium white onion cut into ¼-inch-thick slices (about 1½ cups)

1½ teaspoons minced garlic

¾ cup chopped tomato

1 cup packed oyster mushrooms, roughly chopped

6 ounces fresh, canned, or defrosted frozen huitlacoche

Salt

2 to 3 tablespoons chopped fresh epazote leaves

12 warm corn tortillas

¼ cup *queso añejo*, for garnish

Roast the chiles directly over a gas flame or 4 inches below a very hot broiler until blackened on all sides, about 5 minutes for open flame and about 10 minutes for broiler. Cover with a kitchen towel and let stand 5 minutes. Peel, remove stem and seeds, and then rinse briefly. Chop into ¼-inch pieces.

In a large skillet, heat the oil over medium heat. Add the onion and fry, stirring regularly, until lightly browned, 7 to 10 minutes. Stir in the garlic and cook about 2 minutes more. Increase the heat to medium-high, add the tomatoes, and cook, stirring occasionally, until the juices have reduced, about 4 minutes.

Add the poblanos to the tomato mixture along with the oyster mushrooms and the huitlacoche. Simmer, stirring often, until reduced and quite thick, about 10 minutes. Season with salt to taste, usually about 1 teaspoon, and mix in the epazote.

Spoon the mixture onto the warm corn tortillas and top with *queso añejo*.

OAXACAN WILD MUSHROOM QUESADILLAS

BY JANE B. MASON, COLORADO | YIELD: 4 SERVINGS

Foraging was always on my bucket list, but it wasn't until I moved to Colorado and discovered morels growing under the cottonwoods on my property that I realized the opportunity had presented itself. Shortly thereafter, I met Trent and Kristen Blizzard of Modern-Forager.com, who have generously taught me much about fungi and foraging. Now I try to forage wherever I find myself! Years ago, I tasted these mushroom quesadillas in an Oaxacan market. Don't let the simplicity of this recipe fool you—that is entirely the point. You can find fresh epazote and masa flour at Hispanic grocery stores, but in a pinch, cilantro can replace the epazote, and you can use premade corn tortillas.

2 tablespoons, plus 1 teaspoon neutral oil, divided

¼ cup diced white onions

6 ounces coarsely chopped fresh wild boletes, or cultivated mushrooms (like white buttons) or a combination

3 cups instant yellow corn masa flour

Several stems fresh epazote, minced, or 1 tablespoon dried

7 ounces (about 2 cups) grated Oaxaca, mozzarella, or Monterey Jack cheese

Fresh salsa (optional), for garnish

Heat 2 tablespoons of oil in a skillet over medium heat. Add the onions and sauté 1 minute, then add the mushrooms. Sprinkle with salt and cook about 10 minutes, until the mushrooms give up their water, the water evaporates, and the edges are browned. If necessary, lower the heat to avoid burning. Remove from the heat, cover, and keep warm.

In a large bowl, combine the masa flour and 2¼ cups water. Stir into a soft dough. Shape the masa dough into golf ball–sized balls, then place between two pieces of parchment paper or plastic wrap and roll into tortillas using a rolling pin. Don't worry about making them perfectly round. Alternatively, use a tortilla press.

Heat remaining 1 teaspoon of oil in a cast-iron skillet over high heat. Place a tortilla in the skillet and cook for 1 minute, until it dries out a bit, then flip it over and place a small pile of grated cheese, mushrooms, and a sprinkle of epazote on one half. Fold it over and continue cooking, flipping once, until the cheese is fully melted. You can cook as many as you can fit in the skillet at one time—I usually start a new one once the previous one is filled, folded, and set off to the side.

Serve as they come out of the skillet, topped with a bit more epazote and salsa, if you like.

MUSHROOM TEMPURA

BY DON PINTABONA, NEW YORK | YIELD: 4 SERVINGS

I fell in love with tempura of all sorts while training as a cook in Japan in the late 1980s. I especially loved visiting tempura shops that had been passed down through many generations. There I tasted some mushroom types for the first time, prepared in this traditional manner. When it comes to the batter, the recipe below works great, but I highly recommend you also check out Welna Tempura Batter Mix. It's very good and so easy!

FOR THE TEMPURA

4 ounces maitake mushrooms

4 ounces Bunashimeji (beech mushrooms)

4 ounces enoki mushrooms

3 cups neutral oil, like safflower, for frying

1 egg, beaten

1 cup ice-cold water

1½ cups pastry flour, sifted, divided

Salt

FOR THE DIPPING SAUCE

¾ cup *bonito dashi* broth, or ¾ cup hot water mixed with 1 teaspoon *bonito dashi* powder

3 tablespoons soy sauce

2 tablespoons mirin

2 teaspoons sugar

3 slices fresh ginger, sliced to the size of pennies

2 ounces daikon radish, grated on the big holes of the grater

TO MAKE THE TEMPURA:

Brush the mushrooms clean and tear into small clusters (and, in the case of maitake, cut away the tough stem).

In a large nonstick skillet, heat frying oil over medium-high heat to 350°F.

Mix the beaten egg with the ice water, then slowly add 1 cup of sifted flour. Blend gently; don't overwork the batter. It is important to keep the batter very cold, so you can add ice cubes to it, but don't let those cubes slip into the hot oil!

Place the remaining ½ cup of pastry flour in a shallow bowl. Dredge the mushrooms in the flour, shaking off the excess. Then dip the mushrooms into the egg batter several times until fully coated.

Fry the mushrooms in batches. Do not overcrowd the skillet. Using tongs, carefully swish the battered mushrooms lightly on the top of the oil, forward and backward, to release the excess batter. Leave mushrooms in the oil to cook until lightly browned, a few minutes, then flip over with a slotted spoon to cook the other side until golden brown, a few more minutes. Between batches, use your slotted spoon to strain out the bits of excess batter in the oil.

Drain mushrooms on paper towels. Lightly salt and serve with dipping sauce.

TO PREPARE THE DIPPING SAUCE:

Combine the *bonito dashi*, soy sauce, mirin, sugar, ginger slices, and grated daikon in a small bowl.

WOODLAND WILD MUSHROOM STRUDEL

BY SEBASTIAN CAROSI, OREGON | YIELD: TWO 9-BY-3-INCH STRUDELS

Growing up in an area like the Pacific Northwest, you quickly realize how much food is truly at your feet. The area on and around Mount Saint Helens yields many different kinds of mushrooms throughout the year. I like to make this simple mushroom strudel with my finds, and its flavor defines the day's hunt. Sometimes I serve this dish with an herbaceous salad made from miner's lettuce, chickweed, dandelions, and young hemp leaves tossed in a citrus vinaigrette. I've been experimenting with incorporating fresh cannabis and hemp into my recipes for many years to take full advantage of this unknown culinary and nutritional plant.

FOR THE STRUDEL

6 tablespoons salted butter, divided

1 pound mixed fresh wild mushrooms (like chanterelles, morels, porcini, matsutake, or black trumpets) or 1 pound cultivated mushrooms, roughly chopped

1 cup diced sweet onions

2 teaspoons chopped garlic

Salt and freshly ground black pepper

1 tablespoon chopped fresh thyme leaves, divided

½ teaspoon chopped fresh rosemary, divided

1½ tablespoons all-purpose flour

1 cup heavy cream

Pinch of freshly ground nutmeg

¼ cup dried wild mushroom mixture, rehydrated in ¼ cup hot water

1 cup panko breadcrumbs

Eight 9-by-14-inch sheets of thawed phyllo dough

FOR THE MUSTARD CREAM SAUCE

1 tablespoon salted butter

½ tablespoon minced sweet onion

½ teaspoon minced garlic

Pinch of fresh thyme leaves

1 cup heavy cream (or less for a tighter sauce)

Salt and freshly ground black pepper,

1 tablespoon whole grain mustard

TO MAKE THE STRUDEL:

In a large skillet, melt 2 tablespoons of butter over medium-high heat. Add the mushrooms, onions, garlic, and salt and pepper to taste. Cook, stirring occasionally, until the mushrooms release their juices, the liquid evaporates, and the mushrooms start to brown, 10 to 12 minutes. Add half the thyme and half the rosemary and continue to cook 2 to 4 minutes longer to meld the flavors. Sprinkle the flour over the mushrooms, stir until incorporated, then add the heavy cream, nutmeg, and rehydrated dried wild mushrooms plus the water they were rehydrated in and turn down the heat to low. Simmer, stirring often, for 15 to 20 minutes, until the cream is reduced by one-quarter. Add the panko and stir vigorously to incorporate well. Remove from the heat, check the seasoning, and stir in the remainder of the thyme and rosemary. Pour the mixture into a bowl, cover with plastic wrap, and refrigerate for 2 to 3 hours.

Preheat the oven to 375°F.

In a small pot, melt the remaining butter over medium-low heat. Add salt and freshly ground black pepper to taste.

Line a sheet pan with parchment paper. Have ready the melted butter and a pastry brush.

On a flat surface such as your countertop, gently place one sheet of the phyllo dough with the 14-inch side in front of you. Brush the sheet with melted butter, then place another sheet of phyllo on top, brush with butter, and continue for a total of four layers of phyllo, with butter brushed between each one.

Remove the mushroom mixture from the refrigerator and place half of it in a rough line on the long side of the phyllo. Roll the mushroom filling and phyllo into a log, folding in the ends of the pastry as you go. Repeat with the remaining four layers of phyllo and the remaining mushroom mixture. Place the two strudels on the sheet pan seam-side down and brush the top and sides with the remaining melted butter.

Bake for 20 to 25 minutes, or until the strudels are golden brown. Remove from the oven and let rest 10 minutes before cutting.

TO MAKE THE MUSTARD CREAM SAUCE:
Heat the butter in a small saucepan over medium heat. Add the onions, garlic, and thyme, and sweat for 4 to 6 minutes, or until the onions are translucent. Whisk in the heavy cream and mustard and incorporate well. Reduce the cream mixture over medium heat, stirring occasionally until it is reduced by half, about 10 minutes. For a thicker sauce, more like a tartar sauce, reduce for an additional 3 to 5 minutes. Add salt and pepper to taste.

Serve the sauce in a puddle on the plate with the sliced strudel on top.

LAKE PRESPA BAKED MUSHROOMS

BY NENI PANOURGIA, NEW YORK | YIELD: 4 SERVINGS

As an anthropologist, I travel a lot both for fieldwork and conferences, and everywhere I go, I keep my antennae up for new recipes. I had this dish while I was visiting Lake Prespa, at the shared border of Greece, Albania, and North Macedonia. It was served in the village of Psarades, which sits right on the lake. The lake teems with life—from fish, turtles, and birds to water chestnuts, which can be harvested easily by just wading in the shallows. When I asked for the recipe, I was told that there wasn't one: you just put everything together in the oven. After I returned in New York, I tried to replicate the dish. This version is just like the one I had in Greece. It's best to make this dish in an earthenware pan. Otherwise, use a baking pan about 9 by 12 inches that will hold the mushrooms snugly.

2 pounds fresh mixed cultivated and/or wild mushrooms, cleaned and chopped into quarter-sized chunks

½ cup chopped juicy tomatoes (about 1 medium tomato)

¼ to ½ cup white wine

Pinch of dried oregano

2 small red or green bell peppers, or a combination, chopped in chunks (about 8 ounces)

1 tablespoon sweet *bucovo* or 1 teaspoon smoked paprika

2 teaspoons hot *bucovo* or ½ teaspoon hot paprika

Salt and freshly ground black pepper

¼ cup olive oil

¼ cup thinly sliced shallots

2 tablespoons sliced garlic

½ cup chopped fresh flat-leafed parsley

Preheat the oven to 450°F.

In a large pan, combine the mushrooms, tomatoes, white wine, oregano, bell peppers, sweet *bucovo*, hot *bucovo*, salt, pepper, olive oil, shallots, and garlic. Make sure that there is enough liquid to cover the bottom of the pan. If there is not, add a few tablespoons of water. Cover the pan with aluminum foil, leaving a couple of openings on either side for steam to escape. Bake for about 20 minutes, then give the mixture a good mix. Continue cooking, checking the mushrooms periodically for doneness (they are ready when they are fork-tender) another 25 minutes or so. Do not overcook; you are looking for tender mushrooms in a little sauce.

Remove from the oven, mix in the parsley, and cool. Serve at room temperature with sliced feta cheese and bread, if you like.

SQUASH AND MUSHROOM PIE (*KOLOKYTHOPITA ALMYRI*)

BY NENI PANOURGIA, NEW YORK | YIELD: 4 SERVINGS

Growing up in Athens, Greece, there were two kinds of savory pies that my mother made: cheese pie (in many different forms) and spinach pie (in one form, containing a combination of greens, including spinach, chervil, Good King Henry, and sorrel). I don't think that a pumpkin ever saw the inside of our house. But corruption lurks everywhere. A friend's mother used to make savory pumpkin pie, for which I was willing to beg. The origins of this dish are in the Peloponnese peninsula in southern Greece, where winter squash is used for savory cooking. It is similar to a spinach pie in preparation, although both the texture and the taste are very different. The addition of mushrooms is my innovation. I call for white button mushrooms here, but you can use oyster mushrooms or boletes instead.

7 tablespoons olive oil, divided

8 ounces finely chopped white button or cremini mushrooms, or a combination of both

1 large (about 4 cups) butternut squash, steamed and peeled, then cooled and cut into 1-inch chunks

2 eggs, whisked

2 cups mixed grated mixed cheese (like Comté, cheddar, mozzarella, and smoked Gouda)

5 ounces feta cheese, crumbled

¼ cup dried spearmint (don't skimp on this!)

3 tablespoons breadcrumbs

Salt and freshly ground black pepper

6 tablespoons unsalted butter

1 pound fresh 18-by-14-inch phyllo pastry or 1 package frozen phyllo pastry, defrosted

2 tablespoons all-purpose flour

Heat 3 tablespoons of olive oil in a medium skillet over medium-high heat. Add the mushrooms and cook until they have released their water and the water has evaporated, about 7 minutes. You should have about 2 cups of cooked mushrooms.

In a large bowl, add the squash and mash it well with a fork. Add the mushrooms, eggs, grated cheese, feta, spearmint, and breadcrumbs. Combine well. Season with salt and pepper to taste. (Remember: Feta can be salty, so be careful.)

Melt the butter and 2 tablespoons of olive oil in a small saucepan over low heat. Have ready an 8-by-8-inch square baking pan and a pastry brush.

Unroll the phyllo pastry. Place 4 sheets of phyllo in front of you lengthwise. Cut strips 4 inches wide along its full length. At the end of the phyllo, you will have 2-inch-wide strips; reserve to patch any bald spots.

Preheat the oven to 400°F.

Continued on page 63...

Brush some of the butter mixture on the bottom of the baking pan and lay down two 4-inch-wide strips of phyllo side by side, letting the ends of the pastry hang over the side of the pan. Brush the phyllo with more of the butter mixture, add two more 4-inch-wide strips perpendicular to the first layer, and brush with more butter mixture. Continue in the same way, laying down two 4-inch-wide strips for every layer and alternating the direction of the pastry, until you have used all the wide strips of phyllo and brushed each layer with the butter mixture. If you run out of warm butter, just top up with more olive oil. If you need to patch an opening or tear, use a piece from the reserved 2-inch-wide strips.

Pour the squash-and-mushroom mixture into the baking pan on top of the phyllo layers and smooth the top with a spatula. Fold the overhanging phyllo pastry over the top, one strip at a time, brushing with the butter mixture between each layer. Brush the top liberally with the butter mixture.

In a small bowl, combine the flour, remaining 2 tablespoons of olive oil, and 2 tablespoons of water into a paste about the consistency of pancake batter. Drizzle the mixture over the top of the pie. This will make it extra crunchy.

Bake for 20 minutes, until the phyllo is golden brown.

Allow the pie to rest for at least 1 hour before serving

MONGETES AMB BOLETS
(BEANS WITH MUSHROOMS)

BY CHAD HYATT, CALIFORNIA | YIELD: 4 SERVINGS

As a professional chef, I've always loved wild foods, and that led me to write The Mushroom Hunter's Kitchen *(2018). Lately I've been working on projects related to regional Spanish food, especially food from Catalonia, where my wife grew up. The Catalans are obsessed with wild mushrooms, and this dish is one of the many ways they are cooked. You can make this dish with any kind of beans, like large lima beans or favas. This recipe calls for wild mushrooms, which tend to have a higher water content than cultivated ones. If you use cultivated mushrooms (which are very good in this dish), you do not need to cook them as long, as they will release less water.*

12 ounces dried cannellini beans, soaked overnight in cold water, drained

1 small onion, peeled and left whole

¼ cup chopped flat-leafed parsley, divided

2 large garlic cloves, peeled and left whole, plus 1 tablespoon minced garlic, divided

2 bay leaves

Salt

½ ounce dried wild mushrooms (like porcini or lobster mushrooms)

2 tablespoons toasted pine nuts (see note)

1½ pounds fresh mixed wild mushrooms (like porcini and saffron milk caps), cut into big chunks

4 tablespoons olive oil, divided

Extra-virgin olive oil, for garnish

NOTE: To toast pine nuts, place the nuts in a dry skillet over medium-high heat. Shake often and allow the nuts to pick up a golden color, a few minutes. Do not brown!

Place the drained beans in a large pot and cover with about 6 cups of water. Add the onion, the whole garlic cloves, and the bay leaves. Bring to a boil over medium-high heat, then reduce the heat to low, partially cover, and simmer the beans, skimming off the scummy foam until the beans are fork-tender, about 1 hour. When the beans are done, remove from the heat and season with salt to taste. Drain the beans and reserve the onions and cooking water in separate containers.

Place the dried mushrooms in a bowl and cover with about 1 cup of the bean cooking water. When the mushrooms are rehydrated, about 20 minutes, drain and set aside, reserving the soaking water. Strain the soaking water and set aside.

Place the cooked onion in a blender or food processor. Add the pine nuts and about 1 cup of the bean cooking water. Carefully blend until smooth. Alternatively, you can transfer the onion, nuts, and cooking water to a bowl and blend them with an immersion blender.

Heat a large, heavy-bottomed pot over a medium-high heat. Add enough of the fresh wild mushrooms to cover the bottom of the pot and add a small pinch of salt. Cook until the mushrooms release their water and the water evaporates, about 10 minutes. Add 1 tablespoon of olive oil and continue cooking, stirring occasionally, until the mushrooms are browned. Remove the mushrooms from the pot and set them aside.

Continued on page 66 . . .

Repeat in batches, adding more olive oil as needed, until all the mushrooms are cooked.

When the last batch of mushrooms is browned, add all of the mushrooms back into the pot, along with the rehydrated mushrooms, 2 to 3 tablespoons of the parsley, and the tablespoon of minced garlic. Stir in the onion pine nut sauce from the blender and the remaining mushroom soaking water. Turn the heat down to medium and simmer the sauce and mushrooms for 1 minute, stirring to combine, then add the beans. Check the seasoning and add salt to taste, if needed. Cook for a few more minutes, to meld the flavors. If the sauce seems dry, add ½ cup of the bean soaking water. The sauce should be about the consistency of a thin apple sauce.

Garnish with a small drizzle of extra-virgin olive oil and the remaining chopped parsley, and serve with good crusty bread, if you like.

If there are leftovers, stir in the remaining reserved bean cooking water. This will keep them from drying out. Leftovers can be stored in an airtight container in the refrigerator for a couple of days.

ULTIMATE MUSHROOM HALLOUMI BURGER

BY SARAH JONES, GLOUCHESTERSHIRE, UK | YIELD: 4 SERVINGS

My mushroom journey came to life while watching Star Trek: Discovery. *The first episode introduces the "Mycelial Network," and I got very excited because I knew about this stuff. Growing up in the 1970s, my dad worked in organic farming and horticulture, and he taught me about soil microbiomes. Then I saw* Fantastic Fungi *and I was inspired to start a mushroom garden. I love experimenting with food, and, although I don't eat meat, my husband loves a good burger, so I came up with this recipe. The Halloumi cheese, which is traditionally made from sheep or goat milk or a combination of the two, adds a tart, salty richness to the dish. You can use* queso fresco *or cheese curds as a substitute. Any burger bun will work for this recipe, but I like homemade sourdough buns flavored with smoked paprika and green olives (recipe not included).*

5 tablespoons neutral oil (like rapeseed), divided

2 tablespoons garlic puree or minced fresh garlic

2 teaspoons smoked paprika

Salt and freshly ground black pepper

4 large portobello mushrooms, about the size of a burger

4 slices of Halloumi, about the size of a credit card, patted dry

1 large ripe avocado

1 large beefsteak tomato

4 burger buns

In a flat dish, mix the oil, garlic puree, smoked paprika, and salt and pepper to taste. Liberally smear this mixture all over the mushrooms. Allow to rest a few minutes.

Heat a large skillet over medium heat. Add the Halloumi slices and dry fry until softened and nicely browned, a couple of minutes, then remove and set aside.

In the same skillet, add the mushrooms and cook for 15 to 20 minutes, turning frequently, until they are softened and browned and any liquid has cooked off.

While the mushrooms cook, slice the avocado and tomato. Split the burger buns, toast lightly, and top with sauces of your choice. (I like yellow mustard and sriracha; my husband likes barbeque sauce and mayonnaise.)

Layer each burger bun with mushroom, Halloumi, avocado, and tomato. Hold the burgers together with a toothpick, if necessary.

Serve with chips, Padrón peppers (pan-fried and sprinkled with sea salt), a salad, or coleslaw, if you like.

THE KITCHEN MYCOLOGIST

HOW A LITTLE MYCOLOGY CAN MAKE YOU A BETTER MUSHROOM COOK

I think the most significant realization I had reading and testing the recipes shared by the Fantastic Fungi community is that when it comes to cooking, mushrooms really don't have anything to do with plants. We often lump mushrooms with vegetables, but they are very different organisms, and if you want to get the most out of cooking and eating them, it helps to understand them on their own terms. I think that's why mushroom hunters tend to be good mushroom cooks: They are often accomplished amateur mycologists. Fungi are so different from other life-forms that eaters of mushrooms have their own name: plant eaters are *vegetarians*, meat eaters are *carnivores*, and mushroom eaters are *mycophagists*.

Understanding a bit of the biology of mushrooms can inform how you cook them. Let's start at the beginning: what are mushrooms? They are the fruiting bodies of some species of filamentous fungi, that is, fungi that grow in long, one-cell-thick threads called *hyphae*. When you kick open a rotten log, that cottony stuff you see is massing hyphae. (*Hypha*, from the Greek word meaning "web," is the singular form.) There are thousands of pounds of this stuff in every acre of soil, living lives as decomposers, as mutualists trading services with other organisms, and as pathogens.

Molecular tools like DNA sequencing suggest that there are about 3 million species of fungi—many times more species than plants—which includes yeasts and molds, but only about 120,000 have been identified so far. In North America, about 10,000 of those species produce mushrooms, about 30 of which are commonly eaten. (The rest fall on a spectrum between poisonous and edible-but-not-incredible, or their edibility is unknown or unacknowledged.) Think of the fungus/mushroom relationship this way: the fungus is like an underground apple tree, and the mushroom is like the apple—the fruit or flower of a fungus. It's the vessel for fungal spores.

When you pick or buy mushrooms, it's helpful to use the same measures to decide what's good to eat as you do when picking or buying fruit. You wouldn't pick a squishy, wormy apple, right? I take ethnomycologist Elinoar Shavit's advice: "I don't pick old mushrooms. No exceptions. I don't eat old mushrooms or old cabbages or old tomatoes."

Select mushrooms that are firm and fit, not wrinkly or flabby; moist but not slimy; and fresh smelling. An ammonia smell generally is a bad sign, as is, obviously, anything wriggling with worms. Wild mushrooms, however, may be colonized by worms in the soil, leaving a mushroom with a wormy stem but a cap that is clean and good to eat. There may be a worm or two, but they are unlikely to be an issue. It's OK to just cook them up with the mushroom. I mean, if you were to eat a plate of those worms, they would probably taste like the mushroom anyway.

As the Forager Chef, Alan Bergo, who hunts and cooks in Minnesota, explained to me, his old mushroom-hunter friends are far less concerned about finding worms in their mushrooms than others: "Those guys say, 'Alan, I can take a good amount of bug in my food.' But I have another friend who inspects the stem of every mushroom, and if he finds a single worm hole, he'll discard it." Alan takes the middle course: "I always sort my mushrooms by quality. I'll generally dehydrate buggy mushrooms. I'm not eating piles of them fresh."

Picking a wormy mushroom is totally a personal choice. Picking an immature mushroom, however, is considered bad style—though it takes great restraint not to do it—as is picking your mushrooms dirty. When the picking is slow, there's plenty of time to brush the mushroom clean of forest debris, but that's not so easy when you come across a bountiful patch. "I get into a kind of FOMO thing where I am too excited to clean as I pick," says California-based

chef Chad Hyatt. And so, we sometimes end up bringing home dirty mushrooms. Whether to wash mushrooms or just brush them clean is a controversy that shouldn't be. "It's silly," Chad says. "Most of the time, I am gathering mushrooms in a downpour."

Freshly picked mushrooms do not absorb water readily because the mushrooms are covered with a water-repellent coat made from proteins called hydrophobins (though not all mushrooms produce this stuff, like wood ear, which dehydrates and rehydrates quickly). But all mushrooms should be washed prior to eating. Just don't store wet mushrooms in plastic in the fridge or, like a bag of wet raspberries, mold will bloom in a few days. You can wash and dry the mushrooms—professional chefs lay them out on a tray and blow-dry them with a fan—or wipe them off and cover them with a damp towel and refrigerate. They should hold for a couple of days.

Molds are fungi, and fungal spores are floating around pretty much everywhere, including your fridge. When a spore, which is like a very light seed, lands on the food it likes to eat, it will germinate and grow into hyphae, which branch and rebranch, each tip probing the habitat in search of food. This aggregate of hyphae is called a *mycelium*, and like us, the mycelium gets its energy from eating other organisms or the products of other organisms' manufacture. They specialize in extracting and absorbing nutrients from their environment by degrading the bonds between complex molecules like fats, carbs, and proteins and consuming the smaller molecules of which those fats and carbs are made.

The mycologist Amy Tuininga once explained it to me this way: if you were a fungus that wanted to eat a steak, you'd lie on the beef and your stomach acid would seep out and break down the meat, and then you'd absorb the nutrients back into your stomach. As long as you had steak to eat, you could keep growing, which is why fungi are among the largest and oldest living organisms. (An endless steak could feed an endless fungus endlessly.)

Say the fungus living on the steak encounters a mycelium from the same species, and they are genetically copacetic. They then can merge, like streams coming together to form a river, resulting in a secondary mycelium that may produce a mushroom whose spores contain genes from each donor. The spore is distributed by wind or some other means, and if it lands on another steak, it will germinate and grow in every direction it has food to grow into. So, when you see a disk of mold on your yogurt, you can't just assume the mold is the shape of a coin that can be lifted out. The blue part of the mold is the sporulating part, but the rest of the mycelium may be growing in three dimensions in that cup of yogurt. As a result, you must scoop as deep as the mold is wide to get the entire fungus.

Many of these mushrooms don't grow in the sense of adding cells; they swell. When it rains, the mycelium pumps water into the nascent mushroom and it expands. Mushrooms are 90 percent water (by comparison, our bodies are 78 percent water), and that's evident when you cook them: Add heat, and what was a pound of mushrooms shrinks to about 2 cups—less than 2 ounces when dried. Indeed, mushrooms preserve quite well, but with a pH around 6, they are low acid, which means they must be dried until they are cracker crisp, and 90 percent of their moisture is removed. Not all mushrooms like to be dried, but others love it: drying concentrates the flavor of porcini, shiitake, and morels, for example. But dried chanterelles tend to rehydrate tough and leathery.

Mushrooms can be preserved in jars, but to safely water-bath canned mushrooms, you must acidify them. Otherwise, you must pressure-can. Unfortunately, the USDA data for canning mushrooms exists only for "domesticated" species—aka the white button (*Agaricus bisporus*)—and canning wild mushrooms is not recommended. But all mushrooms can be frozen. Partially cook them first, as some mushrooms develop off flavors when frozen raw. If you sauté, do so until they let go of their water, and freeze the mushrooms with the water, which is flavorful and worth having when it is time to cook. You can also parboil.

In general, we consider a mushroom cooked when it has released its water and the water has evaporated, about ten minutes. When you cook mushrooms with vegetables, it's helpful to remember that the mushrooms will dump water into your pan, which can end up steaming the vegetables. That's great if it's what you intend, but if not, cook your mushrooms separately and add them to your dish after they have released their water and their flavor has become more concentrated. You don't need fat to cook mushrooms—it's the heat that pushes out the water—so you can dry-cook and then add the fat afterward for flavor. You can even dry-cook them, then boil them, then cook them some more in whatever dish you are making. It may seem counterintuitive, but mushrooms are quite hardy.

Ever seen a mushroom pushing up through asphalt? Kind of incredible, considering they are mostly water. But the reason they can do it is because as the mushrooms swell with water, tough cell walls contain the pressure. Mushroom cell walls are partly made of chitin, a sugar derivative that is structurally like cellulose (which is what plant cell walls are made of) but functionally more like keratin (which is what our fingernails are made of). If you leave mushrooms in the fridge only to find they become tough and leathery, that's because as the water in the mushrooms evaporates (it's dry in there), the ratio of chitin to water increases.

The tough nature of mushrooms is evident in cooking, too. When you boil a small potato for twenty minutes, it just disintegrates, but if you boil a similarly sized piece of a dense mushroom, it will retain its firmness: "Mushrooms can handle moist cooking better than most vegetables," explains Chad. "People often apply assumptions they have about vegetables to mushrooms, but they just are not the same at all."

The presence of chitin is just one of many indicators that remind us that fungi are closer on the tree of life to animals than they are to plants. Indeed, you can cook mushrooms a lot like meat for great results. A meaty mushroom like wild hen of the woods can be "hammered with heat," says Alan. (Cultivated specimens tend to be more delicate.) Grilled in slabs, they cook like a steak, while a thin-walled mushroom like a black trumpet would shrink to a chewy plug.

Mushrooms brown like meat as well. Vegetables caramelize when carbs interact with heat to create that yummy sweetness. But mushrooms don't technically caramelize. Like meats, they undergo the Maillard reaction, in which the amino acids and sugars in the mushroom interact with heat to create that awesome savoriness. In general, mushrooms pair beautifully with meat and meat-favoring herbs like thyme and rosemary. They also pair well with dairy and dairy-friendly spices like nutmeg and cinnamon, and they are a great substitute for meat in recipes, as you will see in this book.

"The fun part is how versatile mushrooms are," says Alan. The challenge, though, is understanding how that versatility plays out in the kitchen. Many of us approach cooking mushrooms in a uniform way: we cook white button mushrooms the same way as maitake, for example. And that's a shame, because just as you wouldn't cook corn the same way as kale, so, too, do mushrooms need to be appreciated for their uniqueness to get the most out of them. One way to do that, recommends Chad, is to sniff: "If they smell fruity, like an apricot, think of what apricots cook well with." He also recommends that the first time you cook with a new species of mushroom, just cook a bit on its own, with no flavorings, to determine its taste and texture. "You just need to get to know them," says Chad, "to know what they can do."

All that fungal diversity means there are a lot of mushroom tastes to try. But it also means that not all mushrooms can be treated the same way in the kitchen. Only a few species are OK to eat raw. Morels, for example, should be thoroughly cooked, as a morel carpaccio can cause severe gastro upset. *Gyromitra esculenta*, the false morel, can be eaten if pretreated properly (but you won't find instructions on how to eat that mushroom in this book, because the specifics of rendering otherwise toxic mushrooms safe to eat are anecdotal.)

Successful mycophagy, then, is enhanced by a little basic mycology. I'll never forget watching California-based mycologist Ken Litchfield put an *Amanita phalloides* in his mouth and chew while I gasped in horror—*A. phalloides* can melt your liver in a matter of days. But then, with a smile, he spit it out.

His message was clear: it's all about knowing your mushrooms.

MUSHROOMS
WITH EGGS

BLACK TRUMPET DEVILED EGGS

BY JILL WEISS, NEW YORK | YIELD: 12 PIECES

One Saturday years ago, I got home earlier than normal, so my husband and I went on a walk in the woods. I looked down one side trail and saw a carpet of orange. I had never seen chanterelles in person, but I recognized them from the show Iron Chef. *On another side trail, I saw a carpet of black trumpets. We saw so many varieties of mushrooms that the next day we joined the Mid-Hudson Mycological Association, and two weeks later, I went on a walk with them and was instantly hooked on mushroom hunting. I still am. This recipe, which is a favorite, also makes a great egg salad.*

1 tablespoon unsalted butter

¼ cup minced onion

1 teaspoon minced garlic, or less if you are not a huge garlic fan

¼ cup finely chopped black trumpet mushrooms, fresh or rehydrated dried, about 1 ounce

Salt and freshly ground black pepper

6 large hard-boiled eggs

2 tablespoons mayonnaise, plus more if needed

1 teaspoon Dijon mustard

Pinch of smoked paprika or Aleppo pepper, for garnish (optional)

Heat the butter in a small pan over medium heat. Add the onion and garlic and cook until soft, a few minutes. Add the mushrooms and continue cooking for about 5 minutes. If the garlic begins to brown, reduce the heat to medium-low. Continue cooking until the fresh mushrooms look like a dark paste or the rehydrated mushrooms look crumbly, a few minutes more. Add salt and pepper to taste.

Peel and cut the eggs from pole to pole. Carefully scoop out the yolks and place them in a small bowl. Add the mushroom mixture, mayonnaise, and mustard, and mix until smooth. The yolk-and-mushroom mixture should be thick but soft; if it is stiff, add a little more mayonnaise.

Spoon the filling into the egg whites or use a piping bag with a wide tip to fill.

Garnish with the paprika or Aleppo pepper, if using.

PORCINI AND SWEET CORN CUSTARD

BY CHARLES LUCE, NEW JERSEY | YIELD: 6 SERVINGS

My father taught me about mushrooms when I was a boy, and hunting them was a rite of spring. But I got seriously interested in fungi during a bachelor-party backpacking trip when one of the guys had a bag of dried black morels, which we cooked over the campfire. Those outdoor meals took my interest to a whole new level. I now forage mushrooms regularly and am always in search of new ways to prepare my finds. This recipe combines Jack Czarnecki's Creamed Corn with Cèpes and America's Test Kitchen's Corn Custard. The dish is best with sweet corn. Unfortunately, porcini and corn seasons rarely coincide, so during the hot months, I freeze corn to have on hand, and then I hope for a grand porcini autumn. This recipe serves 6 as a side dish, but 4 can make a meal out of it.

5 tablespoons unsalted butter, divided, plus 2 teaspoons for greasing baking dish

½ pound fresh porcini mushrooms, washed

2 cups heavy cream, divided

6 cups fresh sweet corn kernels, or 24 ounces frozen

2 teaspoons salt

1 teaspoon soy sauce

1⅓ teaspoons granulated sugar

5 large eggs

1 cup whole milk

4 teaspoons cornstarch

¼ teaspoon ground cayenne or Chimayó pepper

NOTE: Alternatively, you can use six 10-ounce-capacity ramekins. Baking time may decrease slightly if using ramekins.

Grease a 2-quart baking dish (see note). Prepare a bain-marie by lining a turkey roasting pan with a clean kitchen towel and filling a teakettle with water.

Remove the porcini stems and chop them into ½-inch chunks. Slice the caps into bite-sized pieces. Melt 2 tablespoons of butter in a large skillet over high heat. After 1 or 2 minutes, when the butter finishes sizzling and begins to change color, add the porcini. Sauté the mushrooms without stirring, about 2 minutes, until golden brown on one side. Reduce the heat to medium, stir the mushrooms, and cook for another 5 minutes, until the mushrooms are soft and any liquid has evaporated. Add ¼ cup of the cream, stir, and remove from heat. Pour the mushrooms and cream into a medium bowl and set aside.

Preheat the oven to 350°F.

Return the skillet to the stove and add the remaining 3 tablespoons butter. Melt the butter over high heat. Add the sweet corn and cook, stirring occasionally, until the liquid released by the corn is reduced by half, a few minutes. Add the remaining 1¾ cups of cream, salt, soy sauce, and granulated sugar, reduce the heat to medium-high, and continue to cook, stirring, until the liquid thickens and you can drag a clean track on the bottom of the skillet with your spoon, a few minutes more. Add the porcini and their cream and stir. Cook another minute to meld the flavors, then remove from heat.

Transfer the porcini-and-corn mixture to a large bowl. Whisk in the eggs, milk, cornstarch, and cayenne pepper and stir until thoroughly blended, then transfer to the prepared baking dish.

Place the baking dish into the bain-marie and place the bain-marie into the oven. When the kettle boils, carefully pour the hot water into the bain-marie until it comes about halfway up the sides of the baking dish. Take care not to spill any water into the porcini-and-corn dish. Cook, uncovered, for 30 to 45 minutes, or until custard is set at the edges, barely jiggly in the center, and lightly spotted with brown.

Remove the bain-marie from the oven and carefully remove the baking dish from the bain-marie. Set the baking dish on a cool counter or wire cooling rack until the baking dish is cool enough to handle. Serve immediately. Leftovers (if there are any!) can be refrigerated or frozen.

BAKED EGGS WITH PORCINI AND PEAS

BY ANNALIESE BISCHOFF, MASSACHUSETTS | YIELD: 4 SERVINGS

This nontraditional egg coddler recipe is adapted from the brochure that came with some Wilhelm Wagenfeld coddlers I purchased from Jenaer Glas in England. You can make this dish in coddlers or in 4½-ounce ramekins. It is wonderful with spring boletes and fresh peas, although frozen peas work well, too.

3 tablespoons unsalted butter or extra-virgin olive oil, divided

2 large eggs

3 tablespoons organic heavy cream

¼ teaspoon fresh grated nutmeg

½ cup finely chopped shallots

1 cup sliced porcini mushrooms, fresh or rehydrated dried, about 4 ounces

½ cup fresh peas

½ teaspoon salt

¼ teaspoon freshly ground mixed or black peppercorns

½ cup grated Gruyère or aged Gouda cheese

1 white marinated anchovy filet, minced (optional)

1 ounce mixed fresh herbs (like basil, flat-leafed parsley, green scallions, and chives)

1 ounce pea shoots or other microgreens (such as baby arugula or watercress)

Preheat the oven to 300°F.

Use 1 tablespoon of butter to grease four egg coddlers or ramekins. Place the eggs in a medium bowl. Whisk by hand, or use an electric mixer on low and slowly add the cream. Continue to beat until the mixture is foamy, 1 minute or so. Sprinkle in the nutmeg.

Melt the remaining 2 tablespoons of butter in a medium skillet over medium heat. Add the shallots and sauté until softened, about 1 minute. Add the mushrooms and continue to sauté for 4 more minutes, or until they release their water. Then add the peas, cook for 1 minute, and take off the heat. Season with the salt and pepper.

Fold the mushroom mixture into the eggs and cream. Stir in the grated cheese and anchovy, if using. Next, add the fresh herbs and pea shoots and gently mix to combine. Pour into the egg coddlers or ramekins. Lock the coddlers, or, if using ramekins, cover with foil.

Place the coddlers or ramekins in a large pan for a water bath. Fill the pan with enough hot water to come two-thirds up the sides of the containers. Bake for 40 to 45 minutes, until the eggs are set.

Serve immediately with a green salad and a baguette, if you like.

CHEESY BAKED EGGS WITH MUSHROOMS

BY CHARLOTTE GREENE, MASSACHUSETTS | YIELD: 4 SERVINGS

I have always been fascinated by mushrooms, but for most of my life I believed wild mushroom identification and foraging were out of my personal reach. However, as my grandmother—a mushroom hunter who foraged in Latvia in the early twentieth century—got older, I decided to give it a try as a way to connect with her. Nervous about look-alike mushrooms and intimidated by scientific jargon, I joined the Boston Mycological Club rather than striking out on my own. There I found a generous and supportive community, which helped me grow into an amateur mycologist. This recipe is a favorite special-day breakfast in our house. It can be easily scaled up or down.

4 tablespoons salted butter, divided

8 ounces cremini or other mushrooms (like oyster or shiitake), or a combination, roughly chopped

Salt and freshly ground black pepper

½ cup finely chopped yellow onions, about 4 ounces

1 tablespoon all-purpose flour

½ cup heavy cream, divided

½ tablespoon chopped fresh sage, or ½ teaspoon dried sage

½ tablespoon chopped fresh thyme, or ½ teaspoon dried thyme

½ tablespoon chopped fresh rosemary, or ½ teaspoon dried rosemary

4 to 8 large eggs

4 ounces shredded Gruyère cheese

2 ounces grated Parmesan cheese

Fresh herbs, for garnish

Preheat the oven to 350°F.

Grease four 6-ounce ramekins with 1 tablespoon of butter and place them into a deep baking dish for a water bath.

Place chopped mushrooms in a medium dry skillet over medium heat with a pinch of salt and pepper, and cook until they release their liquid, most of the liquid evaporates, and the mushrooms begin to brown, 7 to 10 minutes. Add the onion and 1 tablespoon of butter to the skillet with a little more salt and pepper. Cook until the onions are translucent, a few minutes.

Push the mushrooms and onions to one side of the skillet. Heat the remaining 2 tablespoons of butter on the empty side of the pan until it foams, then mix the flour into the foaming butter and cook for about 30 seconds, stirring constantly to avoid burning, until the mixture thickens into a roux. Then add the mushrooms. Add ¼ cup of heavy cream and all of the herbs to the skillet. Stir the ingredients together and adjust the seasoning.

Divide the mushroom mixture equally among the four ramekins. Crack one or two eggs on top of the mushrooms, depending on your appetite and how much room is left in the ramekins. (Leave at least ½ inch of space for cream and grated cheese.) Season the eggs with a pinch of salt and pepper.

Divide the remaining ¼ cup of cream equally among the ramekins. Sprinkle with the Gruyère and then Parmesan cheese.

Place the ramekins into a baking dish. Carefully pour boiling water into the baking dish until the water comes halfway up

their sides. Place the baking dish in the oven for 10 to 15 minutes, depending on how soft you like your egg yolks. Then turn the oven to broil and continue to cook for a few minutes, until the cheese is golden brown.

Be careful when removing the ramekins from the water bath, as they will be very hot. Transfer the ramekins to plates for serving. Garnish with the fresh herbs of your choice and serve with buttered toast points, if you like.

CREAMED EGGS WITH MUSHROOMS

BY EUGENIA BONE, NEW YORK | YIELD: 4 SERVINGS

Sweet and soft creamed eggs—consisting of sliced hard-boiled eggs combined with ample béchamel cream sauce—are a Southern and Midwestern staple in the United States. Regional and household variations abound, with the sauce flavored by sherry or capers or—in the case of the mushroom hunter—mushrooms! This dish is traditionally served over toast or (my preference) biscuits. A wide variety of cultivated and wild mushrooms can be used, or you can use a mix of mushrooms.

5 tablespoons unsalted butter, divided

4 ounces mushrooms (one species or a mix), coarsely chopped

2 cups whole milk

1 egg yolk

1 cup finely minced white onions

¼ cup all-purpose flour

Pinch of *Urfa biber* (Turkish chili pepper), or cayenne pepper

4 large hard-boiled eggs, peeled and sliced into thin slices (see note)

Salt and freshly ground pepper

2 tablespoons grated Parmesan cheese, or feta cheese, crumbled

1 tablespoon sweet or smoked paprika

NOTE: Slice the hard-boiled eggs thin, but not so thin they disintegrate in the dish.

Preheat the oven to 350°F.

Melt 1 tablespoon of butter in a medium skillet over medium-high heat. Add the mushrooms and cook for about 10 minutes, until the mushrooms have given off their water and the water has evaporated. Set aside.

In the meantime, whisk together the milk and egg yolk in a measuring cup or small bowl with a spout. Set aside.

To make the béchamel sauce, melt the remaining 4 tablespoons of butter in a medium saucepan over medium-high heat. Add the onions and sauté until they become transparent, about 6 minutes. Do not brown the onions; if necessary, lower the heat. Add the flour and chili pepper, stir to coat the onions, and sauté for about 5 minutes to cook off the raw taste of the flour.

Lower the heat to medium-low and slowly add the milk-and-egg mixture, whisking constantly. The mixture will boil up at first and seem chunky, but keep adding the milk-and-egg mixture and whisking. As the béchamel thickens, about 6 minutes, pour in the last of the milk even more slowly, and whisk until smooth. The finished consistency should be like gravy. Remove from the heat and add the mushrooms. Combine well. Fold in the sliced eggs, being careful not to break them up. Add salt and pepper to taste.

Pour the egg-and-mushroom mixture into a 1½-quart casserole dish, sprinkle with Parmesan cheese and paprika, and place in the oven uncovered. Cook until the sauce is bubbling around the edges and is just barely golden on top, about 15 minutes.

Serve over or with toast or fresh biscuits. For a tidier presentation, you can prepare this dish in individual ramekins. Ramekins will take a few minutes less to cook.

MUSHROOM AND PROSCIUTTO FRITTATA

BY CHAMBLISS GIOBBI, NEW YORK | YIELD: 4 SERVINGS

I do most of the cooking for our family, because I work in my home studio all day. The kind of artwork I do is so focused that I find cooking dinner every night rather relaxing. We don't eat as much meat as we used to, and mushrooms provide that same carnal satisfaction. We typically eat this frittata with a salad in the evening. It has a strong mushroom flavor, and the prosciutto adds an extra touch of decadence.

4 tablespoons olive oil, divided

2 cups leeks (white sections only), washed and diced

1 pound assorted mushrooms (like cremini, maitake, and shiitake), sliced

1 cup dry white wine

½ cup chopped fresh parsley

6 eggs

1 cup grated Parmesan plus more for sprinkling on top

1 teaspoon chopped fresh thyme

1 teaspoon chopped fresh rosemary

Salt and freshly ground black pepper

¼ pound sliced prosciutto

NOTE: I usually remove the frittata from the skillet by running a knife along the edge, then slipping a spatula under the frittata and rotating the skillet to free it. Just make sure you angle the spatula edge down so as not to leave a thin layer of frittata still stuck to the bottom of the skillet. After unsticking the frittata, place a plate face down over the top of the skillet and flip. Remove the skillet and place another plate face down over the frittata and flip again. The frittata will now be ready to be served.

Heat 2 tablespoons of oil in a well-seasoned 12-inch skillet (or nonstick pan) over medium-low heat. Add the leeks and cover the pan. Cook the leeks slowly for about 10 minutes, until soft. Do not brown. Add the mushrooms and turn up the heat to medium. Cook for about 6 minutes, until the mushrooms release their liquid. Then turn the heat down to low. Cook the mushrooms another 4 minutes or so, until their liquid has mostly evaporated. Add wine, cover, and simmer for 10 minutes, until the mushrooms and leeks are very soft. Remove the cover, turn up heat to medium high until the liquids evaporate, about 4 minutes. Take off the heat, let cool, add the parsley, and set aside in a large bowl.

In a medium bowl, beat eggs and Parmesan together and add the thyme and rosemary. Season with salt and pepper, but not too much, as the prosciutto will add saltiness. Add the egg mixture to the mushroom mixture, then divide into thirds.

Wipe out the skillet and add the remaining olive oil over medium-low heat. Pour in a third of the mushroom egg mixture. Place a thin layer of prosciutto on top, then another third of the mixture, followed by another layer of the prosciutto, then the remaining mixture. This last portion may be less than a third, but it's fine as long as the prosciutto is covered. Sprinkle more Parmesan on the top, cover, and cook over low heat for 10 minutes, until all but the middle of the frittata is firm.

Heat the broiler in your oven and place the frittata underneath, cooking only for 1 or 2 minutes. The top should be barely brown. Let the frittata rest for 15 minutes before serving (see note).

MUSHROOM AND WILD ONION QUICHE

BY GARY LINCOFF AND IRENE LIBERMAN, NEW YORK | YIELD: 1 DEEP-DISH QUICHE, 4 TO 8 SERVINGS

Gary's very first enterprises were wild-food dinners on Saturdays and walks to gather the wild foods on Thursdays. Soon after he started that, we went on our first mushroom walk together and he started teaching at the New York Botanical Garden. At the early wild-food dinners, we included dried morels rehydrated in the cream we used for the quiche, and we sometimes made our crust from the recipe in Euell Gibbons's Stalking the Wild Asparagus *(not published here). When I went to check the recipe, I saw that Gary had quoted the poet Gerard Manley Hopkins in the book's frontispiece:*

FOR THE PASTRY

1½ cups all-purpose flour plus more for rolling out the dough

6 tablespoons cold unsalted butter, cut into little pieces

¼ teaspoon salt

1 large egg yolk

FOR THE FILLING

2 tablespoons olive oil, divided

4 ounces sliced wild mushrooms (like chicken of the woods or maitake)

2 cups thinly sliced yellow onion

1 cup minced wild onion grass, or 2½ cups chopped ramps

5 eggs

2 cups half-and-half

1 teaspoon salt

⅛ teaspoon freshly ground black pepper

Pinch of nutmeg

Pinch of cayenne pepper

1 cup grated Swiss or Gruyère cheese (about 4 ounces)

¼ cup sour cream

What would the world be, once bereft
Of wet and of wildness? Let them be left,
O let them be left, wildness and wet;
Long live the weeds and the wilderness yet.

TO MAKE THE PASTRY:

Place the flour in the bowl of a food processor. Cut in the butter and add the salt. Pulse to combine ingredients, then add the egg yolk. Continue pulsing until the dough starts to come together. If the dough is dry and crumbly, add cold water, a scant tablespoon at a time, until the dough comes together. Alternatively, you can cut the butter into the flour by hand and mix in the salt, the cold water, and the egg yolk with a fork. Form the dough into a ball, cover with wax paper, and chill for about 30 minutes.

TO MAKE THE FILLING AND ASSEMBLE THE QUICHE:

In a skillet, heat 1 tablespoon of olive oil over medium-high heat and add the mushrooms. Cook until the mushrooms release their water and the water evaporates, about 10 minutes. Transfer the mushrooms into a bowl and set aside.

In the same pan, heat 1 tablespoon of olive oil over medium heat and add the onions. Sauté slowly until the onions are soft, about 10 minutes. Add the onion grass (or ramps) and cook until wilted, a few minutes more. Transfer onions to the mushroom bowl.

Continued on page 88...

Preheat the oven to 400°F.

Roll out the pastry dough on a floured surface with a rolling pin. When the dough begins to retract at the edges, you have rolled it out to its maximum size. Roll the dough up onto the rolling pin and transfer it to a 9-inch-diameter, 2-inch-deep pie dish.

Pat the dough into the sides of the pie dish. Trim the pastry to the dish edge and place the dish on a cookie sheet

Pour the sautéed mushrooms and onions onto the pastry and distribute evenly.

In a small mixing bowl, whisk the eggs with the half-and-half, salt, pepper, nutmeg, and cayenne and pour over the mushrooms and onions.

Place the quiche in the middle of the oven and bake for 10 minutes, then reduce oven temperature to 325°F and continue to bake for about 30 minutes, until the custard sets. Remove the quiche from the oven.

Preheat your broiler.

In a small bowl, combine the cheese and sour cream. Carefully spread the mixture over the top of the quiche. Place the quiche under the broiler and broil until lightly browned, a few minutes.

Let the quiche rest for about 5 minutes before serving.

DUCK EGGS WITH MORELS

BY OLGA KATIC, SOUTH CAROLINA | YIELD: 4 SERVINGS

I grew up mushroom hunting with my relatives in Bosnia and Herzegovina, but when I met microbiologist Tradd Cotter in 2004, mushrooms became my life. This recipe came from my experimentation with morels many moons ago. You can prepare the eggs in this dish poached on top of the morel sauce or cooked sunnyside up or scrambled and then baked in tins with the sauce. Whatever way you choose, the recipe is delicious. Duck eggs are huge, so if you use chicken eggs instead, make two per person. If you make this recipe with fresh morels, replace the rehydrating water with chicken or duck stock.

1 ounce dried morels or 1 pound fresh morels

2 tablespoons olive oil

1 teaspoon minced garlic

Salt and freshly ground black pepper

¼ cup chicken stock (if using fresh morels)

¼ cup dry red wine

1 tablespoon unsalted butter

⅓ cup heavy cream

¼ cup grated Parmesan cheese

¼ teaspoon vanilla extract

¼ cup chopped fresh flat-leafed parsley

4 duck eggs

Place the dried morels in a medium pot, cover with 4 cups of water, and bring to a boil over a medium-high heat. Immediately take the morels off the heat and allow them to rest for about 5 minutes. When the morels are rehydrated, remove them and reserve the water. If the mushrooms are large, chop them in half; if bite-sized, leave them whole. Pass the reserved water through a fine sieve and set aside. If using fresh morels, no need to do anything but wash and chop in half if they're large.

Heat the olive oil in a medium skillet over medium-high heat. Add the rehydrated or fresh morels and cook for a few minutes, until they release their water. Add the minced garlic and continue cooking for a few more minutes. Add salt and pepper to taste. By now, the pan should be drying out; add ¼ cup of the reserved morel water (or stock) and continue cooking until the water evaporates, a few minutes. Then add the red wine and continue cooking, scraping the browned bits with a wooden spoon, until the wine mostly evaporates.

Add the butter and let it melt, 1 or 2 minutes, then add the heavy cream, Parmesan cheese, and vanilla extract. Cook for 1 to 2 minutes, stirring, to combine. Add the parsley, cover, and take off the heat.

To poach the eggs, remove the skillet cover and make four (or eight) indentations in the morel sauce with the back of a large spoon. Gently crack the eggs into the depressions in the sauce, cover, and cook over medium-low heat for about 6 minutes, or until the whites are set. Season the eggs with salt and pepper and serve with buttered toast, if you like.

POACHED EGGS WITH CHANTERELLE AND HAM CREAM SAUCE

BY JACK CZARNECKI, OREGON | YIELD: 4 SERVINGS

I grew up in a mushroom hunter's kitchen. My parents turned the Reading, Pennsylvania, restaurant they inherited from my grandfather into a destination restaurant specializing in mushrooms. I kept the restaurant going until my wife and I moved to the Willamette Valley in Oregon and opened the Joel Palmer House Restaurant, a mushroom-forward restaurant now helmed by my son Christopher. I fell in love with Oregon truffles and started Oregon White Truffle Oil, which is run by my son Stephan and his wife, Meghan. And I spend as much time as I can walking in the woods, hunting for mushrooms. I published a version of this recipe in my book, Joe's Book of Mushroom Cookery *(1986).*

2 tablespoons unsalted butter

½ cup finely chopped smoked ham

½ cup minced onions

2 cups chanterelles chopped into bite-sized pieces (about 6 ounces)

Salt and freshly ground black pepper

1 cup sour cream

2 tablespoons milk

4 English muffins, split into halves, or toast

1 tablespoon distilled vinegar

8 large eggs

2 tablespoons minced flat-leafed parsley, for garnish (optional)

Melt the butter in a medium skillet over a medium-high heat. Add the ham and cook until it sizzles, less than 1 minute. Add the onions and cook until translucent, about 5 minutes. Add the chanterelles and cook until they release their water and the water mostly evaporates, 8 to 10 minutes. Add salt and freshly ground black pepper to taste. Take the pan off the heat. Thin the sour cream with the milk and stir into the mixture.

Toast the English muffins and place them on individual plates. Top each English muffin with a heaping spoonful of chanterelle ham sauce.

Fill a large deep nonstick skillet with a couple of inches of water. Add a pinch of salt and bring to a simmer over a medium heat and add the vinegar. Gently crack each egg into a ramekin and then slide it into the water. Poach in batches if necessary to avoid crowding the eggs. Cover and poach the eggs for about 3 minutes. Remove with a slotted spoon and gently place one egg on top of each English muffin.

Serve immediately, garnished with parsley, if you like.

THEY ARE WHAT THEY EAT

HOW MUSHROOMS GROW AFFECTS WHEN YOU EAT THEM, AND WHAT THEY TASTE LIKE

When I go to a restaurant with my husband, and I point out there is wild mushroom risotto on the menu, he always gives me his "Don't do it" look. That's because he knows one of the mushroom community's favorite games is Risotto Gotcha: I like to ask the waiter which wild mushrooms are in the risotto. Usually, she will name domesticated ones that seem wildish, like cremini—the same species as the white button—or hen of the woods. Hens are a great tell, because they are cultivated year-round but available wild only in the late summer and fall, so if your wild mushroom risotto contains hen of the woods in June, they are most likely cultivated. It's empowering to know something about the foods we eat, even if all the knowledge does is help you determine whether to order the risotto.

Why mushrooms grow when they grow, and where, and why some are so costly has a lot to do with the way a fungus eats. Fungi have three main trophic, or nutritional, lifestyles: Saprobic fungi scavenge their carbon from dead or dying things (mainly plants); parasitic fungi get their carbon by theft (also mainly plants, though there is a large group that kills insects); and mutualistic fungi get their carbon by trading nutrients or some other service with living things (again, mainly plants). Sounds tidy, right? It's not. We draw lines around nature, but nature doesn't necessarily color in the lines.

There are fungi that can alter the way they get their food depending on the circumstances, like a farmer who switches to hunting when her irrigation water runs dry. But most of the mushrooms you see in the market are saprobes. They are the rotters that break down plants and absorb the nutrients, but in so doing they also nourish soil and its myriad of ever smaller creatures. If it weren't for saprobic fungi, we might be buried under miles of plant debris.

Some people are freaked out by the rotters, because their presence indicates death. But looked at another way, they resurrect life by cycling nutrients from the dead back into a system that supports the living. I know there are folks who think saprobic mushrooms are somehow dirty because they grow on decaying matter, but they're not. The fungus disassembles whatever it is growing on—say, a pile of manure—and absorbs its nutritional components, like carbon, water, phosphorus, and nitrogen, and uses those nutrients to grow and, in some cases, produce mushrooms.

Most cultivated mushrooms, like oysters and white buttons, are saprobes that fruit without too much fuss and whose preferred food is easy to come by. Cultivation, according to Dr. Tom Volk, an esteemed mycologist at the University of Wisconsin–LaCrosse, is the exploitation of a fungal lifestyle by finding the biological triggers that make it fruit. Maybe that trigger is as simple as providing fresh air, or lowering the temperature, or reducing nutrients. Assuming there is a market for the species, the simpler and cheaper the trigger, the more likely it's going to be cultivated.

But in some cases, that trigger is complex. Mycologist Tradd Cotter, proprietor of the mushroom research facility Mushroom Mountain in South Carolina, suggested that to get some mushrooms to fruit, you might have to replicate the microbiome of its food habitat. For example, *Stropharia rugosoannulata* (the wine cap) doesn't fruit in a sterile culture, whereas oyster mushrooms have no problem with it. The presence of live bacteria isn't a condition for fruiting oysters, but it is for wine caps. "Think of it like this," says Tradd. "What if you needed something else besides your mate to make a baby? That's how it is with some mushrooms. The fungi are actively growing, but maybe bacteria trigger the process for fruiting."

China is perhaps the first country to have cultivated mushrooms: *Auricularia auricula* (around

600), *Flammulina velutipes* (800–900), *Lentinula edodes* (1000–1100), *Volvariella volvacea* (1700), and *Tremella fuciformis* (1800). Japan, according to Dr. Kenji Ouchi, general manager of the research laboratory at mushroom producer the Hokto Kinoko Company, started cultivating shiitake in the mid-1600s. The practice of cultivating enoki mushrooms in glass jars to create the distinctive pale and leggy mushrooms in the markets (in the wild, enoki is tough and orange) began in 1928, and since then, other mushrooms have been cultivated.

The first mushrooms to be cultivated in the West were the *Agaricus bisporus*, the white button mushroom. (Cremini and portobello are also *A. bisporus*, just different ages and colors.) The specifics are murky, but they were probably first cultivated around 1650 in France. Farmers collected wild mycelium and transplanted it to cultivation beds, where they grew out the mycelium, then dried and sold it in bricks to mushrooms farmers. (Some fungi can be dried and then resurrected with food and water—think baking yeasts.)

William Swayne Jr., the son of a nineteenth-century carnation grower in Pennsylvania, is generally considered the first US cultivator. He utilized the empty spaces underneath his father's flower bleachers, because unlike plants, *A. bisporus* doesn't need sunlight to grow. But the mycelium that he bought from Europe easily died, due to the stress of travel or microbial stowaways that might have hitched a ride across the ocean.

Large-scale mushroom cultivation didn't happen until the US Department of Agriculture got involved and financed the development of pure spawn, mycelium grown out from a selected spore. Pure spawn allowed growers to be confident in the species they were getting and, what's more, select for genes that coded for attributes like taste and insect resistance. The word *spawn* comes from the French *espandre*, meaning "to expand." And indeed, it does. One piece of pure spawn about the weight of a house fly and the size of a watch battery can be grown out on sterile mulch and produce as much as 100,000 pounds of mushrooms.

In the United States today, a variety of cultivated mushrooms are on the market, and should consumer appetites continue the upward trend they are exhibiting now, more cultivated types may come online. Traditionally, Pennsylvania hosted the

most mushroom farms in the country, but now there are mushroom farms in almost every state in the Union, with many in California, New York, and North Carolina. Pennsylvania State University, however, remains the industry's primary research institute, and market improvements are being made all the time. For example, in 2016, Penn State used CRISPR gene-editing technology to design a white button mushroom that doesn't brown.

Many tasters consider cultivated mushrooms less intensely flavored than their wild sisters. Certainly, that's due to the amount of time it takes a mushroom to get from farm to table. (But a homegrown *A. biosporus*? Awesome.) There's another reason, however: As Tom Volk says, mushrooms are what *they* eat. Cultivated fungi grown on sawdust are exposed to the nutrients available, and that's reflected in the nutrient load of the mushroom. *Grifola frondosa*, the maitake, or hen of the woods, mushroom, for example, is cultivated on bags of oak chips. In the wild, it grows at the base of mature oak trees, where it may encounter a host of micronutrients. I find the flavor of wild maitake deeper and more gamey, and the texture tougher, like the difference between a lean wild turkey and a juicy domesticated one.

Additionally, cultivated fungi may not encounter the environmental triggers that a wild fungus is accustomed to, like mycophagic insects. Without the insects around, the fungus won't make antifeedant chemicals, "and that could translate into taste—or lack of taste," says Tom. Similarly, fungi also produce chemicals to ward off or kill bacteria that are competing for food and space. "Most fungi produce chemicals that deter bacteria," Tom says, "and fungi are less likely to produce as much of those chemicals in a cultivated scenario."

There are delicious wild saprobes whose fruiting triggers have yet to be determined, but many of our favorite wild mushrooms, like truffles, chanterelles, and porcini, are the fruiting bodies of mutualists, which are significantly harder to cultivate. That's because mutualist fungi depend on living plant partners. Almost all plants maintain relationships with mutualist fungi; they are key players in a plant's nutritional health. Called mycorrhiza (from the Greek term for "root fungus"), the fungus expands a plant's ability to get micronutrients like phosphorus, nitrogen, and water that it needs but doesn't make on its own. The fungus attaches to root tips and trades these foraged micronutrients for carbohydrates plants make through photosynthesis.

When I was in high school, we learned that plants gather water and nutrients with their roots. Well, not totally. They also utilize nutrients that have been predigested by mycorrhizal fungi. The roots of conifers, which are ancient plants with ancient symbionts, don't help feed the tree at all. The roots stabilize the tree in soil, but it's the fungus that acts as its mouth in the soil. Indeed, squeeze the tip of a pine tree root, and you'll smell mushrooms. There are different kinds of mycorrhizal fungi, but the type that produces most of the prime wild edibles we prefer are ectomycorrhizal: fungi that attach to the plant roots topically (versus intercellularly). About 10 percent of plant families, mainly woody plants like birch and pine, participate in ectomycorrhizal relationships.

Mushrooms that are the fruiting bodies of ectomycorrhizal fungi are rarely cultivated, because to cultivate them, you have to recreate the living ecosystem they depend on. Even if you successfully inoculate a Christmas tree farm with *Boletus edulis* spawn, we still don't know what triggers fruiting. It's possible that there must be a certain kind of bacteria present, or a whole community of microbes. Or let's say the fungus lives in a mutualistic relationship with the Christmas tree, and the tree starts to decline, and its microbial population begins to change. Does *that* trigger fruiting? "In which case," says Tradd Cotter, "what's the difference between an oak and an ash from the fungal perceptive? Shit, the trigger may be a nematode."

In short, there are a lot of possibilities when it comes to figuring out the fruiting triggers of a mutualist fungus. It's not surprising, then, that in almost all cases, it is simply cheaper to collect mycorrhizal mushrooms from the wild—which means every wild mushroom you eat has been picked by hand.

One mycorrhizal fungus we cultivate is *Tuber melanosporum*, the Périgord, or French black truffle, because they fetch so much money. Credit for the first truffle orchard goes to Joseph Talon, a Provençal farmer who planted acorns under truffle-producing oak trees and then transplanted the seedlings onto his property. In time, those trees produced truffles.

What Talon intuited was what we've come to understand as kin recognition and mycorrhizal colonization. Biologist Suzanne Simard has shown that a mature tree in a forest will connect to seedlings by means of mycelia, and the carbohydrate products the mature tree makes is utilized not only by the fungus but also by the immature trees connected to the fungus. This gives the seedlings, with their tiny leaves and puny roots and limited access to sunlight, a kind of leg up. When Talon transplanted those seedlings, he also transplanted the truffle mycelium. After that, it was mostly a matter of time—anywhere from five to ten years—before the mycelium would fruit and produce truffles.

Today, truffle orchardists plant seedlings of truffle-friendly trees, like oak or filbert, whose roots have been inoculated with a slurry of Périgord spore (although other types of truffles are cultivated as well). The capital investment of a truffle orchard can cost up to $10,000 per acre just to get started, and that still doesn't guarantee you'll get truffles. Still, according to Jasmine Richardson, a truffle orchardist from Virginia, most black truffles on the market today are cultivated. Because they sell for about $1,200 a pound, some people think the risk is worth it, and the temptation to master the complicated ecology of the truffle and the tree continues to entice prospective farmers.

No one has yet successfully cultivated the white truffle of Italy, the *Tuber magnatum pico,* though there have been promising studies. This is perhaps because the key to its fruiting lies in the soil. "Maybe you need to get a soil inoculant from Europe and get all the [microbial] players on the field, even though you don't know the number of players or who they are," says Tradd. He went on to compare this to an agricultural version of a human fecal transplant—introducing an array of healthy microbes to a dystopic gut: "I'll wager it is the same with soil."

Parasitic fungi live and sometimes kill on a spectrum, and depending on what they kill, they can be easier or more difficult to cultivate. There are fungi that don't kill plants, but render them unable to reproduce, like *Ustilago maydis,* or corn smut, which causes tumors on the cob. Sounds gross, and it's evil looking when cooked—black and slick—but huitlacoche is a specialty of the Mexican kitchen and tastes like a heavenly combination of corn and mushrooms. Huitlacoche farming is not widespread in the United States, but there are farmers who infect part of their crop for niche sales or allow savvy chefs to come collect naturally infected ears.

There are fungi that parasitize other fungi, like *Hypomyces lactifluorum*, which grows on certain species of mushrooms, particularly species of *Russula* and *Lactarius*. Once parasitized, the mushroom turns lobster red, hence its common name, the lobster mushroom. It is the parasite that gives this mutant mushroom its spicy, seafood-like flavor. To cultivate them, the host mushroom must be grown before the parasite is introduced. Most cordyceps species kill insects, and some are popularly characterized as zombie fungi because they colonize an insect's body and, creepily, influence its behavior. Cordyceps are cultivated primarily for medicinal uses. It's not an easy fungus to grow on its natural food, but some species are grown on rice, and they are edible and tasty in recipes.

How you cook a mushroom doesn't have much to do with what its trophic lifestyle is, though cultivated mushrooms do behave somewhat differently from their wild counterparts. Wild mushrooms tend to have more water in them, for example. Culinary choices are more influenced by morphology and flavor. But *why* you can buy certain mushrooms often and relatively cheaply, and others only at great expense and limited seasonality, most certainly does.

MUSHROOM SOUPS, PASTA, AND RICE

ENOKI MUSHROOM SOUP

BY DIPA CHAUHAN, ONTARIO, CANADA | YIELD: 4 SERVINGS

As a functional-medicine provider, I am very interested in mushrooms and health. I created this Enoki Mushroom Soup recipe because I love both miso and mushrooms and I wanted to blend the two ingredients and flavors in some way. Despite their petite size, enoki mushrooms are rich in vitamins and minerals and high in fiber, in addition to being delicious. If you have any leftovers, don't worry: The enoki hold up very well to reheating.

1 tablespoon avocado oil

5 ounces enoki mushrooms, chopped into 1- to 2-inch pieces

8 ounces extra-firm organic tofu, diced (optional)

One to two 10-inch scallions, finely chopped

1 teaspoon minced garlic

6 cups mushroom broth, or water

3 tablespoons red miso paste

2 ounces fine vermicelli rice noodles

2 tablespoons chopped cilantro, for garnish

Salt

Chili oil, for garnish (optional)

In a medium saucepan, heat the avocado oil over medium-high heat. Add the mushrooms, tofu, scallions, and garlic and cook for 6 minutes, stirring frequently, until the enoki are soft. Add the broth or water and the miso paste. Turn the heat up to high and stir to dissolve the miso. When the miso has dissolved and the soup is boiling, add the rice noodles. Turn the heat down to medium-low and cook for 3 to 5 more minutes, until the noodles are tender.

Divide the soup equally into four bowls and garnish each bowl with a pinch of the cilantro, salt, and a dash of chili oil, if you like.

SPARGELSUPPE WITH MORELS

BY EUGENIA BONE, NEW YORK | YIELD: 4 SERVINGS (AS A FIRST COURSE)

Spargelsuppe: *That's German for "white asparagus soup." This one is super elegant and doesn't call for cream. White asparagus are, to quote* Cook's Illustrated, *"simply green asparagus that have never seen the light of day." Soil is mounded over the asparagus as it grows, blocking the sun. As a result, the plant's chlorophyll and its associated greenness never develop. White asparagus stalks should be peeled, as their skin is bitter, but underneath, they are sweet and tender. They are a springtime treat, often expensive, and marvelous with the other treasure of the season, morels.*

1 pound white asparagus

3 tablespoons unsalted butter, divided

½ cup minced white onion

3 cups chicken stock, plus 2 tablespoons if needed

20 small fresh or dried morels (see note)

Dash of dry sherry

2 tablespoons dry white wine

Salt and freshly ground black pepper

Chopped parsley or chives, or minced onion grass, for garnish

NOTE: If using dried morels, rehydrate them in water for 15 minutes, then drain.

Using a vegetable peeler, peel the lower ¾ of the asparagus stalks. Chop the asparagus coarsely, leaving 1 inch of the tips intact. Set the tips aside.

Heat 2 tablespoons of butter in a medium soup pot over medium-high heat. When the butter is melted, add the onion and cook until it is soft, a few minutes. Add the chopped asparagus, without the tips, and continue cooking, stirring often, until the asparagus begins to soften, about 5 minutes. Don't let anything get brown! Turn the heat down a bit if needed. Add the chicken stock, cover, and cook over medium heat, just barely bubbling, for 30 to 35 minutes, until the asparagus is very soft. Take the soup off the heat.

In the meantime, while the soup is cooking, heat the remaining tablespoon of butter in a medium skillet over medium heat and add the morels. Cook the morels until the fresh morels give up their water or the rehydrated morels soften, a few minutes, then add a dash of sherry and continue cooking until the morels are fork-tender and the liquid has mostly evaporated, about 10 minutes altogether. If, when cooking rehydrated morels, the pan dries out before the morels are cooked, add 2 tablespoons of chicken stock and continue cooking until the morels are tender.

Puree the asparagus soup in batches or, as I usually do, remove the vegetables and puree just them, then stir the puree back into the stock. Add the asparagus tips and return the soup to medium heat. Cook gently until the asparagus tips are tender, about 15 to 20 minutes. Add the white wine and season with salt and pepper to taste.

Serve the soup with a share of the morels on top of each portion. A little fresh chopped parsley is nice, or fresh chopped chives. Or I'll often garnish with a little minced onion grass if I find it growing in the yard, which I often do in the spring.

DRYAD'S SADDLE SOUP WITH STUFFED MATZO MEAL DUMPLINGS

BY ELINOAR SHAVIT, MASSACHUSETTS | YIELD: 8 SERVINGS
(WITH ABOUT 25 PLAIN DUMPLINGS OR 16 STUFFED DUMPLINGS)

*In the hands of a creative cook, the Dryad's Saddle mushroom (*Coriolus squamosus*), often considered a weed among mushrooms, can be turned into a delectable culinary treasure. I am an ethnomycologist specializing in mycological and cultural research. I am often inspired by the resourcefulness of people around the world who find ways to prepare nourishing and even brilliant culinary creations from the humblest of foraged ingredients. I was inspired to slow-cook the dried Dryad's Saddle mushrooms with aromatics, and the resultant broth was remarkably rich and delicate. I pair it with pillowy matzo meal dumplings, plain or stuffed with mushrooms, and it has since become my family's favorite Passover soup.*

FOR THE BROTH:

4 cups low-sodium vegetable or chicken stock

14 cups water

dried young Dryad's Saddle mushroom slices (about 6 ounces)

2 tablespoons extra-virgin olive oil

2 medium to large onions (about 15 ounces), ends trimmed, quartered

3 cloves garlic, skin on, halved lengthwise

2 bay leaves

5 sprigs fresh thyme

1 tablespoon McCormick Perfect Pinch Italian Seasoning or similar mix of dried herbs

1 large leek (about 12 ounces), both white and green parts cut in chunks

4 medium to large carrots (about 10 ounces), peeled and cut in chunks

2 to 3 celery ribs (about 4.5 ounces), cut in chunks

1 parsnip root (about 4 ounces), peeled and cut in chunks

1 green bell pepper (about 6 ounces), seeds and stem removed, quartered

½ bunch fresh parsley (about 1.5 ounces) with stems

2 large fresh dill sprigs with stems

1 tablespoon ketchup

2 tablespoons Osem Chicken Style Consomme powder or 2 Knorr Chicken Flavor Bouillon cubes (see note)

¼ teaspoon black peppercorns

Salt

2 tablespoons fresh parsley for garnish, finely chopped

FOR THE MATZO MEAL DUMPLING DOUGH:

1 cup Manischewitz matzo meal

2 teaspoons baking powder

1 teaspoon salt

Pinch of freshly ground black pepper

Pinch of freshly ground nutmeg

4 large eggs

4 tablespoons olive oil, canola oil, or a mix of oil and chicken schmaltz

2 tablespoons finely chopped parsley

FOR THE DRYAD'S SADDLE MUSHROOM STUFFING:

1 tablespoon olive oil

1 tablespoon unsalted butter

1 cup tightly packed, finely chopped fresh and tender pieces of young Dryad's Saddle mushrooms, or other mushrooms

3 tablespoons minced shallot or onion

½ teaspoon finely chopped fresh thyme

⅛ teaspoon finely minced garlic (oven-roasted is best)

2 tablespoons dry white wine

2 tablespoons orange juice

½ teaspoon Dijon mustard

Pinch of freshly ground black pepper

Pinch of freshly ground nutmeg

¼ teaspoon Lipton Onion Recipe Soup & Dip Mix, powder only

9 tablespoons Dryad's Saddle broth or other stock

⅛ teaspoon lemon zest

1 tablespoon finely chopped parsley

7 drops dark-roasted sesame oil

FOR THE DUMPLING COOKING WATER:

12 cups water

6 teaspoons kosher salt

2 sprigs parsley

Continued on page 104...

TO MAKE THE BROTH:
In a medium saucepan, bring to a boil the vegetable or chicken stock along with 2 cups of the water. Place the dried Dryad's Saddle mushroom slices in a bowl, pour the boiling stock and water over the slices, and cover the bowl.

In an 8-quart stock pot over high heat, heat the olive oil and onion, garlic, bay leaves, thyme sprigs, and Italian seasoning. Sauté for 3 minutes.

Add the Dryad's Saddle mushroom slices and their soaking liquid and then all remaining ingredients, except salt and chopped parsley for garnish. The water in the pot should cover the solids by 1 to 2 inches. Bring to a boil, lower the heat to medium-low, partially cover the pot, and simmer for 2½ hours.

Add salt to taste, cover, and let cool in pot for 1 hour. Strain and reserve the stock and a few carrot chunks to slice for garnish. Discard the remaining solids.

TO MAKE THE MATZO MEAL DUMPLING DOUGH:
Place the dry ingredients in a bowl and whisk to combine. In a separate bowl, whisk the eggs, oil, and parsley. Incorporate the wet ingredients into the dry ones, cover, and refrigerate for 1 hour.

TO MAKE THE DRYAD'S SADDLE MUSHROOM STUFFING:
Heat oil and butter in a medium pan over medium heat, add mushrooms, shallots, and thyme, and sauté for 2 minutes. Stir in garlic, white wine, orange juice, Dijon mustard, black pepper, and nutmeg. Sauté until liquid is absorbed, about 1 to 2 minutes.

Dissolve the consommé powder in 9 tablespoons Dryad's Saddle stock or other stock and add to the pan. Partially cover the pan and sauté until the liquid is absorbed, about 3 to 5 minutes. Add lemon zest, parsley, and sesame oil, then stir, remove from heat, and let cool.

NOTE: To make plain matzo meal dumplings, place the ingredients for the dumpling cooking water in a 6-quart stock pot, bring to a boil, partially cover, then lower to a bubbly simmer.

With damp hands, divide the dough into 25 pieces. Roll a piece of dough into a ball and slide it gently into the simmering water. Repeat with the rest of the dough pieces. Partially cover the pot and cook in the simmering water for 30 minutes. Remove from heat and cover.

TO MAKE THE MUSHROOM STUFFED MATZO MEAL DUMPLINGS (SEE NOTE):

With damp hands, divide the matzo meal dumpling dough into 16 pieces, and roll each one into a ball. Press a dough ball into the palm of the hand to form a 1/3-inch-thick disk. Place 1 teaspoon mushroom stuffing in the center of the disk, fold the dough to completely cover the stuffing and squeeze gently to reform into a ball. Gently slide it into the simmering water, and repeat with the remaining dough. Partially cover the pot and cook in the simmering water for 30 minutes.

To serve the soup and dumplings, place 3 plain or 2 mushroom-stuffed dumplings in a bowl, ladle hot Dryad's Saddle broth over the dumplings, garnish with the reserved carrot slices and chopped parsley, and serve piping hot.

LOBSTER MUSHROOM CHOWDAH

BY GRAHAM STEINRUCK, WASHINGTON | YIELD: 4 SERVINGS

I was cleaning out a warehouse in Denver when I found a little book by Gary Lincoff called National Audubon Society Field Guide to North American Mushrooms. *I was already into magic mushrooms, but the sheer number of species was news to me. Then, one summer, I was walking around in Colorado's Indian Peaks Wilderness, and there were mushrooms everywhere. Not so long after that, I found a used copy of Vera Evenson's* Mushrooms of Colorado and the Southern Rocky Mountains, *and that was the game changer. I had to know more about these things. Now, as a professional chef specializing in wild foods, one of my main focuses is mushrooms, as in this recipe, which is inspired by my grandmother Jeanne's seafood chowder. You can make this soup thicker by adding cornstarch, though it doesn't need it.*

1 tablespoon olive oil

1 cup chopped sweet onion

½ pound fresh lobster mushrooms, diced, or ½ ounce dried lobster mushrooms, rehydrated in warm water, drained, and diced

2 to 3 stalks celery, diced

1 tablespoon minced garlic

Salt and freshly ground black pepper

⅓ cup dry vermouth

4 cups vegetable or mushroom stock

2 to 3 medium (12 ounces) white potatoes, peeled and diced

1 cup (2 ears) fresh corn kernels

2 cups heavy cream, or 1 can (13.5 ounces) full-fat coconut milk

1 tablespoon butter (optional)

1 tablespoon cornstarch mixed with 1 tablespoon cold water (optional)

Pinch of cayenne pepper

2 tablespoons chopped fresh flat-leafed parsley, for garnish

Heat the olive oil in a large pot over medium heat. Add the onions and cook for a few minutes, until they are translucent. Add the lobster mushrooms and cook for another 1 or 2 minutes, until the moisture has released from the mushrooms. Add the celery and garlic and cook for 1 minute, then add salt and pepper to taste. Add the vermouth and deglaze the pan with it, scraping up the browned bits of mushroom with a wooden spoon. Allow the vermouth to evaporate, 1 minute or so more, then add the stock, potatoes, corn, and more salt and pepper to taste. Add enough water to just cover the ingredients in liquid. Bring to a simmer and then lower the heat and cook on medium-low heat until the potatoes are fork-tender, about 20 minutes.

Add the cream (and butter and cornstarch-and-water mixture, if using) and the cayenne pepper. Bring to a simmer, stirring often, until slightly thickened, about 10 minutes. Be careful not to get the soup too hot, or the cream will curdle. Check the seasoning, ladle into bowls, and garnish with chopped parsley.

I love this with buttered toast, and Grandma Jeanne likes to dump a shot of vermouth on top of each serving.

SMOKY BLACK BEAN AND HUITLACOCHE SOUP

BY SEBASTIAN CAROSI, OREGON | YIELD: 4 SERVINGS

I learned about huitlacoche when I lived along the Colorado River and a corn farmer who was half Hopi, half Latino turned me on to this pathogen of corn. For him, it was a good problem to have. The fungus, which forms tumors or galls on the ears, has a unique flavor that is at once mushroom and corn. In the past few years, I have seen local corn farmers here in Oregon selling ears infected with the fungus. For some people, huitlacoche is a luxury ingredient—it's known as the truffle of Mexico—but for others, it's just home cooking. The first way I tasted it was in a squash blossom quesadilla, but it is also excellent in this black bean soup.

FOR THE SOUP

¼ cup rendered bacon fat

1½ cups diced sweet onions

½ cup diced carrots

¼ cup chopped garlic

12 ounces dried organic black beans

2 tablespoons chipotle adobo

1 fresh California bay leaf or dried bay leaf

1 tablespoon ground cumin

1 teaspoon dried Mexican oregano

½ teaspoon ground coriander

½ teaspoon dried epazote

2 teaspoons salt

6 cups chicken stock or water

¼ cup chopped fresh or canned
   huitlacoche

FOR THE GARNISH

½ cup diced avocado

1 tablespoon fresh squeezed lime juice

1 teaspoon minced red jalapeño pepper

1 tablespoon minced fresh cilantro

½ teaspoon thinly sliced green jalapeño
   pepper

1 tablespoon extra-virgin olive oil

½ cup crema or sour cream (optional)

TO MAKE THE SOUP:

Heat the bacon fat in a large soup pot over medium heat. Add the onions, carrots, and garlic. Sweat the vegetables, stirring often, until the onions are translucent, 10 to 12 minutes. Add the black beans, chipotle adobo, bay leaf, cumin, oregano, coriander, epazote, salt, and stock and stir to combine. Bring to a boil, then reduce to medium-low heat and let cook at a very gentle boil for about 2 hours, or until the beans are extremely tender and creamy.

Remove the bay leaf, add the huitlacoche, and stir well. Cook for about 5 minutes to heat and distribute the huitlacoche flavor throughout the soup.

Using a handheld immersion blender (or a food processor or blender), puree the soup if you like. Adjust the seasoning (Remember: Beans soak up a lot of salt.)

TO MAKE THE GARNISH:

Gently combine the avocado, lime juice, red jalapeño, cilantro, green jalapeño, and olive oil in a small bowl. Note that this salad is spicy, so alter the jalapeño portions to your taste.

To serve, ladle soup into four bowls and garnish each bowl with a little pile of the avocado salad. Serve with crema or sour cream, if you like.

MATSUTAKE DOBIN MUSHI

BY LANGDON COOK, WASHINGTON | YIELD: 4 SERVINGS

I've been hunting matsutake for years, and through my research for my book, The Mushroom Hunters, *the second book in a trilogy on wild foods. I have tried many different ways to prepare them. I first tried this dish at Shiro's, a beloved sushi parlor in Seattle, and I later learned how to make* dobin mushi *from a great Japanese chef, Taichi Kitamura. A* dobin *is a small Japanese teapot, and* mushi *means "to steam." Matsutake is a traditional way to flavor this subtle soup, which is typically made with* kombu dashi *(kelp broth) and shellfish.*

4 cups *kombu dashi* (kelp broth) stock (see note)

8 Manila clams, or 2 tablespoons clam juice

8 medium shrimp, peeled, and shells reserved

2 tablespoons sake

1 teaspoon shoyu (soy sauce)

¼ teaspoon salt, or to taste

2 small to medium matsutake buttons, thinly sliced

4 baby bok choy (or other mild green), halved, about ½ pound

5 to 6 ounces pound whitefish fillet (such as cod or halibut), cut into 12 thin, bite-sized pieces

2 yuzu, halved, or 4 lime wedge

NOTE: Whether using *dashi* powder, packets, or dried kelp to make the stock, follow the instructions on the package. The stock can be prepared one day in advance and refrigerated.

Heat the *kombu dashi* clams (or clam juice if using instead) and shrimp shells in a medium pot over medium heat. Simmer without bringing to a boil until the clams open (if using), or about 5 minutes. Strain the *dashi*, discard the shrimp shells, and reserve clam meat for another use or cook's treat. Season the clear broth with sake, soy sauce, and salt to taste. Simmer over medium-low heat until the alcohol has cooked off, a few minutes.

If using *dobin mushi* teapots, divide equal portions of sliced matsutake, greens, shrimp, and fish between the teapots, then add the hot broth, and replace lids. Place the teapots in a bamboo steamer over a pot of boiling water and steam for a few minutes. (You can also steam in a wok with a rack and lid.) This gentle steaming allows the matsutake to fully infuse the broth while the shrimp, fish, and greens poach. If you are not using teapots, add mushrooms, greens, shrimp, and fish to the *dashi* pot, cover, and gently simmer a few minutes, until the fish is cooked through, then ladle into small bowls and cover with foil or small plates.

Serve each teapot (or bowl) with a half yuzu or lime wedge. Remove lids to inhale the autumn aroma.

CRAB AND CORDYCEPS BISQUE

BY SEBASTIAN CAROSI, OREGON | YIELD: 4 SERVINGS

My family comes from Abruzzo in Italy, where it was a way of life to forage, but when my parents immigrated to the United States, they became detached from the woods. I got into food because I wanted to showcase my farmer, forager, and Italian roots. Mushrooms are one of the most versatile foods on the planet. Cordyceps, the mushrooms used in this recipe, are part of my diet and part of my medicine. Combining them with the particularly sweet and meaty Pacific Northwest Dungeness crab seemed like it was meant to be.

FOR THE SOUP

6 tablespoons salted butter

1 cup finely diced sweet onion

½ cup finely diced carrots

½ cup finely diced fennel (save fronds for garnish)

½ cup finely diced celery

1 tablespoon minced garlic

¼ cup all-purpose flour

5 cups shrimp stock, water, or fish stock

1½ cups chopped roasted red bell peppers (I like piquillo peppers)

2 tablespoons tomato paste

¾ pound fresh Dungeness or other crab, divided (reserve 2 ounces for garnish)

½ teaspoon Old Bay Seasoning

Salt and freshly ground black pepper

½ teaspoon chipotle adobo, pureed

¼ ounce whole dried cordyceps

1 cup heavy cream

FOR THE CRAB SALAD GARNISH

1 tablespoon lemon juice

1 tablespoon olive oil

1 tablespoon finely chopped chives

1 tablespoon mayonnaise

Fennel fronds, minced, and whole chive blossoms, for garnish (optional)

TO MAKE THE SOUP:

Heat the butter in a 5-quart sauce pot over medium-high heat. Add the onions, carrots, fennel, and celery and cook until the onions are translucent, about 8 minutes. Add the garlic and continue cooking for an additional 2 minutes to soften. Sprinkle the flour over the vegetables and stir to coat thoroughly. Add the stock, roasted peppers, tomato paste, crabmeat (reserving 2 ounces for garnish), Old Bay Seasoning, salt, pepper, and chipotle adobo puree. Turn the heat down to medium-low and simmer for 10 minutes to meld the flavors. Add the cordyceps and continue cooking for an additional 15 minutes, stirring occasionally, until they are tender.

To puree the soup, use an immersion blender, or process in batches in a food processor or blender. The soup may be pureed until smooth, but does not have to be. Return the soup to the sauce pot, add the heavy cream, adjust the seasonings, and warm until heated through over medium-low heat.

TO MAKE THE CRAB SALAD GARNISH:

Carefully mix the reserved 2 ounces of crab with the lemon juice, olive oil, chives, and mayonnaise in a small bowl.

Serve the hot soup in bowls, garnished with fresh crab salad, minced fennel fronds, and fresh chive blossoms.

CREAM OF PORCINI SOUP WITH CHICKEN

BY THOMAS JELEN, CALIFORNIA | YIELD: 4 SERVINGS

Mushroom hunting is a hobby I started when I moved to Northern California in 2006. After years of cooking and eating boletes, I made this soup for our Mendocino Coast Mushroom Club dinner, and everybody loved it. This rich soup is perfect to make with homemade chicken or turkey stock and leftover boiled meat. When cooking for a large group (over 6 people), I will bake a whole chicken, strip off the meat to use in the soup, and make at least 2 quarts of stock with the roasted bones. Alternatively, you can boil a bone-in chicken breast in 2 quarts of chicken stock until it is very tender and use that meat in the dish—plus, this method fortifies the stock!

6 cups chicken stock, divided

4 ounces dried porcini

2 tablespoons unsalted butter

2 tablespoons extra-virgin olive oil, divided

½ heaping cup mirepoix of mixed minced celery, onion, and green pepper

¼ cup minced yellow onions

4 large garlic cloves, roasted (see note)

Pinch of coriander seeds

½ teaspoon fresh thyme leaves

Pinch of ground cardamom

Pinch of cayenne pepper

Salt and freshly ground black pepper

1 cup chopped carrot

1 cup rough chopped butternut or acorn squash

1½ cups heavy cream

Pinch of nutmeg

Pinch of clove

About 1 cup chopped boiled chicken meat

4 slices fresh porcini, for garnish

Pinch of paprika, for garnish

NOTE: To roast the garlic, place unpeeled whole garlic cloves in a small baking dish and cook in a 400°F oven for 15 minutes, then squeeze the roasted garlic out of its skin.

Warm 2 cups of chicken stock in a small pan over medium heat, a few minutes. Place the dried porcini in a bowl and cover with the warm chicken broth. Let rest for about 20 minutes, until the porcini are rehydrated. Squeeze the broth out of the porcini, reserve the liquid, and chop the mushrooms.

In a large stockpot over medium heat, melt the butter and add 1 tablespoon of olive oil, then add the mirepoix. Cook until tender, about 5 minutes. Add the mushrooms and continue cooking, stirring frequently, until the mushrooms and vegetables begin to brown, another 5 minutes or so. Add the onions, garlic, coriander seeds, thyme, cardamom, cayenne, and salt and pepper to taste, and continue to cook until the onions soften, about 6 minutes. Add 4 cups of chicken stock, the rehydration liquid, the carrots, and the squash and cook, covered, over medium-high heat, stirring frequently, for 10 to 15 minutes, until the carrots and squash are very tender.

Remove the pot from the heat. With an immersion blender or in batches in a blender or food processor, puree the mixture to a smooth consistency. Return the soup to the pot and turn down the heat to medium-low. Add the cream and bring to nearly boiling, a few minutes, then turn off the heat. Stir in the nutmeg and clove, and add the chicken meat.

To prepare the garnish, heat the remaining 1 tablespoon of oil in a medium skillet over high heat. (You can also use a grill pan.) Add the four porcini slices and sauté for a few minutes, until they become a caramel color, then flip them over and brown the other side, 1 or 2 more minutes.

Divide the soup equally among four bowls. Float a porcini slice on top of each serving and dust with paprika.

CHANTERELLE VICHYSSOISE

BY JEAN O. FAHEY, NEW YORK | YIELD: 4 SERVINGS

During the COVID-19 pandemic in 2020, my club, the Central New York Mycological Society, only met outdoors. I was committed to doing a mycophagy program, so I made it into a tailgate event after a masked foray. This soup is one of the dishes I made for the program. Leeks can be sandy, so make sure they are washed well. One way to wash them is to slice them lengthwise and wash between the rings. You can use fresh or frozen mushrooms in this soup, but frozen chanterelles do not need to be defrosted before cooking, as they can get rubbery.

1 tablespoon unsalted butter

3 tablespoon extra-virgin olive oil, divided

3 cups chopped leeks, white part only, well washed

½ cup minced onions

1 pound Yukon Gold potatoes, peeled and chopped

4 cups chicken stock or vegetable broth

½ cup dry white wine

2 to 3 cups sliced fresh or frozen chanterelle mushrooms, 8 to 12 ounces

1 to 1½ cups heavy cream

Salt and white pepper

2 tablespoons minced chives, for garnish

Heat the butter and 1 tablespoon of olive oil in a large soup pot over medium-high heat. Add the leeks and onions and sauté until soft, about 4 minutes. Turn the heat down to medium and add the potatoes, stock, and wine. Cover and simmer until the vegetables are tender, about 15 minutes. Remove from heat.

In a medium skillet, heat the remaining 2 tablespoons of olive oil over medium-high heat. Add the chanterelles, turn the heat down to medium, and cook, stirring frequently, until the mushrooms give up their water and the water evaporates, about 10 minutes.

Remove half of the leeks and potatoes from the soup pot and reserve in a bowl. Puree the remaining vegetables until very smooth, either by using an immersion blender or by pureeing in batches in a standing blender.

Return the puree and reserved vegetables to the soup pot and add the mushrooms. Over low heat, stir in the cream and season with salt and white pepper to taste.

Serve at room temperature or chilled, garnished with chives.

SPAGHETTINI AL LOUIE

BY EUGENIA BONE, NEW YORK | YIELD: 4 SERVINGS

I made this recipe for Louie Schwartzberg, the director of Fantastic Fungi, *so he'd have something a little different to make with his turkey stock after Thanksgiving, but you can make this dish with any kind of stock. The Italians call this kind of dish* pasta a risotto, *or "pasta cooked in the style of risotto." The pasta absorbs the flavors from the stock and leaches out starch, which thickens the stock to create a savory sauce. You can cook the pasta up saucy and soupy with more stock, or tight and dry with less stock. Both versions are delicious and versatile. It is best to use thin spaghetti (spaghettini) or thin linguine (linguine fini); both will absorb the stock most efficiently. Thicker pasta will work, but you will need more stock and the taste will be on the "wheaty" side. Very thin pasta like fidelini is okay, but it absorbs fast and tends to become knotted and overcooked. You can garnish any way you please—with a can of tuna in oil, a combination of fresh herbs, grilled shrimp, sautéed tofu, chopped eggs, and capers—feel free to go crazy! In this case, as this was designed for Louie, it is, of course, garnished with mushrooms. You can use a single species of mushroom or a few mixed together.*

1 pound fresh mixed mushrooms (like shiitake, maitake, white buttons, cremini, and boletes)

4 to 6 tablespoons olive oil

Salt

2 tablespoons minced garlic

Hot pepper flakes to taste

6 cups turkey stock (or other stock, like mushroom, vegetable, chicken, or beef)

12 ounces spaghettini

6 to 8 tablespoons ricotta (optional)

½ cup chopped flat-leafed parsley

Wash the mushrooms and trim off any damaged or dirty parts. Chop them into little cubes, about the size of a shelled peanut. Heat the oil in a large skillet over medium heat. Add the mushrooms and a pinch of salt. Cook, shaking the pan frequently, until the mushrooms sweat, about 7 minutes. Add the garlic and hot pepper flakes to taste and continue cooking until the garlic is soft and the mushrooms start to brown, another 3 minutes or so. Adjust the seasoning.

Bring the stock to a boil in a large pot over medium-high heat. Season the stock to taste. Add the pasta. It will be stiff and stick out of the stock. Be patient; gently push down the pasta and, after about 5 minutes, it will soften and collapse into the stock. Stir often, as the pasta tends to stick together. Cook the pasta in the stock for about 12 minutes, until it is al dente and has absorbed almost all the stock; the stock that remains should have thickened to create a sauce. Add a little more stock or water if the sauce gets sticky. The pasta is best served moist with stock.

Pour the pasta into a serving plate and garnish with the mushrooms, ricotta cheese if you like, and parsley.

PORCINI LASAGNA

BY LANGDON COOK, WASHINGTON | YIELD: 4 SERVINGS

For many of us, making Italian food at home means a night of romance: wine (maybe too much of it); endless antipasto of olives, roasted peppers, and prosciutto; some candlelight. It's an occasion. Having a signature Italian ingredient on hand, such as fresh porcini (translated evocatively as "little pigs"), seals the deal. This recipe is adapted from Marcella Hazan's Essentials of Classic Italian Cooking. *While conventional store-bought mushrooms, such as cremini and portobello, will suffice, it's the sweet, nutty flavor of fresh wild porcini that truly makes this dish.*

FOR THE MUSHROOMS

3 tablespoons olive oil, divided

1 cup diced yellow onion

2 pounds porcini mushrooms, sliced

Salt and freshly ground black pepper

1 tablespoon thyme, chopped

1 tablespoon sage, chopped

FOR THE BÉCHAMEL

4 cups milk

8 tablespoons unsalted butter, plus more
   for greasing baking dish

6 tablespoons flour

1 tablespoon minced garlic

¼ cup chopped flat-leafed parsley, divided

1 teaspoon salt

¼ teaspoon white pepper

⅛ teaspoon nutmeg

12 lasagna noodles

1 cup grated Parmesan cheese

1 cup grated young Asiago cheese, about
   4 ounces, grated on the big holes of
   the grater

TO PREPARE THE MUSHROOMS:

Heat 1 tablespoon olive oil in a medium skillet over medium heat. Add the onions and cook gently until they are soft and translucent, about 10 minutes. Remove to a bowl.

In the same skillet, heat the remaining 2 tablespoons olive oil over medium heat and add the mushrooms. Cook until the mushrooms release their water, the water evaporates, and the mushrooms are fork-tender and light golden, about 10 minutes. Season with salt and black pepper. Return the onions to the pan and add the thyme and sage. Cook together, stirring, for 1 more minute. Remove from heat.

TO MAKE THE BÉCHAMEL SAUCE:

Pour the milk into a medium saucepan and heat to a simmer over medium heat, a few minutes.

In a separate medium saucepan, melt the butter over medium heat. Add flour and stir until a paste forms; the paste should darken ever so slightly without becoming too colored, 3 to 4 minutes. Slowly whisk the hot milk into the flour paste. It will boil and thicken quickly, but as you continue to whisk, the sauce will become smooth. The béchamel is ready when it is thick enough to coat a spoon, about 5 minutes. Stir in minced garlic, 3 tablespoons of chopped parsley, salt, white pepper, and nutmeg. Cover and set aside.

Bring a large pot of salted water to a boil and add the lasagna noodles. Cook for about 12 minutes, until the noodles are al dente. Drain and place in a deep platter. Adding a ladleful of the pasta water will keep the noodles moist and pliant.

Mix the cheeses together in a small bowl.

Preheat the oven to 375°F.

In a greased 13-by-9-inch baking dish, assemble the lasagna. Spread a few spoonfuls of béchamel over the bottom of the dish. Place three noodles lengthwise in the dish, then spread about ½ cup of sauce over the noodles, followed by ⅓ of the mushroom-onion mixture, and ⅓ cup of the cheese mixture. Repeat the layers twice more. Top with a final layer of noodles, the remaining sauce, and the remaining cheese.

Bake uncovered for about 45 minutes, until lightly browned on top and along the edges. Garnish with the remaining parsley and allow to sit for 15 minutes before serving.

CHANTERELLE RAVIOLI IN SAFFRON CORN BROTH

BY MARY SMILEY, DELAWARE | YIELD: 4 SERVINGS (MAKES ABOUT 20 RAVIOLI)

I used to pick chanterelles in Seattle, and every time I found a good patch, it would end up clear-cut and, later, the site of a new house. It wasn't until I lived in Florida that I could find bucketloads of these mushrooms, and they were absolutely gorgeous. I developed this recipe for those beautiful little Floridian chanterelles. Not a soup, this is a pasta dish with the ravioli swimming in a delicate broth. I like to make this dish in the summer, when the chanterelles and corn are in season. You can substitute chicken stock for the corn broth in this recipe, if desired, and the ravioli dough comes from Edward Giobbi's mother (see page 137 for his Polenta on the Board with Mushroom Honey Sauce).

FOR THE PASTA

3 cups all-purpose flour plus a little more, for kneading

Salt

4 large eggs

2 to 4 tablespoons warm water

FOR THE CORN BROTH

4 ears sweet corn, kernels removed and cobs reserved

2 cloves garlic, peeled and halved

Pinch of saffron threads

Salt and freshly ground black pepper

FOR THE CHANTERELLE FILLING

2 tablespoons unsalted butter

2 tablespoons olive oil

½ cup minced shallots

2 tablespoons chopped garlic

1 pound sliced fresh chanterelle mushrooms (like yellowfoot chanterelles)

½ cup Mexican crema or ricotta cheese

½ cup grated Parmesan cheese

1 teaspoon minced fresh rosemary

Salt and freshly ground black pepper

TO MAKE THE PASTA:

Place the flour and salt to taste together in a mound on your counter and make a well in the center. Break the eggs into the well and beat them with a fork, gradually working in half of the flour. When half of the flour has been combined, start working in the remaining flour with your hands. Continue to blend the eggs and flour, scraping the counter occasionally with a pastry scraper so that the ingredients are thoroughly mixed (see note). Gradually add about 2 tablespoons of warm water, kneading constantly. The dough should hold together and not be sticky; add a tiny bit more water or flour as needed. Scatter more flour on your counter and knead the dough until it is soft and pliable, about 15 minutes. Cut the dough in half and roll it into 2 balls. Flatten the balls into 2-inch-thick discs. Rub each disc with oil to prevent drying, wrap them in plastic wrap, and let them rest for 1 hour.

TO MAKE THE CORN BROTH:

Place the corn kernels, cobs, and garlic in a medium soup pot (it's okay to break the corn cobs in half) and add about 4 cups of water, enough to cover the cobs. Add the saffron and bring to a boil over high heat. Then lower the heat to a simmer and cook uncovered for about 50 minutes, until the stock is reduced by half to about 2 cups. Strain, reserving a few corn kernels for garnish, and season with salt and pepper to taste.

Continued on page 122 . . .

CHANTERELLE RAVIOLI IN SAFFRON CORN BROTH

NOTE: I don't recommend you mix the dough in a food processor or with an electric mixer, as this will make the dough tough.

TO MAKE THE CHANTERELLE FILLING:

Melt the butter and heat the oil in a large skillet over medium-low heat. Add the shallots and garlic and cook, for a few minutes, until the shallots become translucent, then add the mushrooms. Cover and cook until the mushrooms release their water and the water evaporates, 10 to 15 minutes. Do not brown. Set aside and allow to cool.

Once the chanterelles are cool, place them in a food processor and pulse to chop, or chop very fine by hand. Do not puree. Add the crema, grated Parmesan, rosemary, and salt and pepper to taste and combine well.

TO ASSEMBLE THE RAVIOLI:

Lightly flour your work surface and roll out each disc into a 20-inch-diameter circle, or use a pasta machine to create sheets. Either way, roll the pasta very thin. To make medium-sized ravioli, spoon 10 heaping tablespoons of filling onto half of the circle, leaving about 2 inches between the mounds. Fold the other half of the pasta circle over to cover the little mounds. (Or you can roll out the pasta in strips about 5 inches wide and 24 inches long. On one strip of dough, add the filling in 1-tablespoon mounds in a row. Cover with the second strip of dough.) Cut between the mounds and press the edges closed with the tines of a fork to create the ravioli. Lay the ravioli on a floured platter, dust with flour, and cover with a kitchen towel. Continue the process with the second cake of dough. Try not to make the ravioli much in advance of cooking them, and do not lay the ravioli on top of each other, as they may stick.

Bring a large soup pot of salted water to a boil over high heat. Slip in the ravioli and boil until they float, then continue to boil for a few more minutes to cook the dough. Using a slotted spoon, remove the ravioli from the pot and place them on a platter.

To assemble the dish, divide the ravioli into four shallow soup bowls and add ½ cup of corn broth to each. Garnish with a few corn kernels and a few grinds of black pepper.

FARFALLE WITH BLACK TRUMPETS AND GORGONZOLA SAUCE

BY MICHAEL WOOD, CALIFORNIA | YIELD: 4 SERVINGS

When I first started collecting black trumpet mushrooms (Craterellus fallax) *in the early 1980s, I was looking for ways to cook them that highlighted their distinctive flavor and texture. (I wrote about them in my book,* California Mushrooms, *and there is lots of information about black trumpets on my website, MykoWeb.com.) At that time, Fettuccine with Gorgonzola Sauce from Marvella Hazan's great* The Classic Italian Cookbook *was a regular dish in my household. I thought that black trumpet mushrooms would go well with the Gorgonzola, and the resulting dish was a hit! Over the years, I have continued to try many variations of a blue cheese sauce with black trumpets and pasta—they are all good. This is one variation on that theme. Try it, but it is really hard to beat the original Hazan Gorgonzola version with freshly made fettucine and the added black trumpets.*

4 tablespoons unsalted butter, divided

2½ cups fresh black trumpet mushrooms, washed, or ½ ounce dried black trumpets, rehydrated in water and drained

8 ounces Gorgonzola dolce cheese, cubed or crumbled

½ cup milk

¼ cup grated Parmesan cheese

12 ounces farfalle or other cut pasta

Salt and freshly ground black pepper

2 tablespoons chopped fresh flat-leafed parsley, for garnish (optional)

Heat 2 tablespoons of butter in a medium skillet over medium-high heat. When the butter is melted, add the black trumpets and cook until they release their liquid and the liquid evaporates, about 10 minutes. Add ¼ to ½ cup of water to avoid burning the mushrooms. Set aside.

Place the cheese in a medium saucepan and heat gently over medium-low heat until it melts. Add the milk and the remaining 2 tablespoons of butter and whisk until smooth, about 10 minutes.

In the meantime, bring a large pot of salted water to a boil over high heat. Add the farfalle and cook for about 12 minutes, until the pasta is al dente. Drain and pour pasta into a serving bowl. Add Gorgonzola sauce and black trumpets and toss. Add salt and freshly ground black pepper to taste. Garnish with parsley, if you like.

PORCINI AND PUMPKIN PAPPARDELLE

BY SEAN SULLIVAN, NEW YORK | YIELD: 4 SERVINGS

My friend Alfredo introduced me to his secret porcini patch here in the woods of East Hampton. The first time we went, I got a eight specimens of wild Boletus edulis, *a satisfying number for a novice mushroom hunter. Subsequent trips have not been as productive. Alfredo's "secret" spot turned out not to be so secret; usually, there was evidence of recent harvesting. In this pasta dish, the pumpkin creates an unctuous backdrop that lets the mushroom flavor shine. You can use fresh pappardelle pasta, but remember, fresh takes much less time to cook. I first published this recipe on my cooking blog about extravagant foods, SpectacularlyDelicious.com.*

3 tablespoons olive oil, divided

1 large yellow onion, chopped, about 8 ounces

1 pound fresh porcini mushrooms, sliced

6 cups fresh cheese pumpkin, ends trimmed, seeds and pulp removed, cut into ½-inch cubes, about 24 ounces (see note)

3 to 4 cups chicken broth

Pinch of nutmeg

Salt and freshly ground black pepper

2 tablespoons unsalted butter

¼ cup chopped fresh flat-leafed parsley plus 2 tablespoons for garnish (optional)

1 teaspoon minced fresh thyme or marjoram

12 ounces dried or fresh pappardelle pasta

½ cup grated Parmesan cheese

NOTE: A cheese pumpkin is preferred for this recipe, as the skin does not have to be peeled; however, any edible pumpkin, properly prepared, can be used.

Heat 1 tablespoon of olive oil in a large, heavy pot over low heat. Add the onions and cook gently for 5 minutes, until they become translucent and soft. Add the remaining 2 tablespoons of oil, the mushrooms, and the pumpkin cubes. Turn up the heat to medium and cook, stirring gently, for 10 minutes, until the mushrooms give up their water and the water evaporates and the mushrooms begin to turn golden. Watch to make sure the squash doesn't start to brown on the bottom. If it does, lower the heat. When the mushrooms are golden, add 3 cups of chicken broth, nutmeg, and salt and pepper to taste. The stock should surround, but not cover, the vegetables. If needed, add more stock. Simmer uncovered over medium heat for about 15 minutes, stirring occasionally. Cook until the pumpkin is soft and the sauce has thickened. Stir in the butter and the chopped parsley. Set aside.

Bring a big pot of salted water to a boil over high heat and add the pasta. Cook for about 12 minutes, until the pasta is al dente. Drain and add pasta to sauce. Add the Parmesan cheese and toss. Garnish with parsley, if you like, and serve.

HEN OF THE WOODS SPAETZLE

BY CATHERINE GAVIN, NEW JERSEY | YIELD: 4 SERVINGS

My family and I started to learn about foraging during the summer of 2020 but found that many people were skittish about positively identifying wild mushrooms, so it took us a while to teach ourselves. The first and only wild edible mushroom I've found was a 4½-pound hen of the woods. I used part of her in this recipe. The great things about spaetzle are that you don't need a lot of ingredients to make it, it seasons well, and even if you mess it up, it'll still be delicious! Having a spaetzle maker is helpful but is not necessary to make this dish. You can use a colander.

FOR THE SPAETZLE

2 cups all-purpose flour

1 teaspoon salt

½ teaspoon ground nutmeg

3 medium eggs

½ cup milk

1 tablespoon salted butter

FOR THE MUSHROOMS

2 tablespoons salted butter

4 ounces maitake (hen of the woods) mushrooms, cleaned and sliced lengthwise

1 tablespoon minced garlic

Salt and freshly ground black pepper

¼ teaspoon dried thyme, or 1 teaspoon fresh thyme leaves

¼ cup dry white wine (I like pinot grigio or chardonnay)

2 tablespoons fresh lemon juice

1 tablespoon chopped fresh curly parsley

NOTE: The batter will dry quite hard on your utensils, so I recommend you rinse them while the last batch of dumplings is cooking.

TO MAKE THE SPAETZLE:
Sift the flour, salt, and nutmeg into a large mixing bowl. In a separate bowl, combine the eggs, milk, and ¼ cup of water and whisk until smooth.

Using either an electric mixer or mixing by hand, slowly add the wet ingredients to the dry ingredients, mixing all the while until fully combined, 1 minute or so. Continue mixing for an additional minute to make sure all the flour is fully incorporated. Let the mixture rest for 30 minutes. The batter will be thick, gooey, and glossy.

In the meantime, bring a large stockpot of water to a hot simmer over medium heat. Do not boil. Have a colander or spaetzle maker ready.

After the batter has rested for 30 minutes, place the colander or spaetzle maker over the simmering water and add one-third of the batter. Using a large spoon, slowly swirl the batter in the colander, pushing miniature dumplings through the holes until they fall into the water. If using a spaetzle maker, follow the instructions included with the device.

Allow the dumplings to cook for 4 minutes, stirring to break up any clumps, until they float and are cooked through. Remove the cooked dumplings with a slotted spoon and transfer them to a large bowl, stirring in the butter to keep them from sticking together. Repeat the dumpling-making process two more times, or until the batter is gone (see note).

TO MAKE THE MUSHROOMS:

Toss out the cooking water and return the stockpot to medium-low heat. Melt the butter and sauté the mushrooms for 3 minutes, then add the garlic, salt and pepper to taste, and the thyme and continue to sauté for a few minutes. Add the wine and continue cooking, stirring occasionally until the mushrooms release their water and then begin to crisp up and are fully cooked, about 7 more minutes.

When the mushrooms are done, add the cooked spaetzle and sauté together for an additional minute to meld the flavors. Add the lemon juice and stir.

Serve garnished with fresh parsley.

LINGUINE WITH LION'S MANE WHITE CLAM SAUCE

BY JEAN O. FAHEY, NEW YORK | YIELD: 4 SERVINGS

I am the president of the Central New York Mycological Society and the mycophagist for both my club and the Mid York Mycological Society, so I test wild mushroom recipes all the time. I adapted this dish from one by George and Sharon Yager of the Mid York Mycological Society. It is my favorite Hericium (lion's mane) recipe. I like to serve it with garlic bread, a mixed green salad, and a glass of pinot grigio.

1½ tablespoons extra-virgin olive oil

8 ounces fresh *Hericium* mushrooms, cleaned and torn into bite-sized pieces (see note)

5 medium garlic cloves, peeled and crushed

2 tablespoons minced shallots

Two 6.5-ounce cans minced clams with juice or 24 small live clams

½ cup dry white wine

1 tablespoon chopped fresh flat-leafed parsley

¼ teaspoon dried oregano

1 teaspoon dried red pepper flakes

Salt

12 ounces linguine pasta

Grated Parmesan cheese, for garnish

NOTE: Clean the *Hericium* by removing any bits of wood debris. If using wild *Hericium*, dissolve 1 teaspoon of salt in a large bowl of cold water and soak for 15 minutes to get rid of any bugs, then drain. Tear into bite-size pieces.

In a large skillet, heat the olive oil over medium-high heat. Add the *Hericium* and cook, stirring frequently, for 8 to 10 minutes, until the mushrooms turn golden brown. Add the crushed garlic cloves and shallots and cook for 30 seconds. Then reduce the heat to low and add the clams, the clam juice, and ½ cup of water. Simmer very gently for 15 minutes to reduce the liquid. Add the wine, parsley, oregano, and red pepper flakes. Simmer an additional 15 minutes, until the wine reduces and the flavors meld.

(If using live clams, cook the *Hericium*, garlic, and shallots as above, then add ½ cup of water and simmer gently for 15 minutes. Add the wine, parsley, oregano, and red pepper flakes and the clams. Cover and steam the clams until they open, a few minutes, then remove and set aside. Continue to simmer the sauce an additional 15 minutes, until the wine reduces and the flavors meld.)

While the sauce is simmering, bring a large pot of salted water to a boil over high heat. Add the linguine and cook for about 12 minutes, until it is al dente. Drain and add pasta to sauce. Check the seasoning and add salt to taste. Gently toss and garnish with the whole clams, if you used them, or just the clam meat if you prefer, and grated Parmesan cheese. Serve immediately.

TAGLIATELLE WITH MORELS AND DUCK CONFIT

BY PAM KRAUSS, NEW YORK | YIELD: 4 SERVINGS

Some of my fondest memories of my grandfather are of foraging for mushrooms together in western Pennsylvania , and then serving up what we had gathered simply sautéed in butter alongside baby lamb chops and peas. Those experiences instilled a lifelong love of foraging and of the meaty, earthy flavor and melting texture of mushrooms. These days, I go in search of more exotic specimens than we found when I was young, but the joy of the hunt and of cooking up the spoils remains the same. Confit duck legs are widely available in supermarkets or online and can be stored in the refrigerator for a good long while, making this a quick and easy dish that tastes like it took a lot more time than it did.

2 confit duck legs

2 tablespoons unsalted butter

3 shallots (about ⅓ cup), halved lengthwise and thinly sliced

Kosher salt

9 ounces fresh morels, whole if small, or halved if larger (see note)

Freshly ground black pepper

¾ teaspoon chopped fresh rosemary

2 tablespoons tomato paste

1½ cups duck or chicken stock

10 ounces long pasta (like tagliatelle or pappardelle)

4 ounces (½ cup) fresh peas, boiled until tender and drained, or frozen peas

2 tablespoons plain Greek yogurt, sour cream, or heavy cream

Juice of ½ lemon

4 tablespoons grated Pecorino cheese (optional)

NOTE: You can use cremini instead of morels or use them in combination.

Shred the duck meat into small, bite-sized pieces, discarding the skin and bones. Set aside.

Melt the butter in a large, straight-sided skillet over medium-high heat. When the foam subsides, add the shallots and a pinch of salt and cook, stirring, until they start to soften, a few minutes. Add the mushrooms in a single layer and cook, without stirring, for 3 to 4 minutes, or until they begin to brown. Stir well and cook another 5 to 6 minutes, until the mushrooms begin to give up their water. Sprinkle with the chopped rosemary and salt and pepper to taste and continue to cook until most of the liquid has cooked off, a few minutes more. Add the tomato paste to the center of the pan and cook, stirring, for 1 minute, or until it has darkened a bit. Stir in the stock and reduce the heat to a strong simmer. Cook until the liquid has reduced by about a third, 5 to 7 minutes. Add salt to taste, if needed.

Bring a large pot of water to a boil for the pasta. Salt the boiling water generously and add the pasta. Cook about 12 minutes, or until al dente. Reserve ½ cup of the pasta water, then drain the pasta well.

Stir the duck meat and the frozen peas into the mushroom mixture and cook until heated through, 2 to 3 minutes. Stir in the yogurt, cook for 1 more minute, then taste for seasonings. Add the lemon juice and stir well. Mix in the drained pasta and toss to coat, adding some of the reserved pasta-cooking water to loosen, if needed. Toss over medium-high heat until well combined, then transfer to serving plates. Sprinkle each serving with 1 tablespoon of cheese, if using, and serve immediately.

RIGATONI WITH MUSHROOM BOLOGNESE

BY SPIKE MENDELSOHN, WASHINGTON, D.C. | YIELD: 4 SERVINGS

At our company, Eat the Change™, we promote planet-friendly eating, celebrating the incredible variety of flavors and ingredients the Earth has to offer. In this recipe, I "plant-ify" a rustic classic, using meaty mushrooms instead of beef, veal, or pork. The deep umami qualities of the browned mushrooms make for an indulgent and healthy alternative.

½ cup olive oil plus more to drizzle

1 pound mixed cultivated and/or wild mushrooms, coarsely chopped

Salt and freshly ground black pepper

1 cup diced white onion

1 tablespoon minced garlic

2 leafy thyme sprigs, about 4 inches long

½ cup dry white wine

2 cups peeled, seeded tomato puree (see note)

8 large whole basil leaves

1 pound rigatoni

½ cup chopped flat-leafed parsley, for garnish

NOTE: if using canned tomatoes, select peeled whole tomatoes canned in water. Do not drain; puree the water as well.

In a large pan, heat the olive oil over medium-high heat until smoking, 2 to 3 minutes. Add the mushrooms and a pinch of salt. Cook, stirring frequently, until the mushrooms release their water and the water begins to evaporate, a few minutes. Add the onions, garlic, and thyme, turn the heat down to medium, and cook, stirring frequently, until the mushrooms and onions are golden, about 8 minutes. Deglaze the pan with the wine and black pepper to taste, and cook until the wine has mostly reduced, about 5 minutes. Add the tomato puree and basil, lower the heat to medium low and simmer, stirring often, until the sauce thickens and becomes aromatic, about 8 minutes. Remove the thyme sprigs and check the seasoning.

Bring a large stockpot of salted water to a boil over high heat and add the pasta. Cook until it is al dente, about 12 minutes. Drain and add the pasta to the sauce. Remove from the heat, add a drizzle of olive oil, and toss until the pasta is coated with the sauce. Garnish with parsley.

MISO KABOCHA RISOTTO WITH ROASTED MAITAKE

BY ADAM BERKELMANS, KINGSTON, ONTARIO | YIELD: 4 SERVINGS

I experiment with wild mushrooms all the time and share the results on my Facebook page and website, The Intrepid Eater, along with stories about foraging, hunting, fishing, and food travel. I came up with this dish after encountering a massive maitake in a beautiful oak-filled valley. This dish fuses Italian and Japanese ingredients and methods, as both cultures do a great job cooking wild mushrooms. For this recipe, you start with a whole kabocha squash, which weighs about 2 pounds. You can substitute an acorn squash of about the same weight.

FOR THE ROASTED MUSHROOMS AND SQUASH

1 large maitake (hen of the woods) mushroom per serving (about 2 ounces each)

¼ kabocha squash (about ½ pound)

8 thyme sprigs

1 tablespoon olive or vegetable oil

1 tablespoon hazelnut oil (for flavor; it's okay to use 2 tablespoons vegetable oil instead)

Salt and freshly ground black pepper

FOR THE RISOTTO

2 tablespoons oil

12 fresh sage leaves

¾ kabocha squash, seeds and pulp removed (about 1 pound)

1 tablespoon olive or vegetable oil

1 cup chopped onion

3 sage leaves, minced

1 heaping cup arborio, carnaroli, or vialone rice

1½ tablespoons red miso paste

2 teaspoons fish sauce

2 tablespoons grated Parmesan cheese plus more for garnish, about ⅓ ounce

1½ tablespoons salted butter

Salt and freshly ground black pepper

Chili flakes and flaky salt, for garnish

TO MAKE THE ROASTED MUSHROOMS AND SQUASH:
Preheat oven to 400°F.

Carefully clean the maitake, then pull off one large piece per serving, inspecting it once more for debris or insects. Transfer it to a baking sheet. Cut the one-quarter portion of kabocha squash in half, then into quarters. Take one-quarter, trim the top and bottom ends off, and scrape out any seeds or pulp (see note). Slice the squash into ½-inch-thick crescents. Transfer the squash to the baking tray with the mushrooms. Lay the thyme sprigs on top of the mushrooms and squash and drizzle the two oils over them. Using your hands, toss the mushrooms and squash with the oil until they are well coated. Season generously with salt and pepper to taste, and toss again.

Set the baking tray in the middle of the oven and cook for 30 minutes, flipping at least once. Cultivated maitake may take less time, so keep an eye on them. After 30 minutes, check on them frequently, to make sure the mushrooms and squash develop some color and crispness but don't burn. Once they are browned and crispy, remove from the oven and set aside.

TO MAKE THE RISOTTO:
Heat 2 tablespoons of oil in a small skillet over medium-high heat. Add the sage leaves and cook, flipping once, for about 2 minutes, or until the leaves are crispy and verging on brown. Remove from the oil and drain on paper towels, sprinkling with salt while they're still hot.

Continued on page 136 . . .

MISO KABOCHA RISOTTO WITH ROASTED MAITAKE

NOTE: Consider saving the kabocha seeds for another use! They can be washed, seasoned, and thrown into the cooling oven to dry-roast after you take out the mushrooms. They can be stored in an airtight container for about a week in the pantry, a month in the fridge.

Take the remaining three quarters of the squash and scrape out the seeds and pulp. With a vegetable peeler or paring knife, peel off the skin and dice the squash into ½-inch pieces. They will be cooked down, so don't worry about their exact shape or size.

Heat 1 tablespoon of oil in a large skillet over medium-high heat. Add the chopped onion and cook, stirring often until it begins to soften, a few minutes. Add the diced squash and minced sage and cook for another 2 to 3 minutes.

Have ready 4 to 5 cups of water. Add the rice and about ½ cup of water to the skillet and lower the heat to medium. Continue stirring the rice every 30 seconds or more, adding ½ to 1 cup of water every time the liquid in the pan begins to dry up. The rice will slowly absorb the water and begin to become creamy, and the squash will soften. After about 10 minutes, the squash will be soft enough to smash down as you stir the risotto. The squash should be fully integrated into the sauce, with no visible chunks left at the end.

Once the squash has been incorporated, and the rice looks creamy (about 20 minutes altogether), add the miso paste and fish sauce. At this point, start tasting the risotto—it should be creamy and smooth, yet al dente when you bite into an individual kernel. Remove the risotto from the heat and stir in the grated Parmesan cheese and butter. Add salt and pepper to taste.

To serve, scoop a serving of risotto onto a plate or bowl. Top with a few pieces of roasted squash, a piece of roasted maitake, 3 fried sage leaves, chili flakes, flaky salt, and shaved Parmesan cheese.

POLENTA ON THE BOARD WITH HONEY MUSHROOM SAUCE

BY EDWARD GIOBBI, NEW YORK | YIELD: 4 SERVINGS

The best polenta I have eaten anywhere was made by my mother. She prepared the polenta loose rather than thick, then poured it onto a large (about 30-by-30-inch) poplar wood board. Poplar was used because it has no taste, and the wood keeps the polenta warm. Once the polenta was spread on the board, it was topped with a sauce made with tomatoes, wild birds like squab, homemade sausages cut into bite-sized pieces, and wild mushrooms. My mother used mostly honey mushrooms picked by my father and dusted with pecorino cheese. The board was placed in the middle of the table, and we ate the polenta with spoons directly from the board. In the Le Marche region in Italy, where my mother was from, they say this is the only way to eat polenta. This is her recipe without the wild birds.

½ cup salt pork or pancetta, chopped with a heated knife into dice-sized cubes

½ pound fresh Italian sausage

1 cup chopped onion

2½ cups tomatoes, peeled, seeded, and chopped (see note)

⅓ pound sliced honey or boletus mushrooms, or 1 ounce dried boletes (see note)

1 teaspoon dried basil

Salt and freshly ground black pepper

1 cup finely ground yellow cornmeal or instant polenta

1 quart water

2 teaspoons salt

Grated pecorino cheese for garnish

NOTE: If using tomatoes canned in water, strain off the extra water. Do not use tomatoes canned in puree.

NOTE: If using dried mushrooms, soak them in warm water for about 15 minutes, until they are soft, and drain.

Place the salt pork or pancetta cubes in a large skillet over medium heat, uncovered. As the pork renders, add the whole sausages and brown, turning occasionally, about 15 minutes. (This is when my mother would add the wild birds, which she would cut into quarters.) When the sausages are browned, discard the salt pork or pancetta. Add the onions and cook until they soften, about 5 minutes. Take the pan off the heat and set aside.

In a medium saucepan, add the tomatoes and cook them over medium-high heat for several minutes, until they are bubbling and aromatic. Slice the sausage into ¼-inch pieces and add to the tomatoes. Add the mushrooms, basil, and salt and pepper to taste. Simmer over low heat, partially covered, for 45 minutes.

While the tomato-sausage mixture simmers, prepare the polenta. Bring 1 quart of salted water to a boil in a medium pot over medium heat. Slowly pour the cornmeal into the water with one hand while you stir with the other. When all the cornmeal is in the pot, turn the heat down to low and stir frequently until the polenta is cooked, at most 20 minutes. You can tell the polenta is done when the texture is creamy and the corn is tender. If the polenta becomes thick and heavy, add water, ½ cup at a time. The consistency should be like grits. If using instant polenta, follow manufacturer's cooking instructions.

Pour a ½-inch thick layer of cooked polenta onto a 12-inch-wide board (or a large, flat platter) and then pour the tomato-sausage sauce on top. Garnish with a generous amount of grated pecorino and serve immediately.

CHANTERELLE RISOTTO

BY KELLY DEMARTINI, CALIFORNIA | YIELD: 4 SERVINGS

I started foraging for mushrooms as part of my love for hiking. As an artist, I am fascinated by the morphology and ecology of mushrooms—and I love to eat them. I have honed this dish to perfection, thanks to a few years of really bountiful California golden chanterelles, which allowed me to experiment with the recipe. This recipe is also excellent made with black trumpets or any other kind of mushroom. In a good season, feel free to increase the number of chanterelles in this dish.

4 cups chicken stock or vegetable broth

1 bay leaf

5 tablespoons unsalted butter, divided

1 tablespoon olive oil

⅓ cup minced shallots or yellow onions

Salt

12 ounces chanterelle mushrooms, chopped

1 heaping cup arborio or carnaroli rice

1½ cups dry white or red wine, or vermouth

½ cup grated Parmigiano-Reggiano cheese

Freshly grated nutmeg

White pepper

In a medium saucepan, heat the chicken stock and bay leaf over low heat and let simmer, covered.

In a medium Dutch oven or heavy-bottomed pot, heat 1 tablespoon butter and the olive oil with a pinch of salt over medium heat. Sauté the shallots until they are translucent, about 5 minutes. Do not let them brown. Add the chanterelles and another pinch of salt and continue cooking, stirring occasionally, until the mushrooms have given up their liquid and started to brown, about 10 minutes.

When the liquid from the mushrooms has evaporated, add 2 tablespoons of butter and the rice and turn up the heat to medium-high. Stir well with a wooden spoon, until the rice becomes translucent and starts to make a crackling sound, 1 to 2 minutes. Add the wine and stir vigorously. The wine will boil and then be absorbed by the rice.

Once the wine has been absorbed, lower the heat to medium-low and add 1 cup of the stock. Stir again until the rice has absorbed the stock, then add another cup of stock. Continue until you have used all the stock, about 20 minutes, but do not allow the last cup of stock to be fully absorbed, as this moisture will make the risotto creamy. Do not overcook: The risotto should be loose enough to undulate when you shake the pan. Take the risotto off the heat and add the rest of the butter and the grated cheese. Add a pinch of ground nutmeg and stir briefly to combine.

Season to taste with salt and freshly ground white pepper and serve immediately.

MATSUTAKE GOHAN

BY DR. GORDON WALKER, CALIFORNIA | YIELD: 4 SERVINGS

Matsutake is one of my favorite mushrooms, because its flavor is so unique—a fleeting warm spiciness combined with a fresh shellfish minerality. I first made this dish on a live social broadcast and made up the recipe as I went. Fortunately, it turned out great! I'm a wine and yeast researcher, but I've been fascinated by fungi since I was a kid. As a science communicator, I share engaging educational content about mushrooms through my @fascinatedbyfungi social media accounts. This Matsutake Gohan is a savory, satisfying one-pot meal. In essence, it is a well-seasoned rice with steamed toppings. This recipe calls for soaking the rice for an hour and soaking the mushrooms in mirin and sake before you start cooking. The gohan can be made in a pot, but a rice cooker is definitely the easiest way to make it.

2 cups short-grain sushi rice (like Calrose)

½ pound fresh matsutake buttons, thinly sliced

½ cup mirin or sake

2 tablespoons dashi powder

½ tablespoon shoyu (soy sauce)

Salt

½ pound rock cod or other meaty white fish fillet, cut into chunks

15 to 20 ginkgo nuts, boiled, shelled, and peeled, or ½ cup boiled edamame beans

2 cups water

1 tablespoon *umeboshi* paste, or a few chopped *umeboshi* plums

2 scallions, chopped

1 tablespoon sliced pickled ginger plus more for garnish

Seaweed or sesame rice seasoning, for garnish

Japanese chili flakes, for garnish

Scallion sliced on the bias, for garnish

NOTE: Prior to making this recipe, I often soak very clean matsutake in a jar of mirin or sake for a week or more in my fridge.

Wash and soak the rice in a large bowl of cold water for one hour. In the meantime, slice one of the mushrooms and place a couple of slices in a small bowl or measuring cup with the mirin or sake (see note). Let the mushrooms soak an hour as well.

Drain the rice and place it in either a 4- to 6-quart Dutch oven or the inner pot of a rice cooker. Strain the mirin and pour into the rice, setting aside the mushrooms. Add water, *dashi* powder, and shoyu, and stir to combine. Check the liquid level: It should be about 2 inches above the rice.

Salt the fish and arrange it over the rice. Over the fish, arrange the ginkgo nuts, *umeboshi* paste (or chopped plums, if using), scallions, pickled ginger, and the matsutake slices that you soaked in mirin (or sake). Lay the raw sliced matsutake on top.

If using a rice cooker, cook for 25 to 30 minutes, until the rice is fluffy and the fish is opaque, then let it rest for 10 to 15 minutes with the cooker turned off. If cooking on a stovetop, bring the rice to a boil over medium-high heat, then cover and drop the heat to very low. Cook for about 35 minutes, until the rice is fluffy and the fish is opaque, then let it rest for another 10 to 15 minutes.

To serve, add the garnishes, then dig into the *gohan* with a rice paddle and fluff sections of rice together with the garnishes. Once mixed, transfer to a serving bowl. Salt to taste and add more of any of the garnishes you like. Serve with seasoned nori wrappers or *shizo* leaves if you like, and fill with handfuls of rice as you would a taco.

THE WILD ONES

AND THE ONES THAT MAKE YOU WILD

Not so long ago, I attended a political event in New York City and met a candidate running for city council. "I *love* mushrooms!" she said. "I want to hunt for them. Can I hunt for them in the city?" She certainly can. There are mushroom clubs all over North America, and our own urban New York Mycological Society is active in the local parks. We used to hold forays in the summer and fall and mushroom dinners and lectures in the winter, but as our late and dearly missed club scientist, Gary Lincoff, pointed out, you can forage any time of year. And indeed, there were plenty of winter walks where members followed Gary into snowy Central Park in search of sticks colonized by scabby *Ascomycetes*. He loved them all, bless him.

But most people hunt for edibles, and there seems to be two kinds of hunters: There are those who pick for pleasure and sometimes profit, an odd assortment of gourmands, amateur mycologists, wild-food advocates, and people who just like to tromp around in the woods. Many of the recipes in this book are by just this sort of person—me included. The other kind of mushroom hunter is the commercial picker, for whom picking is a job. When the American wild-mushroom industry exploded in the 1980s—in great part due to the discovery of matsutake, a mushroom highly valued in Asian markets—more and more southeast Asian pickers appeared on the scene, many the descendants of Vietnam War refugees.

Langdon Cook, the author of an excellent triptych of wild-food books, including *The Mushroom Hunters*, has been following the community of professional mushroom foragers for years. He noted that the pickers "knew how to work in the woods. A lot of them had survived in the jungles, running from the Khmer Rouge." Wild-mushroom gathering allowed these populations to make a living despite not speaking the language, and it was something the whole family could do. This was the case along the mushroom trail—which follows the fruiting of culinary wild mushrooms primarily in the Pacific Northwest—up until about 2010, when Spanish fruit pickers began mushroom hunting in California, Oregon, and Washington.

Today, it's a mix: There are still large groups of Southeast Asian pickers, "but it's sort of balkanized," Langdon explains. The matsutake pick in central Oregon is dominated by Southeast Asians, especially Laotians. The chanterelle pick along the coast might have more Spanish-speaking pickers. "The bottom line: Primarily, immigrants do the picking," continues Langdon. "At least 1,000 people and as many as 4,000 pick matsutake in central Oregon. They are a big part of the local economy."

Three conditions are necessary for commercial picking: climate, habitat, and accessible territory in which to find mushrooms. The primo mushrooms are most plentiful in wet, forty- to sixty-year-old forests, where the mycelial network is robust, but competition from multiple fungal species and other critters in the soil is still low. (Old-growth forests, by contrast, are packed with fungal diversity, which is very important, but not ideal when you are looking for a large fruiting of a single species.) Forests in the Northeast, which have been cleared in waves for timber, agriculture, roads, and real estate development, are less prolific—and mature trees tend to be on private property. The great picking in North America happens in the northwestern and Pacific Northwest states.

But there have been changes, maybe due to climate change, that observers like Langdon have noted. In some places, the fruiting seasons seem to have shifted earlier, and in general the mushroom seasons are not as dependable. And that may be because weather patterns, once predictable, are now more erratic. "Mushroom hunting is a little more up for grabs now," says Langdon.

The North American wild-mushroom harvest is much less significant than markets elsewhere, like China and eastern Europe, according to Langdon. Certainly, American consumers are becoming more knowledgeable about wild mushrooms like porcini, chanterelles, morels, and truffles than they were even ten years ago. Within the United States, savvy consumers in places like Northern California can find an array of seasonal wild mushrooms in their markets, and restaurant menus reveal a growing interest in them.

Years ago, I attended a book event for chef and author Jack Czernecki's *A Cook's Book of Mushrooms*. He served wild candy cap mushroom syrup over cheesecake. I'll never forget the first time I tasted a sweet mushroom! It really opened my mind to the possibilities of wild mushrooms. After I wrote a newspaper piece about European truffles, Jack invited me to come to Oregon to sample local truffles at the Joel Palmer House, a restaurant in Dayton, Oregon, that he opened and is now owned by his son, Christopher.

That offer dovetailed nicely with a trip I had discussed with Britt Bunyard, the editor of *Fungi* magazine, ever since we started to debate the practical reality of preserving the volatile aromatics of truffles. I doubted that the premier European truffles, *Tuber melanosporum* and *T. magnatum*, could produce aromatics after a set amount of time, and I asserted that those aromatics could not be captured by lipids for any longer than the amount of time the truffles were emitting those compounds in the first place. Britt said that when he visits Oregon, the truffles there produce aromas capable of being captured in fats for months. I was skeptical, and so we decided to visit Oregon in late February to meet with Jack, observe a truffle hunt, experiment with truffle aromatizing, and, hopefully, settle the argument once and for all.

Britt had carried on about how we would do a road trip, a kind of fungal *Fear and Loathing*-type thing, but during the planning stage, I learned he wasn't even renting a car, but instead had made plans for an extended stay with two (it turns out, gracious and lovely) members of the Oregon Mycological Society that I had never met. Pam Buessing and Don Moore live in Hillsboro, at the head of the Willamette Valley in a suburb set among mature trees, where every square foot of their lot is devoted to food, whether it's gardening or the peckings of a small flock of chickens.

Our first excursion was to Jack's place. I had rented a small car, but because I was a little bit hesitant backing out of Pam and Don's driveway (the property was gardened right up to the edge of the tarmac) that was reason enough for Britt to backseat-drive all the way to Dayton. Britt and I tend to act like squabbling siblings. We needle each other relentlessly. He's also brilliant and kind. But whatever. Every time I braked, he would feign whiplash. Every time I turned, he would sway way over in the passenger seat and pretend he was getting carsick. There were a few stoplights when I considered giving him the heave-ho. But I didn't. We had truffles to learn about.

Up until the 1990s, nobody knew much about the truffles in Oregon, even though Portland native James Beard, in a burst of blustery patriotism, had announced in 1983 that American truffles were as good as European ones. What got the ball rolling was Oregon State University's sophisticated College

of Forestry, said Jack in an interview, and especially the work of mycologist Jim Trappe and his son, Matt. They helped a market emerge through organizations like the Oregon Truffle Festival. Currently, Oregon white truffles (*T. oregonense*), which have an addictive smell—something like a garlicky armpit—cost about $100 to $200 a pound, and black truffles (*Leucangium carthusianum*), with a scent like a cross between a pineapple and a fart, cost $250 to $800 a pound; they are rarer.

Granted, those descriptors are a bit nasty, but the value of the truffle as a food product lies in those feral smells. Truffles are mushrooms that evolved to grow underground, possibly because of environmental stresses. But when truffles went subterranean, they lost their primary means of spore dispersal—wind—and so needed another way of getting their spore out and about.

That's where the incredible aromatics of truffles come in. When their spores are mature, truffles produce volatile aromatics that attract animal vectors to dig them up and eat them, then spread the spore in their scat. There are thousands of truffle species worldwide, and different species have evolved to attract different animals in their ecosystem. (The notion that truffles are aphrodisiacs is misleading, by the way: If you feed the object of your desire a truffle, it doesn't make her attracted to you. It attracts her to the truffle.) The big-ticket truffles, like *T. melanosporum*, evolved to attract swine. Our Oregon white truffle evolved to lure squirrels.

Not all culinary truffles use animal vectors. The desert truffle, of which there are a few species, is probably the truffle of the ancient world. It is mentioned in Pliny and the Bible, and it grows in association with the hardy rock rose family. They are found on every continent except Antarctica. The truffle ripens just beneath the sand, and when desert winds blow, it exposes the truffles and its spore. Desert truffles taste, according to Elinoar Shavit, like a combination of Asian pear and a mild cheese like brie and have the texture of a Jerusalem artichoke when uncooked and a stewed potato when cooked. The flavor of desert truffles is in the fruit body. Not so the European truffles—the fungus doesn't have much taste at all: All the action is in the smell.

Capturing that elusive aroma is the goal of many. But according to truffle oil producer and retailer Rosario Safina, commercial truffle oil didn't even exist in Italy prior to the invention of bismethythiomethane, a chemical that imitates the smell of *T. melanosporum* and *T. magnatum* and costs about forty cents to flavor an eight-ounce bottle of oil. (Rosario says his products are made from real truffle.) My cousin, Maria, who lives in Tuscany and whose husband, Mario, was a truffle hunter, made truffle oil with the broken bits and pieces he couldn't sell. But she didn't make the oil to extend the shelf life of the truffle; she did it to extend the amount of truffle flavor with which she had to cook.

Britt thought maybe Oregon truffles are different. The first thing we noticed pulling up to Jack Czernecki's house was his "trufflemobile" parked in the driveway: a muddy SUV loaded with rakes and grimy gloves, cardboard boxes, and water bottles. Jack is a legendary character in the mushroom world, sturdy and optimistic as a well-built barn. The Czarnecki family have been mycophiles for generations. Their restaurant in Pennsylvania, Joe's Tavern, was famous for its mushroom-forward menu. In 1996, the Czarneckis bought the historic Joel Palmer House, which has become a kind of a bucket list destination for mycophagists. The Joel Palmer House probably serves more Oregonian truffles annually—20 to 50 pounds a year—than any restaurant in the world. It's also that rare restaurant that features a mushroom-tasting menu.

Jack is a truffle raker, and raking for truffles is somewhat controversial, because it can damage the roots of trees and the mycelium of the fungus. It is slightly brutal and totally fun. In fact, I did get truffle fever working a quiet alley of Christmas trees. Inside, the branches were dead and crackling, casting purple shade, the duff pappy and aromatic with humid pine needles. To rake for truffles, you must very tenderly comb the soil around the tree until a white truffle bounces up, like a marble made of gray skin. But even with the lightest scraping, it is easy to rip the tree's root hairs, to tear the mycelium, to rattle the quiet. Raking is indiscriminate, and immature truffles may be revealed. In Jack's opinion, it's OK to harvest immature truffles because they ripen aboveground.

The notion of ripening is particular to truffles in the fungal world. It's not clear what mechanisms are at work when a truffle releases its aromatics, but recent research suggests that bacteria may play a role in the formation of those compounds. Jack and others think maybe the aromatics are a by-product of a decaying truffle, and the aroma is produced by mycophagic bacteria. Whatever it turns out to be, the chemicals in the aromatics produced by American truffles pretty much overlap with European truffles, though the admixtures are different depending on the species.

We also hunted truffles with Britt's friend Toby Esthay and his dog, Appa. Toby is tall and thin, with a long, reddish beard, intense and erudite, the kind of fellow who doesn't trust you until suddenly he does, though you might not know why, and then he reveals his poetic side. We entered a misty stand of farmed Douglas fir about fifteen years old. It was always misting in Oregon—a gentle, enveloping moisture that makes your hair curl and your skin feel like velvet.

We walked behind Toby as he prompted his dog: "Find some!" he'd say, pointing under trees with the dinner spoon he carried for digging. I watched the dog crisscross the forest, nose to the ground and in the air, and Toby explained that scents are like water flowing between the trees, and once Appa crosses the path of truffle scent, she follows it to its source. I could practically visualize the scents floating through the woods, like colored ribbons. When Appa started digging, Toby would nudge her aside and reveal the truffle with his spoon. We also hunted black truffles with a now-defunct outfit called Umami Truffle Dogs. I was thrilled that on the day we hunted, John Getz came along. Getz is a legendary forager, having been there when the Pacific Northwest woods were first exploited for matsutake export.

With our load of truffles, we tested different fats for truffle-aroma absorption. We wrapped the truffles (whites and blacks separately) in paper towels and added them to plastic containers with butter, mild cheeses of all sorts, cream, coconut milk, eggs, avocado, yogurt, curds, and hazelnuts. Every day, we changed the paper towels because the truffles released so much moisture, and every time we opened the fridge, we'd get hit with a blast of truffle aroma that almost made our eyes water, a kind of dirty socks–meets–piña colada smell. It was intoxicating, disgusting, exhausting, wonderful. Of course, the question remained to be answered: Would they last? Pam had kindly packed a container of our infused products for me to take home, and, considering how aromatic they were, I had great hopes. The next morning, I backed out of their driveway, unfortunately running over a lovely patch of just-blossomed crocuses.

Back in New York, I tested the various products we had tried in aromatize. The eggs broke in my luggage, but Pam told me her eggs didn't have any flavor anyway. The cheese was flavorful when I first opened the package, but that quickly dissipated. The butter was aromatic when I spread a pat on toast, but by the time I took a second bite, the flavor has disappeared, like a dream in the morning. Britt, on the other hand, said his products were good for days.

Anecdotal conclusions aside, I think it is fair to say aromatic truffles, like so many things, are at their most delicious fresh, what Elinoar calls "a costly condiment." But because of their short shelf life, it's easy to get ripped off buying retail. It's best to purchase wild truffles from a hunter, wholesaler, or local grower and to make sure you know what you are paying for: The truffles should smell strong, and you should have enough on your plate to overwhelm the senses—I think one-fourth of an ounce shaved over a plate of pasta should do it.

Other seasonal wild mushrooms are more durable. Porcini, chanterelles, matsutake, morels, black trumpets, and many other less well-known wild mushrooms may be available in your market now, or someday. Alternatively, you can join a mushroom foray. Or, as Gary Lincoff suggested to his students many times, you could always just walk around the block and see what's growing under the trees. There may be something edible, but there is *always* something interesting.

MUSHROOMS
WITH FISH

CHANTERELLE AND CRAB SALAD

BY SANDY INGBER, FLORIDA | YIELD: 4 SERVINGS

I was the chef/owner of the Grand Central Station Oyster Bar and Restaurant in New York for thirty-one years, and this is a version of a special we sometimes served. Today, I serve this salad at home in the summer, when the heirloom tomatoes are at their best. You can also substitute good hothouse tomatoes in this recipe. If you use small chanterelles (2 inches tall or less), you can use them whole in this dish. The croutons in this recipe can be made ahead.

FOR THE CROUTONS

¼ cup unsalted butter

1 tablespoon garlic, minced

6 cups day-old bread or focaccia, crusts removed, and cut into ½-inch cubes

Sea salt (preferably gray salt) and freshly ground black pepper

6 tablespoons Parmesan cheese, finely grated

FOR THE SALAD

2 pounds ripe heirloom tomatoes, peeled, seeded, and large diced

½ cup plus 3 tablespoons olive oil

1 pound fresh chanterelles, cleaned and dried, left whole if small, or cut into bite-size slices

Sea salt (preferably gray salt) and freshly ground black pepper

¼ cup red onion, thinly sliced

2 teaspoons garlic, minced

2 tablespoons fresh lemon juice

2 tablespoons chopped fresh basil leaves

1 tablespoon chopped fresh tarragon leaves

2 cups baby arugula

1 pound jumbo lump crabmeat

Shaved Parmesan cheese, for garnish

TO MAKE THE CROUTONS:

Place a cookie sheet in the oven and preheat the oven to 375°F.

Melt the butter in a large skillet over medium heat and cook until it foams, a few minutes. Add the garlic and cook until fragrant, stirring frequently, 30 seconds to 1 minute. Add the cubed bread and toss to coat. Season with salt and freshly ground black pepper to taste.

Transfer the bread to the hot baking sheet and immediately sprinkle with the Parmesan cheese. Place the baking sheet back in the oven, shaking the pan periodically to rotate the croutons until they are crisp and golden on the outside but still soft within, about 8 or 9 minutes.

Allow the croutons to cool. You can store the croutons in an airtight container for up to a month.

TO MAKE THE SALAD:

Place the tomatoes in a sieve to remove excess liquid while you prepare the rest of the ingredients.

Heat 3 tablespoons of the olive oil in large skillet over high heat. Add the chanterelles and cook them until they release their liquid and the liquid evaporates, around 6 to 10 minutes. Avoid crowding the pan, cooking in batches if necessary. Season with salt and freshly ground black pepper to taste and set aside.

In a large bowl, combine the tomatoes, onion, garlic, remaining ½ cup of olive oil, lemon juice, basil, and tarragon. Add salt and freshly ground black pepper to taste. Now add the croutons and toss well.

Divide the salad among 4 plates. There may be some dressing at the bottom of the bowl—if so, reserve it. Top each serving with ½ cup of arugula, ¼ pound of crabmeat, one-quarter of the warm mushrooms, and a few shaves of Parmesan cheese, and drizzle the remaining dressing over the top, if any.

MUSSELS, PORCINI, AND POTATOES

BY GRAHAM STEINRUCK, WASHINGTON | YIELD: 4 SERVINGS

A few years ago, I was eating mussels on the Pacific coast. I had just been in Colorado hunting boletes, and I thought, wow, porcini would be so good with mussels. Mollusks and mushrooms epitomize the ecosystem of the Pacific Northwest. There is a depth of flavor with a mussel, a saltiness that complements the sweet earthiness of the porcini. It's a taste of forest and ocean combined. Since then, I've made this dish with morels, and it works just as well. I like to eat the mussels straight out of their shells. It's deliciously messy.

1 pound skin-on new or fingerling potatoes (I like Ozettes from Washington state)

Salt

1 tablespoon olive oil, divided

1 to 2 fresh andouille or chorizo sausages, or 2½ ounces dried chorizo, sliced into ⅛-inch rounds

8 ounces fresh porcini or other wild mushrooms, cut into bite-sized pieces, or 1 ounce dried porcini, rehydrated in 1½ cups boiling water, drained, and water reserved

¼ cup diced shallots

1 tablespoon minced garlic

½ cup dry white wine

1 cup chicken stock or vegetable broth, or rehydrating water (if using dried mushrooms)

1 tablespoon unsalted butter

2 pounds live mussels, scrubbed and rinsed, with beards removed (see note)

Freshly ground black pepper

¼ cup minced flat-leaf parsley, for garnish

Lemon wedges (optional), for garnish

NOTE: Open mussels that are still alive will close their shells when you handle them. (It takes a minute.) Open mussels that do not close when handled should be discarded, as should mussels with broken shells. Mussels that do not open after cooking should also be discarded.

Rinse the potatoes under cold water. Place them in a medium saucepan and cover with water. Add ½ tablespoon salt, stir, and bring to a boil over medium-high heat. Lower the heat to keep the water at a simmer and cook uncovered for 10 to 15 minutes, until the potatoes are fork-tender when pierced. Strain the potatoes, cut into bite-sized pieces, and set aside.

Heat ½ tablespoon of olive oil in a large, heavy-bottomed stockpot over medium heat. Add the sausage and sauté for about 5 minutes, or until the meat begins to brown. Remove the sausage from the pan and set aside to drain on paper towels. (If using dried chorizo, skip this stage.)

Return the pot to the heat and add the remaining ½ tablespoon of olive oil. Add the mushrooms and sauté for about 7 minutes, until the mushrooms have given up most of their liquid and are starting to brown. Add the shallots and continue to sauté for about 1 minute, until the shallots become translucent. Then add the garlic and cook for another minute. Deglaze the pot with the wine and allow most of the wine to evaporate. Add the stock (or, if using rehydrating water, be sure to strain it well). Bring the stock to a simmer over medium-high heat. Add the butter, potatoes, sausage, and mussels to the pot. Cover with a tight-fitting lid and allow the mussels to steam for about 5 minutes, or until the mussel shells have just opened.

Season the broth with salt and pepper to taste and gently tumble all the ingredients in the pot, making sure not to knock the mussels out of their shells. Ladle into four separate bowls and garnish with parsley and lemon wedges, if using. Serve immediately with buttered toast.

SETAS CON ALMEJAS
(MUSHROOMS WITH CLAMS)

BY CHAD HYATT, CALIFORNIA | YIELD: 4 SERVINGS

*This recipe comes out of the traditional cuisine of Galicia, Spain. Spain, in general, is known for seafood, but if you ask a Spaniard, the best seafood is from Galicia. Oak, beech, and chestnut forests filled with mushrooms cover the hills that tumble to the sea, so the combination of seafood and mushrooms reflects Galician terroir. The saffron milk cap (*Lactarius deliciosus*) is probably the perfect mushroom for this dish, but lots of other mushrooms work—such as edible* Russula *and* Lactarius*—and of the cultivated varieties, I think* nameko (Pholiotya nemko*) and king trumpets (*Pleurotus eryngii*) are good. In general, strong-flavored mushrooms with firm texture are best in this dish.*

4 tablespoons olive oil, divided

1 cup finely diced onions

1 tablespoon minced garlic

Salt

Pinch of saffron threads

½ cup finely diced green bell pepper

¼ cup finely diced red bell pepper

2 pounds assorted mushrooms, cleaned and cut into large pieces

4 tablespoons chopped flat-leafed parsley, divided

1 whole *guindilla* pepper or a small pinch of red chile flakes

1½ cups dry white wine

2 pounds clams, rinsed (see note)

NOTE: You can use any kind of clam, but keep in mind that a large clam, like the littleneck, will take longer to cook than a small clam, like the Manila.

Heat 3 tablespoons of oil in a large Dutch oven or heavy-bottomed stockpot over medium-low heat. Add the onions, the garlic, and a pinch of salt. Sauté, stirring regularly, until the onions begin to soften, a few minutes. Stir in the saffron threads and continue to sauté until the onions are very soft and cooked through but not browned, about 6 minutes. Add the red and green bell peppers and another small pinch of salt. Continue to cook, stirring regularly, until the peppers are meltingly soft, about 20 minutes. Do not brown.

Add the mushrooms, along with another small pinch of salt, and continue to cook on medium-low heat. The mushrooms will give off water; let the water cook down, completely reduce, and reabsorb. If the pot looks dry, add another tablespoon of oil. Keep stirring regularly to make sure nothing burns on the bottom of the pan, about 10 minutes. You don't want to brown the mushrooms and vegetables, but you do want the mushrooms to cook very thoroughly. When the mushrooms are fork-tender, stir in 2 tablespoons of parsley and the *guindilla* pepper and cook for another 1 to 2 minutes.

Turn the heat up to medium, add the wine, and bring to a simmer. Let the wine simmer for 1 or 2 minutes to get rid of the alcohol.

Add the clams and cover the pot. Adjust the heat to keep it simmering gently, and cook just until the clams open. Using tongs, transfer the open clams to a bowl so they don't overcook

while the more stubborn clams continue cooking. Take the lid off the pot and stir things around once or twice to make sure all of the clams are getting cooked in the liquid. As soon as all the clams are opened, up to 10 minutes, remove from the heat, add all the opened clams back into the pot, and adjust salt, if needed.

Garnish with the remaining 2 tablespoons of parsley and serve immediately with hearty, crusty bread, if you like.

MOREL-ENCRUSTED TUNA

BY TIM LEAVITT, WASHINGTON | YIELD: 4 SERVINGS

I started picking mushrooms in Oregon when I was a child, and by middle school, I was selling mushrooms to grocery stores. I studied mycology with David Hosford at Central Washington University, and when I graduated, I worked with Paul Stamets at Fungi Perfecti. I also worked for the USDA surveying mushrooms and creating environmental impact statements. I later started a truffle farm, which, unsurprisingly, failed. Now I am growing and cooking mushrooms. I first published a version of this recipe in my book Cooking Wild Mushrooms for People Who Don't Like Mushrooms. *You can substitute the tuna with scallops or beef, and the morels with dried honey mushrooms or shiitake. Altogether, the dish takes about an hour, although you aren't really doing anything most of the time.*

14 ounces fresh tuna steaks, about 2 inches thick

⅓ cup soy sauce

2 cups dried morels

2 to 4 tablespoons coconut or avocado oil, or other neutral oil

Bring the tuna to room temperature. Pour the soy sauce in a plate with a rim and place the fish in the sauce. Allow to rest about 20 minutes on each side.

While you are waiting, grind the morels into a fine powder using a spice or coffee bean grinder.

Remove the fish from the soy sauce and sprinkle the morel powder all over; pat the powder into the meat with your fingers and then let rest for 25 minutes. This allows the mushrooms to adhere to the meat and reconstitute.

Heat the oil in a cast-iron skillet on medium-low until it just starts to smoke. Sear the tuna for 3 to 3½ minutes on each side (searing for a total of 6 to 7 minutes should be enough to ensure the morels are thoroughly cooked). Avoid moving the fish while it is searing.

Let the tuna rest for a few minutes, then slice. This preparation is wonderful by itself or served as a tataki salad.

RICE PILAF WITH MUSHROOMS AND SHRIMP

BY NENI PANOURGIA, NEW YORK | YIELD: 4 SERVINGS

I am a sworn omnivore — except for escargot, tripe, and reptiles, I will eat almost anything — and a sworn mycophagist. I am also a sworn conservationist, which means that I am loath to throw foodstuffs away until I have used them up to the core of their core. This comes from both growing up in a family that lived through the famine of World War II and a commitment to food and earth justice. I first made this dish using leftover rice. It is a reiteration of a well-known Greek dish, shrimp pilaf, but with the addition of mushrooms, which marry well with the flavors of cognac, cinnamon, and cloves.

¼ cup slivered almonds

¼ pine nuts

24 medium shell-on shrimp

Salt and freshly ground black pepper

3 tablespoons olive oil, divided

4 cloves garlic, peeled

2 bay leaves

6 ounces (about 12 small to medium sized) cremini mushrooms

⅔ cup minced yellow onions

1 tablespoon tomato paste

4 whole cloves

Pinch of cinnamon

⅓ cup cognac or high-quality brandy

1½ cups uncooked basmati rice, or 4 cups cooked rice

NOTE: Different types of rice require different liquid-to-grain ratios. This one is for unwashed, unsoaked basmati.

In a small cast-iron skillet, toast the almonds and pine nuts over medium-high heat until they begin to take on a golden color, about 1 minute. Remove from heat.

Shell and devein the shrimp, preserving the shells for stock. Salt and pepper the shrimp. Transfer to a bowl, and add 1 tablespoon of olive oil. Keep shrimp in the refrigerator while preparing the rest of the ingredients.

Place the shrimp shells in a medium stockpot with 4 cups of water. Add the garlic and bay leaves and boil gently, covered, over medium heat for about 20 minutes, until the water is infused with the shrimp-shell flavor. If the water evaporates, add more water to maintain just under 4 cups of liquid. Strain and measure the stock. You should use 3½ cups of stock for 1½ cups uncooked basmati rice (see note).

In a medium saucepan, heat 2 tablespoons of olive oil over medium-high heat. Add the onions and cook until they start to soften, a few minutes, then add the mushrooms and cook until they release their water, about 5 minutes more. Add the tomato paste, shrimp, cloves, and cinnamon, and stir to distribute well in the pan. Cook until the shrimp are opaque, about 10 minutes. Add the cognac and cook until the alcohol evaporates, 2 to 3 minutes. If using uncooked rice, remove the shrimp from the pan with tongs and set aside.

If using uncooked rice, add the rice grains to the saucepan, turn to coat well with the sauce, and add 3½ cups of shrimp-shell stock. Bring to a boil. Stir to loosen the rice grains, and then turn the heat down to low. Cover and simmer for 20 minutes

without disturbing, then check to see if the rice is tender and the moisture in the pan has evaporated. Remove from the heat, add the reserved shrimp, and cover again for 5 minutes to warm. Uncover, add the nuts, fluff with a fork, and check the seasoning.

If using cooked rice, add the cooked rice to the saucepan and combine until it is heated through, a few minutes. Add the nuts and shrimp, stir to combine, and check the seasoning.

SCALLOPS WITH BLACK TRUMPETS

BY GARY GILBERT, MASSACHUSETTS | YIELD: 4 SERVINGS

Over forty years ago, I went on my first chanterelle hunt in Maine and became hooked. Since then, I've cooked mushroom dishes for countless guests. I regularly teach mushroom ID classes and lead forays, and I have developed a series of mushroom ID flashcards, called MycoCards. This recipe evolved from a basic morel-in-cream-sauce dish, but this version has less cream and the added earthy taste of bourbon. Black trumpets (like Craterellus fallax*) work very well with seafood, and this dish is both beautiful and delicious. You can substitute halibut or lobster meat for the scallops, if you like.*

¾ cup heavy cream

28 large fresh black trumpet mushrooms, cut into bite-sized pieces, or ½ ounce dried mushrooms, broken into bite-sized chunks

10 ounces spinach, stems removed if using large leaves

2 tablespoons unsalted butter, divided

3 tablespoons minced shallots

¼ cup bourbon, or scotch

1 heaping teaspoon minced garlic

1 tablespoon olive oil

Salt

16 large scallops, abductor muscle removed, patted dry with a towel

2 cups cooked rice

In the microwave or a small pot, heat the cream until warm. Pour the warm cream into a large bowl and add the black trumpets. Soak for about 5 minutes, until they are soft. Strain, but do not discard, the cream.

Place the spinach in a medium pot and heat over medium heat until wilted and cooked, stirring periodically to be sure the spinach doesn't stick to the bottom, a few minutes. Squeeze out all the water and set aside to cool.

In a medium skillet, heat 1 tablespoon butter over medium-low heat, add shallots and cook until soft, about 5 to 8 minutes. Add black trumpets and cook, stirring often, for about 5 minutes, until the mushrooms become soft.

Raise the heat to medium and add the bourbon. Stirring frequently, reduce until the alcohol is almost evaporated. Add the garlic and cook for 1 minute, then add the cream. Bring to a gentle boil and continue to stir occasionally until the cream thickens and reduces to about half its volume, about 7 to 10 minutes. Add salt to taste and turn off the heat.

Heat the remaining tablespoon of butter and the olive oil in a medium skillet over medium-high heat. As soon as the fats are smoky hot, add the scallops. Sear them on one side without moving them, a few minutes, then turn each scallop over and brown on the other side, a few minutes more. Remove from the pan immediately. Add salt to taste.

Assemble the dish by placing about ½ cup of cooked rice in the center of each plate. Place one-quarter of the steamed spinach over the rice. Place 4 scallops on top of the spinach, then top each pile with one-quarter of the black trumpets in cream sauce.

SCALLOPS WITH TRUFFLES

BY MARY SMILEY, DELAWARE | YIELD: 4 SERVINGS

Some recipes are just meant to be, and this one happened when I had scallops in the fridge and truffles arriving in the mail. I decided to try them together, since a truffle slice fits perfectly atop a seared scallop. You can make this dish with any culinary truffle species (Tuber estivo is pictured here), but I love it with Oregon black truffles, which have a fruity, almost tropical aroma to them. This could either be served as an appetizer or a main dish. For a main dish, just add a side of rice pilaf or wild rice and a salad.

2 tablespoons unsalted butter

1 tablespoon neutral oil

12 large scallops, abductor muscle removed and patted dry

Salt and freshly ground black pepper

1 ounce ripe Oregon black truffle or other very fresh truffle, cut into paper-thin slices (see note)

2 tablespoons chopped chervil, for garnish

NOTE: To cut truffles very thin, use a mandoline, or, if you like kitchen gizmos, a truffle shaver.

Heat a medium, well-seasoned iron skillet over high heat. Lower the heat to medium-high and add the butter and oil. Heat until the butter is melted (but be careful to avoid burning).

Season the scallops with salt and pepper to taste. Add the scallops to the hot pan and sear for 3 to 4 minutes without touching them, then turn the scallops over in the pan and sear an additional 3 to 4 minutes, until brown. Push a scallop with your finger: If it is firm but not hard and has a nice sear on each side, they should be done. Be careful not to overcook them, or the scallops may become rubbery.

Drain the scallops on paper towels. To serve, top each scallop with a thin slice of truffle, spoon some of the butter from the pan over the scallops, and garnish with the chervil.

TROUT WITH RAMP PESTO AND MORELS

BY JEAN O. FAHEY, NEW YORK | YIELD: 4 SERVINGS

Once the calendar turns to January, I start dreaming of finding morels. In fact, I have a recurring dream of finding morels growing in the corners of rooms. Wild leeks, also known as ramps, are one of the first signs that spring is here, as are the black morels under tulip poplars, followed by the yellow morels under ash trees. They grow in secret places (including in my dreams). After a long winter, the spring needs to be celebrated with fabulous dishes of local foraged and fished food. If you use ramps with their bulbs, the pesto will grind easily. Without the bulbs, you may need to add a tablespoon of pine nuts.

8 ounces whole coarsely chopped ramps, divided

2 tablespoons extra-virgin olive oil, divided

1 tablespoon grated Parmesan cheese

Salt and freshly ground black pepper

½ pound fresh morels, washed well

2 pounds trout fillets (like steelhead or rainbow)

¾ cup dry white wine

Place 6 ounces of ramps in a food processor and add 1 tablespoon of olive oil and the Parmesan cheese. Pulse to puree. Add salt and pepper to taste.

Preheat the oven to 350°F.

In a medium skillet, heat the remaining 1 tablespoon of olive oil over medium heat. Add the morels and sauté gently until they give up their water, a few minutes. Then add the remaining 2 ounces of ramps and continue cooking until the water cooks out and the ramps are tender, about 10 minutes. Add salt and pepper to taste.

Place the trout fillets skin-side down on a buttered rimmed baking pan. Pour the wine over the fish and place in the oven. Bake for 10 minutes until the fish releases its fats and is almost cooked through. Remove the baking pan from the oven and spread the ramp pesto on top of the fish. Pour the sautéed morels and ramp leaves over the fish and return the pan to the oven for 5 to 7 more minutes, until the fish is flaky.

PARMESAN FISH WITH OYSTER MUSHROOM ROCKEFELLER

BY JEAN O. FAHEY, NEW YORK | YIELD: 4 SERVINGS

I find oyster mushrooms in every forest that I visit. Years ago, when I was first learning to hunt mushrooms, I found a log that was covered with oysters. I dragged them home, filled an entire laundry basket with them, and drove around the neighborhood, offering them to all my friends. Now, when I find a mother lode, I leave it on my back porch, and people come and get some. Oyster mushrooms are often plentiful in the fall, growing on dying hardwoods that still have bark. I prepared the first version of this dish for the Northeast Mycological Federation's mycophagy program. Pretty much any whitefish fillet will work.

¾ cup grated Parmesan cheese

½ cup breadcrumbs

½ tablespoon dried parsley

¼ tablespoon dried oregano

¼ tablespoon dried basil

½ cup (1 stick) unsalted butter, divided

12 ounces fresh spinach

2 tablespoons minced shallot

1 pound fresh oyster mushrooms

½ cup milk

2 pounds (4 to 8 filets) white fish fillets, such as flounder or sole

½ cup fresh, chopped flat-leafed parsley

4 large garlic cloves, peeled and squashed

Preheat the oven to 350°F.

In a wide, shallow bowl combine the Parmesan cheese, breadcrumbs, dried parsley, oregano, and basil.

In a large skillet, melt 1 tablespoon of butter over medium heat and add the spinach. Allow it to wilt, about 2 minutes, then stir in the fresh parsley. Transfer the spinach mixture onto a baking pan with edges, and spread it out enough to accommodate the fish fillets, which will go on top.

Wipe the skillet out and melt 1 tablespoon of butter over medium-high heat. Add the minced shallots and sauté a few minutes until they soften, then add the mushrooms. Cook the mushrooms until they release their water and the water evaporates, about 8 to 10 minutes. Remove from the heat and set aside.

Have ready a wide, shallow bowl with the milk in it. Dip the fish fillets in the milk, then dredge them in the breadcrumb mixture.

Place the breaded fish fillets on top of the spinach and spoon the mushrooms over the breaded fish.

Melt the remaining 6 tablespoons of butter in a medium saucepan over medium heat. When the butter is melted, add the garlic and pour it over the fish. Bake for 12 to 15 minutes, until the fish is opaque and flaky.

POMPANO WITH BLACK TRUMPETS AND KEY LIME BEURRE BLANC SAUCE

BY MARY SMILEY, DELAWARE | YIELD: 4 SERVINGS

When I lived in Sarasota, Florida, I went to the Venice Jetty to photograph a very special water bird. I met some supercool old guys at the jetty, one of whom hooked and landed a gorgeous pompano while I took photos. Then he said, "I don't have a cooler," to which I jokingly replied, "Well, you'll have to give it to me, because I'm leaving right now." He wiped off the sand and handed me the fish. WOO HOO! I love, love, love pompano. I rushed home and made this dish. You can substitute the pompano with another whitefish fillet, like sole or flounder, and the recipe works with regular limes if key limes are not available.

FOR THE POMPANO WITH BLACK TRUMPETS

¼ ounce dried black trumpet mushrooms

Four 6-ounce to 8-ounce skinless pompano or other whitefish fillets

Kosher salt and ground black pepper

2½ sticks unsalted butter, chilled and cut into 1-tablespoon pieces, divided

FOR THE KEY LIME BEURRE BLANC SAUCE

⅓ cup white wine

3 tablespoons fresh key lime juice

2 tablespoons finely chopped shallots

2 teaspoons white wine vinegar

½ teaspoon minced garlic

2 tablespoons heavy cream

½ teaspoon key lime zest

1½ teaspoons chopped fresh chives, for garnish

NOTE: For the prettiest results, start sautéing the fish on the presentation side—that is, the side closest to the bone rather than the side closest to the skin. Plate the fish presentation side up.

TO MAKE THE POMPANO WITH BLACK TRUMPETS:
Place the dried mushrooms in a medium mixing bowl and cover with 2 cups hot water. Allow to rehydrate, about 15 minutes. Strain the mushrooms and set aside, reserving the rehydrating liquid.

Season the fish fillets with salt and pepper on both sides.

Heat 4 tablespoons of butter in a large nonstick skillet over medium-high heat. Add the fillets and sauté each side until golden brown, about 6 minutes altogether (see note). Place the fillets on a platter and cover with foil to keep warm.

In a small skillet, heat 1 tablespoon of butter over medium heat. Add the rehydrated black trumpets and cook for 10 minutes, until the mushrooms are very tender. Keep them moist by adding the reserved rehydrating liquid a couple tablespoons at a time; you will need a total of about ½ cup of liquid.

TO MAKE THE KEY LIME BEURRE BLANC SAUCE:
In a small skillet, add the white wine, key lime juice, shallots, vinegar, and garlic. Bring to a gentle boil over medium heat and cook, uncovered, until the liquids reduce to 3 tablespoons, about 4 minutes. Stir in the cream and continue to cook until the liquid is reduced to 3 tablespoons, a few minutes.

Reduce the heat to medium-low and add 15 tablespoons butter 1 tablespoon at a time, stirring until the butter melts, a few minutes. When all the butter is incorporated, remove from

heat and strain the sauce through a metal sieve to create a very smooth sauce. Stir in the key lime zest and add salt to taste. Cover to keep warm.

To serve, pour the mushrooms on top of the cooked fish, add the beurre blanc sauce on top, and garnish with chives. Serve the fish over cooked jasmine rice combined with butter and minced cilantro, if you like.

LET FOOD BE THY MEDICINE

WHY MUSHROOMS SHOULD BE A PART OF A REGULAR DIET

There was a time when mushrooms didn't get much cred. They were thought to be about as nutritious as celery or cucumbers, suffering from the negative-calorie food myth (or misunderstanding) that says that chewing the food burns more calories than the food provides. Mushrooms are indeed very low calorie—7 ounces of white button mushrooms have 44 calories and are 90 percent water—but that doesn't mean they are nutritionally impoverished.

However, these days, maybe mushrooms are getting too much cred. "How the Lowly Mushroom Is Becoming a Nutritional Star," "Are Mushrooms the Future of Wellness?" "Eating This One Food Every Day May Help Weaken COVID-19." These headlines and so many more laud the incredible superpowers of mushrooms. Mushrooms do, indeed, contain a variety of micronutrients, but if you ate nothing but this superfood, you would eventually suffer from malnutrition. So, where does the truth about mushroom nutrition lie? What's hype, and what does the science say?

Mushrooms are a poster child for wellness, meaning they keep you well, as do soluble fiber, fermented foods, and foods loaded with vitamins and essential minerals. That's not the same as saying they cure illness, though plenty of anecdotal evidence claims that various mushrooms or their extracts may reduce tumors or have other curative effects, and a fair amount of research does suggest potential curative effects. (And certainly, some compounds derived from fungi, such as penicillin, definitively cure illness.)

But when I say "anecdotal evidence," I mean there are people who will testify to the effects of these mushrooms, though the effects are not dependably reproducible. When I attended a birthday party over Zoom last summer, a friend asked whether mushrooms could protect him from COVID-19. I could only shrug. Maybe they could; there just isn't empirical data. What some mushrooms may do, however, is keep your immune system primed to fight pathogens should you be exposed.

A plethora of mushroom products on the market fall under the category of *nutraceuticals* (a mashup of the words *nutrient* and *pharmaceutical*): supplements, usually in pill or powder form, that contain nutrients and chemicals derived from mushrooms or their mycelium, like *Hericium*, which some people take for neural regeneration, and functional foods, which are fortified or enriched foods, like chaga coffee. While these are very interesting, it is arguable whether nutraceuticals improve health, and none are regulated for their efficacy or safety by the FDA.

This contrasts with medicinal mushrooms, a category that spans the gamut from disease busters like antibiotics to wellness enhancers—a much more difficult factor to measure, as not getting sick, or not getting as sick as you might have had you not used mushrooms, is harder to quantify than the obliteration of disease. Mushrooms may be prescribed by doctors or nutritionists who make specific dietary recommendations, but whether they heal disease like antibiotics do is not yet established.

The goal of traditional Chinese medicine is to support health by enhancing the immune system and increasing vigor, for example. Small amounts of therapeutic agents like mushroom extracts are taken over long periods of time, often in combination with foods and other therapies like acupuncture, all specifically tailored to the individual. (You could say the definition of Western doctoring is to *respond* to disease, while the definition of Eastern doctoring is to *avoid* disease.)

Most knowledge regarding the medicinal properties of eating mushrooms comes from the literature of the Far East, where certain mushrooms have been collected, cultivated, and prescribed for thousands of years. In the last few decades, the scientific community has shown an eagerness to understand the molecular mechanisms responsible for their actions, if any.

One of the most provocative areas of study is the action of fungal beta-glucans, chains of polysaccharides found in the cell wall of fungi. They may act as antibody generators, or antigens, that provoke immune responses. Proponents of the healing properties of mushrooms have suggested that our bodies are adapted to respond to fungal beta-glucans with an immune reaction. Here's the theory: Our immune systems have evolved to fight off the airborne pathogenic fungi that are ubiquitous in our atmosphere. When we are exposed to the beta-glucans in those pathogenic fungi, our immune systems kick in. However, when our bodies are exposed to the beta-glucans in nonpathogenic fungi, like shiitake mushrooms, this exposure also triggers our immune system, which may offer an advantage in fighting off disease. But synthesizing and administering these metabolites is a different thing than eating mushrooms.

The amino acid ergothioneine, which is present in mushrooms, is also attracting attention. Dr. Kenji Ouchi, a specialist from the Mushroom General Research Institute of the Hokto Kinoko Company, a Japanese mushroom cultivator, wrote that it is known as the "longevity vitamin." What is unknown is whether increasing your intake of ergothioneine by ingesting mushrooms affects health. However, it's not my mission to argue the pros and cons of mushroom-based nutraceuticals here. What I do want to talk about is what role mushrooms may play in your regular diet, like when you have them for dinner. And without doubt, there is an overall benefit to diversifying your diet by regularly including mushrooms—in terms of not only your personal health but also the health of our environment.

So, let's look at the nutrients in mushrooms. Most mushroom research in the United States is conducted by universities affiliated with the mushroom industry, and on *Agaricus bisporus*, the white button mushroom. There are two very good reasons for this: The folks who pay for this research are interested in data that benefits their own products. What's in it for them to study the nutritive values of a chanterelle, which is not cultivated? The second reason is standardization. Wild mushrooms can show differing trace elements of minerals, including heavy metals, and secondary metabolites based on insects they encounter and any number of other factors, depending on what the species is and where the specimen is growing.

A. bisporus is grown in a controlled environment, and it's usually a particular genotype. That kind of standardization allows for testing that can be applied across an industry. But it is probably safe to say these measurements are generally true of most edible mushrooms, whether they grow in a greenhouse or in what Dr. Suzanne Simard calls the forest cathedrals of British Columbia.

Based on *A. bisporus* research, the 10 percent of mushroom left after you take away its water consists mostly of proteins, fiber, sugars, vitamins, and minerals. Let's break it down: Mushrooms contain all nine essential amino acids necessary to produce high-quality protein. When you taste that meaty savoriness, that umami flavor of mushrooms, what you are tasting are those amino acids, particularly glutamate. A serving of button mushrooms, around 3 ounces, provides as much protein as a third of a glass of milk. For every 3.5 ounces of mushrooms you eat, you can expect getting somewhere between 4 and 7 percent of your daily protein value.

The Recommended Dietary Allowance for protein is about a third of a gram per pound of body weight. Certainly, mushrooms aren't as efficient as a steak, where an equivalent amount will supply over 50 percent of your daily value, but in a warming world, mushrooms could become a viable source of some protein without the belching cows and the conversion of forest to field.

Fifty percent of the dry weight of mushrooms is composed of complex carbohydrates, which are sugar molecules strung together. Most of the carbohydrates in mushrooms consist of dietary fiber, mostly insoluble fiber, which can't completely be broken down by digestion. The digestible fiber in mushrooms contains sugars like trehalose (one theory about the role of trehalose is that it may prevent ice formation when a mushroom gets really cold), mannitol, glycogen, and glucose.

The nondigestible fiber in mushrooms—which constitutes the larger share—is composed of sugars like mannins, the aforementioned beta-glucans, and chitin. Chitin is a tough polysaccharide that is a structural component of insect exoskeletons, fish scales, and fungal cell walls. It's the stuff that enables mushrooms to hold together, despite being mostly water, as they push through soil. But we don't digest it.* Like other insoluble fibers, chitin plays a role in moving one's poop along. As Dr. Nicholas Money, a mycologist and author of numerous insightful books about fungi, says, "Some is digested, and some is swept through."

Mushrooms contain a variety of micronutrients necessary for the healthy function of our cells, like potassium (an electrolyte that aids in the balance of fluid in cells, among other duties) and selenium. (Only garlic provides more selenium per gram than mushrooms—in fact, in the rare case of a selenium overdose, excess selenium, when excreted by the breath, smells garlicky.) Mushrooms contain iron, magnesium, and copper, which is bioaccumulated in the soil by the fungus. A serving of mushrooms provides 20 percent of the Daily Value for copper, and 3 percent of the Daily Value for zinc, which has antiviral properties, though not much, but I guess these days we can use all the antiviral help we can get.

Mushrooms also contain vitamins, particularly the B vitamins riboflavin and niacin, and vitamin D2, one of the two forms we commonly see. The other form, vitamin D3, is known as the sunshine vitamin because our skin makes it when exposed to sunlight. Similarly, when mushrooms are exposed to sunlight, they increase their production of vitamin D2. "At my home," wrote Ouchi in an email, "I irradiate mushrooms with ultraviolet rays for about ten minutes before eating them" to benefit from the increase in vitamin D2.

Mushrooms contain fatty acids, mostly of the unsaturated type (think avocados versus pork sausages). Of them, linoleic acid is essential; we need it, but we don't make it. In general, unsaturated fats like those in avocados and mushrooms are far healthier than saturated fats; replacing saturated fats with unsaturated fats in your diet can reduce blood cholesterol levels.

These are all important compounds, but except for vitamin D, most of the nutrients in mushrooms are available in a wide variety of foods. That said, "there are conditions under which people need more," says Nik Money. "A pregnant mother, for example, may be prescribed nutritional supplements." And bottom

line, we need to fold these micronutrients into our diet somehow. Why not mushrooms? There certainly are other benefits if we do.

When we choose to eat mushrooms, we are not choosing something else. "By eating mushrooms rather than, say, processed meats, you are inherently consuming something that is better for the body," Nik adds. When we choose to eat mushrooms, which are low in sodium, we are avoiding high-sodium foods like prepared foods. So, simply by eating this and not that, you are supporting good health. "By enriching our diet with this food source," says Nik, "we are excluding others."

That sounds like the opposite of the proactive boosterism surrounding much of the mushrooms-for-health movement. But in fact, incorporating mushrooms in your diet absolutely displaces other foods, and if you make it your business, they can replace less healthy ones. What's more, mushrooms are minimally processed. This is a good thing. Their environmental impact is low and can even be net positive: A mushroom like the white button basically turns poop into protein in a matter of weeks.

Mushrooms biosynthesize their own food from wood waste or readily available agricultural crop and animal residues like straw and manure, and their spent compost or substrate can be used as a soil conditioner or to grow other species of mushrooms or in environmental bioremediation. When Ouchi wrote me, he said, "Mushrooms play a role as a decomposer on the earth, and we believe that a recycling-oriented society using mushrooms can be realized. The mushroom medium is agricultural waste (inedible parts of crops such as corn, wheat, rice, and soybeans), but the medium residue after cultivating mushrooms, which are health foods, is compost raw materials for orchards and fields, livestock feed, or it is also effectively used as a raw material for biomass fuel."

Another benefit is caloric. Mushrooms are low in calories, about equal to lettuce, and if you replace meals with mushrooms (bearing in mind that cooking them with large amounts of cream and butter won't help keep those calories down), for most people, this will drive weight loss over time. This fact has been exploited by the usual diet-industry shysters. You might have heard of the M-Plan, which is sure to decrease your "tums, bums, and thighs," according to the UK tabloid the *Daily Mail*, but, incredibly, it will not reduce your bust size.

While taking in fewer calories is a well-established way to lose weight, mushrooms, despite how wonderful they are, aren't prejudiced in favor of bosoms. A cup of uncooked white button mushrooms (which cooks down by about two-thirds), yields about 21 calories. (According to one study, of all the mushrooms, the truffle is the most caloric, though eating enough truffles to be worried about the calories is a problem few of us are likely to have.) It's plausible that the amino acids in mushrooms lead to feeling satiated. So, you might feel fuller from a bowl of mushrooms cooked in water and flavored with oil than a bowl of dressed lettuce that has the same number of calories. And, of course, if you are hunting for mushrooms, you are getting health benefits from the fresh air and exercise.

Chemicals in mushrooms, like ergothioneine and glutathione, may play roles in mitigating oxidative stress of cells, which is associated with diseases of aging like cancer and Alzheimer's disease. But while these chemicals may be present in the mushroom, what happens to the chemical when we eat the mushroom has barely been explored, and those studies that do exist show only correlative results—meaning, some people who ate mushrooms didn't get dementia, but it is not clear that they avoided doing so because they ate mushrooms. At this point no one can say with reproducible certainty that *Hericium* mushrooms, if consumed, will regrow your neural cells. But here's the thing: That doesn't mean eating a bowl of *Hericium* mushrooms isn't a healthy way to eat.

Because it is.

* Some research has identified the enzyme chitinase in humans, and animal studies indicate that certain eating behaviors can affect chitinase gene expression, so it's possible that if you are from a culture where eating insects is the norm, you might produce enough chitinase to break down chitin.

MUSHROOMS
WITH POULTRY
& MEAT

DUCK AND SHIITAKE CONGEE

BY GRAHAM STEINRUCK, WASHINGTON | YIELD: 4 SERVINGS

You can go about this dish a few ways: You can start with a whole duck and use all of its parts for the congee. You can buy duck legs and breasts and use chicken stock, in which case, ignore the instructions for making the duck stock, rendering the fat, and making the cracklings, all of which are best done in advance. Or you can use a combination of duck and chicken. It all works in this versatile dish, which really shows off the excellent pairing of duck and shiitake.

FOR THE DUCK STOCK, DUCK FAT, AND CRACKLINGS

1 whole duck (legs and breast meat removed, excess fat trimmed and reserved, skin from all but the legs and breasts trimmed and reserved, and carcass reserved), or 2 duck legs and 1 duck breast (2 lobes)

FOR THE CONGEE

6 cups duck or chicken stock, mushroom broth, or water

½ ounce dried shiitake mushrooms

3 scallions, white and green parts separated, green parts chopped

1 clove garlic, peeled

1-inch piece fresh ginger, peeled

¾ cup jasmine rice

Salt

4 large eggs

1 tablespoon duck fat or olive oil, divided

1 teaspoon sesame oil plus more, for garnish

8 ounces fresh shiitake or other cultivated mushrooms (like *shimeji* or enoki), sliced

Sichuan chili oil or other hot pepper oil, for garnish

Fresh ginger, julienned, for garnish (optional)

TO MAKE THE DUCK STOCK, DUCK FAT, AND CRACKLINGS:

If you start with a whole duck, make the stock first. Chop the carcass into a couple of big pieces and place in a large stockpot. Cover with about 10 cups of water and bring to a boil over high heat. Turn the heat down to medium and simmer for 2 to 3 hours uncovered, occasionally skimming any foam. Strain and allow to cool, then pass through a fat separator (see note). Retain the stock and the fat.

Pour the reserved fat into a medium saucepan. Be sure there is no stock in the fat, or it will splatter. Add the reserved fat trimmings and gently cook over very low heat until the fat has rendered and is clear, about 90 minutes. Cut the reserved duck skin into strips and add it to the rendered fat. Continue cooking until the skin is golden brown and crispy, about 5 minutes. Strain the fat, reserve the cracklings, and pour the fat into a pint-size jar and refrigerate.

Alternatively, you can skip all this and use prepared duck or chicken stock, or mushroom broth, and olive oil for fat, and skip the crackling garnish altogether.

TO MAKE THE CONGEE:

In a large stockpot, add 6 cups of stock, the duck legs, dried shiitake, the white parts of the scallions, garlic, and ginger, and bring to a simmer over medium-high heat. Add the rice and stir. Bring to a simmer again, then turn down the heat to medium-low and maintain a hot simmer. Partially cover the pot, allowing a tiny bit of steam to escape. Simmer for 40 minutes, until the duck meat starts to fall from the bones.

Continued on page 174 . . .

173

DUCK AND SHIITAKE CONGEE

NOTE: If you make stocks often, a fat separator is a very useful and inexpensive tool. Alternatively, you can refrigerate the stock and, when the fat has solidified, remove it with a slotted spoon.

Remove the duck legs. Remove the meat from the bones, shred the meat, and set aside. Return the bones to the stockpot and continue to simmer for 30 minutes more, partially covered, until the rice is like a porridge. Remove the bones, mushrooms, ginger, and scallions and discard. Check the consistency of the porridge. A congee is ready when it's creamy and homogenous (not separating into liquid and rice layers). Add salt to taste. Add the reserved duck leg meat. Cover and keep warm while you prepare the other ingredients.

In a small saucepan, add 1 inch of water and bring to a boil, covered. Add the eggs to the pot and cover. Steam the eggs for 6 minutes, then chill in an ice bath until cool, 5 minutes or so. Remove the eggs from the ice bath, shell, cut in half at the equator, and set aside.

Score the skin of the duck breasts with a knife and allow them to come to room temperature. In a medium skillet over medium heat, add ½ tablespoon of duck fat (or olive oil). Add the duck breasts skin-side down. Reduce the heat to low. Allow the fat in the duck breasts to render slowly and the skin to turn golden brown, about 20 minutes. Flip the duck breasts and continue to cook them for another 5 minutes, until they are medium rare and their internal temperature reaches 125°F to 130°F. Allow to rest for 15 minutes.

In a medium sauté pan over medium-high heat, add the remaining ½ tablespoon of duck fat and 1 teaspoon of sesame oil. Add the fresh mushrooms and sauté until slightly crispy on the edges and most of their water has been given up, about 10 minutes. Remove from the pan and set aside.

TO ASSEMBLE THE DISH:
Ladle the porridge into four bowls. Slice the duck breasts on the bias and place a quarter of the meat on top of the porridge in each bowl, leaving room for a quarter of the mushrooms. Add a halfed soft-boiled egg and scatter the chopped scallion greens and crispy duck skin on top. Garnish with a drizzle of sesame oil and Sichuan chili oil and a sprinkle of julienned ginger, if you like. Serve immediately.

TURKEY BREAST ROULADE WITH SOUS VIDE PORCINI

BY CHARLES LUCE, NEW JERSEY | YIELD: 4 SERVINGS

During a good porcini year, I dehydrate at least half my hoard. This is a recipe that takes advantage of that stash. Half of this recipe—the turkey roulade—comes from the New York Times *adaptation of an Ina Garten recipe. The other half—sous vide porcini—is my own invention. Sous vide is an extraordinary method for extracting maximum flavor from mushrooms: A fistful of dried porcini in a pint jar of heavy cream submerged in a sous vide device's water bath, or simply placed in a low-temperature oven, emerges several hours later a brown, fragrant, fatty, umami bomb. You can also make this recipe with two pounded chicken breasts. The recipe calls for some day-ahead preparation. You don't have to have a sous vide water bath or an immersion circulator, but do have some kitchen twine on hand and, if you've got one, an instant-read thermometer.*

2 to 3 pounds butterflied, boneless, skin-on turkey breast

1 cup buttermilk

½ cup (about ½ ounce) dried porcini slices, lightly packed

½ cup heavy cream

Salt and freshly ground black pepper

2 tablespoons extra-virgin olive oil, divided

1 cup diced yellow onion

3 teaspoons minced garlic

½ teaspoon nigella seeds

1½ teaspoons chopped fresh sage plus several whole sage leaves

1 teaspoon minced rosemary leaves

1½ teaspoon dried thyme leaves

½ cup dry white wine

NOTE: Check out the many videos on tying roasts on the internet; this is one technique better seen than described!

The evening before cooking, place the turkey breast in a large resealable bag and add the buttermilk. Seal the bag, squeezing to eliminate as much air as possible, and refrigerate overnight. Remove from refrigeration about 1 hour before preparing the dish.

Several hours before preparing the meal, place the dried porcini slices in a 1-pint glass jar and add the cream. Use a spoon or fork to push the mushrooms under the cream. Seal the jar tightly and submerge in a sous vide bath set to 170°F, or place in a low-temperature oven set to 170°F or as close as you can get to that temperature. Allow the mushrooms to process for 3 to 4 hours, until they are very soft and the cream is a caramel color. Remove them from the heat and allow to cool. Add salt and pepper to taste.

Position a rack in the center of the oven and preheat the oven to 350°F.

Heat 1 tablespoon olive oil in a small sauté pan over medium heat. Add the onions and sauté until just beginning to brown, a few minutes. Add the garlic and cook 1 minute to soften. Remove from the heat and add the nigella seeds, sage, rosemary, and thyme. Stir and set aside.

Continued on page 176 . . .

Remove the turkey breast from the bag and scrape off as much residual buttermilk as possible. Do not wash. Remove the skin and reserve. If the meat is quite thick, it may be trimmed or pounded to produce an overall thickness of 1 inch or less. Lay the meat out and add salt and pepper to taste, then evenly spread the onion mixture on one side. Spread the porcini and cream mixture evenly over the onion mixture.

Arrange the turkey breast so that the narrow end is next to you, then roll the meat up like a yule log, ending with the seam side up. If the onion and porcini mixtures leak out of the ends, you can either unroll and remove some or reroll the roulade a little looser. Drape the skin over the seam. If it doesn't cover the entire seam, it's OK. Using clean kitchen twine or string, tie the roulade as you would a roast, at 2-inch or 3-inch intervals (see note). Place the whole sage leaves under the twine.

Place the roulade, skin side up, on a small sheet pan or roasting pan. Drizzle the skin with the remaining 1 tablespoon of olive oil, pour the wine into the pan around the roulade, and roast for 1 to 2 hours, or until an instant-read thermometer registers 150°F in the center of the roulade.

Remove the roulade from the oven and allow to rest, covered with aluminum foil, for 15 minutes before serving. Slice roulade and drench each slice in any juices that have escaped, then serve.

CHICKEN WITH MORELS AND SHERRY

BY BRITT BUNYARD, ILLINOIS | YIELD: 4 SERVINGS

I published a version of this recipe in my recent book, The Beginner's Guide to Mushrooms *(2020), because it is one of my favorites. Dried mushrooms allow you to enjoy the flavors of mushroom season even out of season, and I collect many varieties when I'm on the road in support of* Fungi *magazine or the Telluride Mushroom Festival. I learned this recipe from Eugenia Bone, who says it is derived from* poulet au vin jaune, *a French dish that calls for a sherrylike wine from the Jura region of France. You can use other chicken parts in this recipe, like bone-in breasts, or a combination of parts. The recipe also is easily doubled if you're serving more than four.*

2 tablespoons unsalted butter

¼ cup finely chopped shallots

4 to 6 bone-in, skin-on chicken thighs, about 3 pounds

Salt and freshly ground black pepper

1 ounce dried morels or ⅓ pound fresh morels, cleaned, or a combination

1 cup sweet sherry

1 cup semidry sherry

½ cup heavy cream

Fresh tarragon, chopped, for garnish (optional)

In a Dutch oven, heat the butter over medium-high heat and add the shallots. Cook until they are translucent, a few minutes. Remove the shallots with a slotted spoon and set aside.

In the same pot, add the chicken thighs, skin-side down, in a single layer, and add salt and pepper to taste. Cook until the skin is brown, about 12 minutes. Turn the chicken and cook for a few more minutes, until the juices run clear. Turn the heat down to medium-low and add the shallots, morels, and the two sherries. The sherry must cover the chicken. If it does not, add more. (Alternatively, you can increase the liquid by adding chicken stock or water.) Gently bring to a boil over a medium heat. Cover and cook until the chicken is tender, about 20 minutes. The sauce will reduce some; this is good as long as the pan doesn't become dry. Add the cream, stir to combine, and continue cooking, uncovered, until the sauce thickens and the cream has reduced by a third, about 5 minutes more. Adjust the seasoning.

Garnish with fresh tarragon, if you like, and serve over noodles.

CHICKEN THIGHS WITH PORCINI AND LEEKS

BY GARY GILBERT, MASSACHUSETTS | YIELD: 4 SERVINGS

I have been known to visit my favorite porcini patches (somewhere in North America) and subsequently turn my hotel room into a porcini drying factory. This is a simple, inexpensive dish that I make almost weekly with dried porcini. You can vary the amount of cream or broth to suit your taste; the flavors meld together so well, you can easily adapt the ratios.

1 cup chicken stock

¾ ounce dried porcini

2 tablespoons olive oil, divided

2 cups leeks, rinsed well to remove any sand and thinly sliced, or 2 cups onions, sliced

1 tablespoon finely sliced garlic

4 to 6 (about 2¼ pounds) bone-in, skin-on chicken thighs

¼ cup dry sherry or white wine

1 cup heavy cream

½ teaspoon salt and freshly ground black pepper

1 heaping tablespoon dried tarragon

Heat the chicken stock in a small saucepan over medium heat. Add the dried porcini, then take the pot off the heat and allow the mushrooms to rehydrate, about 10 minutes.

In a medium skillet, heat 1 tablespoon of olive oil over medium-low heat. Add the leeks and cook about 10 minutes, stirring often, until they are very soft. Then add the garlic and continue cooking, another minute. Pour the leeks into a bowl and set aside.

Turn up the heat to medium-high. Add the remaining 1 tablespoon of olive oil to the skillet and add the chicken thighs, skin-side down. Cook about 12 minutes without moving them to render the fat and brown the skin. Then move the thighs around so they all get evenly browned and cook another 5 minutes. Turn the thighs over, add the sherry or wine, and cook until the alcohol is mostly cooked off, a few minutes. Add the leeks back to the pan, turn the heat down to medium-low, then add the cream, the stock and rehydrated porcini, the salt and black pepper to taste, and the tarragon, and cover the dish. Cook 40 minutes, until the chicken is tender and cooked through.

Serve on a bed of basmati rice or a pasta, if you like.

SIMPLE MATSUTAKE CHICKEN

BY CHRIS PHILLIPS, KENTUCKY | YIELD: 4 SERVINGS

I am a nature lover—practically a nature worshipper. I was impressed with the Fantastic Fungi *movie and inspired to expand my relationship with mushrooms beyond simple buttons. The matsutake (*Tricholoma matsutake*), which I buy from Northwest Wild Foods (Nwwildfoods.com), sounded a little challenging at first, but I was curious. You can make this simple, delicious dish with fresh matsutakes, but it works equally well with dried. You can make this recipe with split chicken breasts as well, or bone-in chicken thighs, as pictured here. They will take a little longer to cook.*

4 tablespoons ghee, or unsalted butter, divided

8 ounces fresh or 1 ounce dried matsutake (hen of the woods) mushrooms, chopped (see note)

6 boneless, skinless chicken thighs

1 cup rough chopped white onions

1 cup rough chopped red onions

Himalayan or other salt and freshly ground black pepper

½ teaspoon turmeric powder

½ teaspoon mustard powder

Dash of *umeboshi* or other vinegar, for garnish

2 cups cooked basmati rice

NOTE: If dried mushrooms are used, soak them for 20 minutes in warm water before chopping.

Preheat the oven to 350°F.

Grease the interior of a baking dish large enough to hold the chicken pieces in one layer with 1 tablespoon ghee or butter. Add the matsutake in a layer. Wash and dry the chicken thighs and layer over the mushrooms. Add salt and pepper to taste. Then smother with onions, sprinkle with turmeric and mustard powder, and top with the remaining ghee or butter.

Cover with a lid or foil and place in the oven. Bake for 1 hour or until the chicken is falling-apart tender. Check and adjust the seasoning to taste.

To serve, break the chicken up and mix it in with the onions, garnish with vinegar, and serve with cooked basmati rice to soak up the sauce, if you like.

CORNISH GAME HENS WITH CAULIFLOWER MUSHROOM

BY JANE B. MASON, COLORADO | YIELD: 4 SERVINGS

If there's one thing you can say about Sparassis crispa, *it's that it can tolerate a long, slow simmer and still maintain its wonderful chewiness. I created this dish after stumbling upon a 9-pound specimen during a rainstorm on the Northern California coast. Like an iceberg revealing only its tip, the mushroom was mostly buried. It was a lot of work to clean that specimen, but worth the effort! You can prepare this dish in an electric slow cooker or in a Dutch oven.*

2 to 3 ounces dried cauliflower mushrooms

2 Cornish game hens

Salt and freshly ground black pepper

½ lemon, halved

1 teaspoon herbes de Provence, divided

4 tablespoons extra-virgin olive oil, divided

1 cup sliced yellow onions

1 tablespoon minced garlic

¼ cup dry white wine

½ teaspoon dried thyme

1 tablespoon unsalted butter (optional)

1 tablespoon all-purpose flour (optional)

2 to 4 tablespoons heavy cream (optional)

2 tablespoons chopped flat-leafed parsley, for garnish

NOTE: Check out any of the many videos on trussing birds on the internet—this is one technique better seen than described!

Place the dried cauliflower mushrooms into a 2-quart saucepan and cover well with about 4 cups of water. Bring to a boil over medium-high heat, then reduce the heat to medium-low and simmer gently for 5 minutes. Remove from the heat, cover, and cool completely. (I like to do this part the night before and leave it on the stove, covered, overnight.) When cool, drain the mushrooms over a bowl, reserving the broth.

Dry the game hens and sprinkle their insides with salt and pepper. Place 1 piece of lemon and ½ teaspoon of herbes de Provence inside each hen. Truss the birds using kitchen string, (see note), lightly salt and pepper the outside, and set aside.

If using your oven, preheat the oven to 325°F.

Heat 2 tablespoons of olive oil in a medium skillet over medium heat and sauté the onions and garlic together until the onions are translucent, 2 to 3 minutes. Salt to taste and transfer the mixture to a large Dutch oven or slow cooker.

Wipe out the skillet, return it to medium heat, and toss in the mushrooms for a brief dry sauté. After 1 or 2 minutes, sprinkle lightly with salt. When the mushrooms are lightly browned, about 3 minutes more, add a few tablespoons of the reserved mushroom broth and simmer, stirring occasionally, until the broth has evaporated, a few minutes more. Transfer to the Dutch oven or slow cooker.

Continued on page 186 . . .

Heat 2 tablespoons of olive oil in a large nonstick skillet over medium-high heat and brown the game hens, turning until all sides are slightly golden, about 7 minutes altogether. Then tuck them into the Dutch oven or slow cooker on top of the onions and mushrooms. Pour 1 cup of the reserved mushroom broth and the white wine over the top and sprinkle with thyme. Add salt and pepper to taste. If you are using a Dutch oven, cover and place the pot in the oven to cook for 1½ hours. If using a slow cooker, set it on high and cook for 3 to 3½ hours. In either case, cook until the hens reach an internal temperature of 165°F.

Remove the game hens from the pot and let them rest a few minutes. Slice each one in half, place on a baking pan, and slide under the broiler to brown the skin, a few minutes.

To make the gravy, drain the cooking juices into a saucepan (if you use a slow cooker, there will be more cooking juices than if you use a Dutch oven) and add 1 cup of the reserved mushroom broth. Simmer over medium heat, stirring frequently, until reduced by half, about 8 minutes. For a thicker gravy, add 1 tablespoon butter and sprinkle 1 tablespoon flour over the liquid while whisking vigorously to blend. When it is reduced, add cream, if desired, and adjust the seasoning.

Spoon the mushroom-and-onion mixture into four wide, shallow bowls, place half a hen on top in each, pour gravy over and around it, and garnish with parsley. Serve with an extra bowl for the bones, which can be simmered after dinner to produce a rich, delicious broth for later use.

CHICKEN CHANTERELLE PAPRIKASH

BY PAUL SADOWSKI, NEW YORK | YIELD: 4 SERVINGS

The New York Mycological Society grew out of a mushroom class at the New School taught by the avant-garde composer John Cage. One of the students, Laurette Reisman, suggested the group go on a mushrooming trip in Vermont, and so the first chanterelle weekend occurred in the summer of 1962. The society has visited Vermont every summer since. We typically come away from the weekend with a bag or two of chanterelles, which gave rise to this recipe. I was John Cage's music engraver when he died in 1992. I was bereft of a mentor, employer, and friend, and sought to fill the void in my life with mushrooms. The following month, I took a beginner's mushroom class with the late Gary Lincoff, and today I teach that same class at the New York Botanical Garden.

½ cup flour

¼ teaspoon marjoram

Salt and freshly ground black pepper

2½ tablespoons unsalted butter, divided

2½ tablespoons olive oil, divided

1 tablespoon sliced garlic

1½ pounds skinned and boned chicken thighs and breast

1 cup diced red bell peppers, plus 4 teaspoons minced red pepper, for garnish

1 cup diced onion

10 ounces chanterelles (fresh or frozen)

3 tablespoons paprika (smoked, sweet, hot, or a combination), divided

1½ cups chicken stock, and up to ½ cup more, if necessary

¼ cup white wine, and up to ¼ cup more, if necessary

2 cups sour cream

Prepare the seasoned flour. In a shallow bowl, combine the flour and the marjoram, and season with salt and pepper to taste.

Heat 1 tablespoon of butter and 1 tablespoon of oil in a large skillet over medium heat. Add the garlic and cook for 1 minute, until fragrant. Do not brown. Remove the garlic and reserve.

Dredge the chicken in the seasoned flour and add immediately to the pan. Sauté until golden, about 5 to 6 minutes, then remove the chicken and set aside.

In the same pan, add the remaining butter and oil and melt over medium heat. Add the peppers and cook for a few minutes until soft, then add the onions, the chanterelles, and 1 tablespoon paprika. Cook for about 7 minutes, stirring often, until the chanterelles give up their liquid and the liquid starts to evaporate. Add the chicken stock and the wine and bring to a boil. Add the remaining paprika and stir to combine for 1 minute, then return the chicken and garlic to the pan. Cover and cook until the chicken is cooked through, up to 15 minutes. If the pan looks dry, add up to ½ cup stock, wine, or a combination. Stir in the sour cream, lower the heat to medium-low, and continued to cook for about 10 more minutes, or until the sauce thickens.

Serve garnished with the minced red pepper, and over egg noodles or spaetzle, if you like.

PHEASANT WITH LECCINUM AU VIN

BY DEREK MOORE, NEW JERSEY | YIELD: 4 SERVINGS

I'm a chemical engineer who enjoys experimenting with foods that I have encountered throughout my connections and experiences. My first foraging experience was with Leccinum aurantiacum, *which is a mushroom commonly foraged by Eastern Europeans in the United States.* L. aurantiacum *have a rich and fruity flavor, but they spoil quickly and must be cooked the same day they are picked. This dish is based on coq au vin, but it is stripped down to allow the mushrooms to shine.* L. aurantiacum *may be substituted with fresh porcini, and the pheasant with a whole chicken. Here, the pheasant is marinated for a few hours, but overnight is fine.*

1 pheasant (about 2½ pounds) split or cut into 4 portions (see note)

3 cups dry red wine (like burgundy)

Salt and freshly ground black pepper

3 tablespoons olive oil, divided

5 large sprigs thyme

2 cups diced Spanish onion

3 medium carrots (6 ounces), cut into large chunks

8 ounces (about 4 cups) chopped young *Leccinum aurantiacum* or other young boletus mushrooms

2 tablespoons minced garlic

2 cups chicken broth

2 tablespoons cold unsalted butter

NOTE: If you split the pheasant, when cooked it will be tender enough to easily divide into 4 portions.

Place the pheasant in a deep bowl or large resealable bag with the wine, salt, and pepper, and refrigerate for at least 2 or up to 10 hours. Remove the pheasant and pat dry. Reserve the marinade.

Heat 2 tablespoons olive oil in a Dutch oven with a fitted cover over medium-high heat and add the pheasant. Brown the pheasant on both sides, about 8 to 10 minutes altogether. Remove the bird and set aside. Recoat the bottom of the Dutch oven with the remaining tablespoon of olive oil and add the thyme sprigs. Turn the heat down to medium and fry until slightly brown and aromatic, a few minutes, then remove the sprigs and set aside. Add the onion and carrots and cook until the onions become translucent, about 4 minutes. Add the mushrooms and cook about 2 minutes, then add the garlic and continue cooking until the vegetables and mushrooms are golden brown, about 6 minutes. Add the reserved red wine marinade and gently boil until the wine is reduced by half and the alcohol smell disappears, about 5 minutes. Then add the chicken broth and bring to a simmer. Lower the heat to medium-low to maintain a hot simmer. Add the pheasant and the fried thyme sprigs back into the pot, cover, and simmer for 30 minutes, until the pheasant is very tender. Add salt and pepper to taste, stir in the butter, and remove from the heat.

Serve with a starch or grain; mashed potatoes are the classic accompaniment.

MOM'S RED-COOKED CHICKEN WINGS WITH WOOD EAR MUSHROOMS

BY CATHY RESIDENT, TEXAS | YIELD: 4 SERVINGS

When my mom—a physician who trained in Western medicine in China—got lung cancer, she returned to her home country, because there was no treatment available for her in the United States. There, she was able to get medication that extended her life by several years. It was my understanding that the protocols my mother received included medicinal mushrooms. That launched my interest in mycology. This recipe was my mother's; the dish is called red-cooked chicken because the slow braising creates a lustrous caramel color. The wood ear mushrooms, which have many health benefits, add texture and earthy nuance. Tofu can be substituted for the chicken wings.

10 chicken wings

1 ounce fresh wood ear mushrooms, or ½ ounce dried wood ear mushrooms (see note)

4 scallions, 3 sliced diagonally into 1-inch pieces and 1 minced, for garnish

¼ cup Shaoxing wine or dry sherry

2 tablespoons dark soy sauce

2 tablespoons light soy sauce

1 teaspoon sugar

2 slices of fresh ginger, about the size of a quarter

1 teaspoon minced garlic

NOTE: If using fresh wood ear mushrooms, rinse them and trim off any hardened edges. If using dried wood ear mushrooms, soak them for 20 minutes in warm water and then trim.

Place ¼ cup of water and all of the ingredients (except the minced scallions for garnish) into a Dutch oven and bring to a boil over medium-high heat. Cover the pot, turn the heat down to low, and simmer gently for 30 minutes.

Remove the lid, turn the heat up to medium-low, and continue cooking for another 30 minutes or so, turning the chicken wings every 10 minutes until they brown evenly. Remove from heat and serve garnished with the minced scallions. This dish can also be served cold or at room temperature.

MUSHROOM VIN WITH LAMB CHOPS

BY HARRY KOEPPEL, NEW YORK | YIELD: SERVES 4, WITH 2 CUPS OF SAUCE

Mushrooms are crazy versatile, earthy, muddy ingredients that as a chef I find incredibly fun and inspiring to cook with. Mushroom sauces really allow you to explore that range. I'm involved in a sauce company right now called Batchworthy, and on the side, I am creating some of my own sauces called Thought Sauce. (You can find them on my Instagram account, @koeppelharry.) This recipe is really a kind of vinaigrette, hence the name. The sauce recipe is adapted from one I learned as a line cook at Blue Hill in New York City. It pairs well with many foods, but here, I made it with grilled lamb chops and, for a vegetarian option, roasted carrots. The recipe calls for two prepared ingredients, garlic-infused oil and mushroom stock.

FOR THE MUSHROOM STOCK

5 cups water

2 ounces dried shiitake

FOR THE GARLIC OIL

1 head of garlic (about 1½ ounces)

1 pint canola or other neutral oil

FOR THE MUSHROOM VIN

1 tablespoon olive oil

6 ounces onion, thinly sliced (about 2 cups)

1 cup mushroom stock reduction (instructions below)

3 tablespoons garlic puree (instructions below)

2 tablespoons Dijon mustard

2 tablespoons balsamic vinegar

1 tablespoon soy sauce

2 teaspoons Worcestershire sauce

1⅓ cups garlic oil (instructions below)

TO MAKE THE MUSHROOM STOCK:

Add the water and dried shiitake to a medium pot and bring to a boil over medium-high heat. Boil for 10 minutes, until the mushrooms are fully hydrated and the water is brown. Strain out the mushrooms and continue to boil gently, uncovered, until the stock has reduced to 1 cup, for about 20 minutes. Set aside.

TO MAKE THE GARLIC OIL:

Cut the head of garlic in half along the equator, skins on. Combine the garlic and oil in a small pot and cook over low heat. The oil should be hot enough to produce a trickle of small bubbles. Do not overboil. Cook for about 20 minutes, until the garlic is golden brown and very soft. Strain, but retain both the oil and the garlic, and let them both cool down. When the garlic is cool enough to handle, press the soft garlic out of its skin and retain the pulp. You should have about 3 tablespoons.

TO MAKE THE MUSHROOM VIN:

Heat the olive oil in a medium skillet over medium-low heat and add the onion. Cook the onions low and slow until they are caramelized, very soft, and golden, about 30 minutes. Do not brown.

Place the onion, 1 cup of stock, the garlic puree, and the mustard, balsamic vinegar, soy sauce, and Worcestershire sauce into a food processor or blender. Blend until smooth, then slowly add the garlic oil in a thin stream to emulsify the sauce. The sauce holds for about 2 weeks in the fridge. Give it a good shake if it separates.

Continued on page 193...

MUSHROOM VIN WITH LAMB CHOPS

FOR THE LAMB CHOPS

2 pounds loin lamb chops

½ cup white wine

Two 3-inch sprigs rosemary

Salt and freshly ground black pepper

1 tablespoon butter (optional)

1 tablespoon chopped flat-leafed parsley,
  for garnish (optional)

FOR THE CARROTS

2 large, thick horse carrots (about 1
  pound), cut in half from pole to pole

1 cup mushroom or vegetable stock

1 bay leaf

Salt and freshly ground black pepper

1 tablespoon chopped flat-leafed parsley,
  for garnish (optional)

TO PREPARE THE LAMB CHOPS:

Place the chops in a nonreactive bowl or sealable plastic bag with the wine, rosemary, and salt and pepper to taste. Let come to room temperature.

Heat your grill or, alternatively, use a grill pan on top of your stove. If using an outdoor grill, remove the chops from the marinade and place on the grill. Cook for about 5 minutes, until brown, then flip over and cook for another 2 minutes for medium rare. Remove the chops and let rest. If using a grill pan on your oven burners, heat 1 tablespoon of butter in the pan over high heat. Remove the chops from the marinade and add to the pan. Cook for 6 minutes, until brown, then flip over and cook for another 2 minutes for medium rare.

Serve the chops over a puddle of the sauce. Sprinkle with parsley, if you like.

TO PREPARE THE CARROTS:

Place the carrots in a braising pan and add the stock, bay leaf, and salt and pepper to taste. Braise over medium heat for 15 minutes, until the carrots are tender but not soft. Heat your broiler and place the braising pan under the broiler for a few minutes to lightly brown the tops of the carrots, a few minutes.

Serve the carrots over a puddle of the sauce. Sprinkle with parsley, if you like.

MUSHROOM GYOZA

BY EUGENIA BONE, NEW YORK | YIELD: 14 PIECES

These gyoza are seriously addictive. I can't eat just a few. The stuffing combines duxelles—minced mushrooms cooked down to a nubbly paste—and ground pork flavored with ginger, scallions, and soy sauce. You can definitely make these without the meat; just double the amount of duxelles and flavor them as described, or replace the pork with finely chopped cabbage. This recipe makes about a half-pint of duxelles. You will need about ¼ pint for gyoza with sausage, but you will need the whole half-pint if you want to make an all-mushroom version. I call for white button mushrooms here, but you can make duxelles using other species, too, like shiitake or hen of the woods.

1 tablespoon olive oil

10 ounces white button mushrooms, minced (about 3 cups)

¼ cup minced shallots

3 tablespoons white wine, dry marsala, or dry sherry

Salt and freshly ground black pepper

3 ounces ground pork

3 tablespoons minced green scallions, divided

½ teaspoon minced ginger

½ teaspoon minced garlic

2 tablespoons plus ½ teaspoon toasted sesame oil, divided

¼ cup plus ½ teaspoon soy sauce, divided

14 round gyoza wrappers

TO MAKE THE DUXELLES:

Heat the olive oil in a large nonstick skillet over medium heat. If all the mushrooms and shallots can fit in a single layer, then put them all in your pan. Otherwise, prepare the duxelles in batches. If the skillet is crowded, the mushrooms will steam rather than brown, and your end product will be mushy. Sauté the mushrooms and shallots in batches, if necessary, until the mushrooms give up their liquid and the liquid evaporates, about 10 minutes. Stir frequently. Once all the mushrooms are cooked, return them to the pan (if cooking in batches) and add the wine and salt and pepper to taste. Continue cooking until the duxelles become quite dry and the mushrooms begin to take on a golden color, another 10 minutes.

TO MAKE THE GYOZA:

In a small bowl, combine the pork, 2 tablespoons of scallions, ginger, garlic, ½ teaspoon of sesame oil, and ½ teaspoon of soy sauce. It's okay to pulse this in your food processor if you like. Add half of the duxelles, and stir in by hand. The rest of the duxelles can be saved for another recipe. They are great on a grilled cheese sandwich! You can hold duxelles in the refrigerator for a few days if you pack them into a sterilized jar; that is, a jar that has been boiled in water for 10 minutes at sea level, adding 1 minute for every 1,000 feet above sea level.

Continued on page 197 . . .

On your countertop, lay out the gyoza wrappers. Place 1 tablespoon of the pork-and-duxelles mixture onto the lower half of each wrapper and moisten the edges of the wrapper. (I just dip my finger into a small bowl of water and paint the water around the rim.) Then fold the upper half of the wrapper over and, with a strong pinch, seal the gyoza closed.

Heat 2 tablespoons of the remaining sesame oil in a large nonstick skillet over medium-high heat. Add as many gyoza as will fit comfortably in your pan, cooking in batches if needed. Brown the gyoza, about 3 minutes, then flip over and brown for another minute. Most of the browning will happen on the center of the gyoza. Add enough water to cover the bottom of the skillet. When you add the water, it will boil hard for a second before settling down, and some wrappers may open slightly. It's OK. Cover and poach the gyoza for about 3 minutes, until the water cooks out and the gyoza skins are somewhat translucent, yellowed, and wrinkled.

Slip the first batch of gyoza onto a serving plate and prepare any remaining gyoza.

In a small bowl, combine about ¼ cup of soy sauce and the remaining 1 tablespoon of minced scallions for the dipping sauce.

GARBANZO BEANS WITH CREMINI AND UNCURED BACON

BY NENI PANOURGIA, NEW YORK | YIELD: 4 SERVINGS

During the summer of 2020, a tenant in my building forgot she had stored her Tupperware in the oven, which led to a fire that destroyed her apartment. Our building having been built before World War II, the gas lines had developed enough tiny leaks over the years to make the gas company shut down service altogether. Because we didn't have enough electricity to run an electric stove, I spent a year coming up with hot plate–friendly dishes. This is one. You can make it with a wide variety of firm mushrooms, like boletes. Don't use sliced bacon, or the dish will end up fatty. Other canned beans, such as cannellini, can be substituted for the garbanzo beans; just don't use dark beans, because they will affect the color of the dish. If you want to use dried beans, rehydrate them overnight, then boil them gently until creamy and fork-tender.

Two 15-ounce cans garbanzo beans

4 tablespoons high-quality olive oil, divided

1 teaspoon dried marjoram or oregano

1 teaspoon dried thyme

Salt and freshly ground black pepper

1 tablespoon sliced garlic

8 to 10 ounces cremini mushrooms, sliced

1 cup chopped fresh flat-leaf parsley or cilantro, divided

1 teaspoon dried basil

1 cup uncured lean slab bacon, sliced into 1-inch pieces

1 tablespoon lemon juice

20 small grape tomatoes

Drain and rinse the garbanzo beans. Place them in a medium saucepan and add 3¾ cups of water. Add 2 tablespoons olive oil, marjoram, thyme, and salt to taste. Bring to a boil over high heat, then turn down to a robust simmer. Cook uncovered for about 1 hour, until about half of the water has evaporated. Remove from heat.

Warm the remaining 2 tablespoons of olive oil in a large skillet over medium heat and add the garlic. Cook until the garlic starts to sizzle, 1 minute or so, then add the mushrooms and sauté, stirring frequently, until they start to sweat, a few minutes. Add ⅔ cup of parsley, the basil, and the bacon. Continue cooking for about 3 to 4 minutes to merge the flavors. Add the garbanzos with their water, black pepper to taste, and the lemon juice. Cook for an additional 5 minutes and add the tomatoes, leaving them whole. Shake the pan so that all the ingredients are well distributed, and turn the heat off. Let it sit for 5 minutes, then add the remaining parsley.

MORELS STUFFED WITH SAUSAGE AND SAGE

BY SEBASTIAN CAROSI, OREGON | YIELD: 4 SERVINGS

As a professional chef, I rely heavily on the recipes my family has passed down through the generations. But let's look further back: I think that when we eat wild foods, we relive deeply satisfying ancestral memories. The morel is more than just a wild food; it is among the most delectable of edibles. For me, good eating provides plenty of motivation to fill my basket with wild morels. I've used this family recipe, which is of Italian origin, many times.

12 ounces ground pork

¼ cup golden raisins, plumped in hot water and chopped

¼ cup panko breadcrumbs

2 tablespoons grated Parmesan cheese

2 tablespoons peeled and grated sweet onions

2 tablespoons toasted and chopped pine nuts (see note)

1 tablespoon minced fresh sage leaves, 2 to 3 large fresh sage leaves, and 8 to 12 very small fresh sage leaves, divided

1 tablespoon chopped fresh flat-leafed parsley

2 teaspoons finely chopped garlic

1 teaspoon minced fresh thyme

¼ teaspoon wild fennel pollen (optional)

20 medium morels (any *Morchella* species except *M. verpas*), washed

2 tablespoons vegetable oil

1 tablespoon rendered bacon fat

4 tablespoons salted butter

Salt and freshly ground black pepper

2 tablespoons balsamic vinegar

NOTE: To toast pine nuts, place the nuts in a small, heavy skillet over medium-high heat. Shaking the pan frequently, toast the nuts until they begin to take on a golden color. Remove from the heat promptly.

Combine the pork, raisins, breadcrumbs, cheese, onions, pine nuts, minced sage, parsley, garlic, thyme, and fennel pollen, if using, in a medium mixing bowl. Mix and set aside.

Fill a pastry bag fitted with a small regular tip with the pork filling. Pipe the filling into the morels, place on a baking tray, and refrigerate for up to 3 hours. Alternatively, roll the pork mixture into meatballs a little smaller than your morels and stuff the caps. You may have to slit open the stems to do this.

Preheat the oven to 400°F.

Heat the vegetable oil and bacon fat in a large cast-iron skillet over medium-low heat. Add the stuffed morels and brown them for 4 minutes or so, then add the large sage leaves and continue cooking for another 2 to 4 minutes. Place the skillet into the hot oven and cook the morels for 8 to 10 minutes until the pork filling has lost its pink hue.

Remove the skillet from the oven and place it back on the burner. Add the butter and small sage leaves and heat over medium heat for a few minutes, until the butter is browned.

Season the morels with salt and pepper to taste, and drizzle with the balsamic vinegar.

MUSHROOM SAUSAGE ROLLS

BY EUGENIA BONE, NEW YORK | YIELD: 6 ROLLS

I saw a version of this recipe in the British newspaper the Guardian *and knew I had to try it with my own mushroom duxelles. (I make a batch every so often and keep it in the refrigerator.) These rolls are very easy to make, and it's very hard to eat just one. They are a great party food, late-night snack food, or lunch-while-standing-at-the-counter food. To make life easier, I use premade frozen puff pastry. (Pepperidge Farm is fine.) This recipe makes about a half-pint of duxelles. I call for* Agaricus bisporus *here, but you can make duxelles out of other species, too, like hen of the woods.*

1 tablespoon olive oil

10 ounces white button mushrooms, minced (about 3 cups)

¼ cup minced shallots

3 tablespoons white wine, dry marsala, or sherry

Salt and freshly ground black pepper

One 10-by-10-inch sheet defrosted puff pastry, plus flour for rolling

3 tablespoons Dijon mustard

12 ounces sausage meat (either loose meat or sausages with casings removed)

1 small egg, beaten

NOTE: You can hold duxelles in the refrigerator up to ten days if you pack them into a sterilized jar; that is, a jar that has been boiled in water for 10 minutes at sea level, adding 1 minute for every 1,000 feet above sea level.

TO MAKE THE DUXELLES:
Heat the olive oil in a large nonstick skillet over medium heat. If all the mushrooms and shallots can fit in a single layer, then put them all in your pan. Otherwise, prepare the duxelles in batches. If the skillet is crowded, the mushrooms will steam rather than brown, and your end product will be mushy. Sauté the mushrooms and shallots in batches, if necessary, until the mushrooms give up their liquid and the liquid evaporates, about 10 minutes. Stir frequently. Once all the mushrooms are cooked, return them to the pan (if cooking in batches) and add the wine and salt and pepper to taste. Continue cooking until the duxelles become quite dry and the mushrooms begin to take on a golden color, another 10 minutes (see note).

Preheat the oven to 350°F.

TO MAKE THE ROLLS:
Lay the sheet of puff pastry on a lightly floured board. Sprinkle some flour over the pastry. With a rolling pin, gently roll out the pastry until it is 1 to 2 inches larger on all sides. Cut the pastry into six pieces, each about the size of a Tarot card (or about 2 x 4 inches). Brush off any extra flour, and then brush the mustard on the surface of each piece of pastry.

Continued on page 204 . . .

Season the sausage meat and divide it into six oblong meatballs. Place a sausage ball close to the top of each pastry piece. Spread 1 tablespoon of duxelles along each meatball. Roll the pastry from the top down, encasing the sausage and duxelles. With your brush, add a little beaten egg to the edge of the pastry to seal the dough.

Place the rolls seam down on a baking sheet. (I use a Silpat® on my baking sheet to avoid sticking.) Brush the tops of the rolls with a little more beaten egg. Cut a couple of slits in the rolls so steam can vent during cooking, and pop them in the oven for about 30 minutes, until they are golden brown. Keep an eye out: They burn easily.

These rolls hold great in the refrigerator for a day or so and can be reheated in a low oven.

KARBONĀDE

BY CHARLOTTE GREENE, MASSACHUSETTS | YIELD: 4 SERVINGS

My grandmother grew up foraging mushrooms in Latvian forests, where foraging is still an extremely popular pastime, and she is the reason I decided to take the plunge into the world of wild mushrooms. She turns 103 in January 2022, and I learned to cook this quintessential Latvian pork and chanterelle dish to feel closer to her. Traditionally, panko is not used in this dish—just a dusting of flour—but I love the texture it adds. For a schnitzel-style fried cutlet, add 1 tablespoon of vodka to the eggs and grind the panko to a fine dust.

2 pounds pork tenderloin, cut into eight 4-ounce slices and pounded into thin cutlets

Salt and freshly ground black pepper

4 large eggs

1 tablespoon canola oil plus several cups, for frying

3 cups all-purpose flour

3 cups panko, or other breadcrumbs

12 ounces chanterelles, or honey or cremini mushrooms, or a combination, chopped into bite-sized pieces

3 tablespoons salted butter

½ cup (about 4 ounces) chopped yellow onions

1 tablespoon lemon juice

¾ cup heavy cream

2 to 4 tablespoons chopped fresh dill

NOTE: If you are using honey mushrooms, add the butter first (for a sweeter taste), and cook until they release their liquid, the liquid evaporates, and the mushrooms begin to brown, about 10 minutes.

Season both sides of the pork cutlets with salt and pepper. Beat the eggs and 1 tablespoon of oil in a shallow bowl, and season it with salt and pepper. Place the flour and panko into two separate shallow bowls.

Working one at a time, dip the cutlets first into the flour, then into the egg-oil mixture, and finally into the panko, shaking gently after each dip to remove any excess.

Place the chanterelles in a dry pan over medium heat (see note). Cook until the mushrooms release their liquid, the liquid evaporates, and the mushrooms begin to brown, about 10 minutes. Add the butter and onions to the skillet. Season with salt and pepper and cook until the onions are translucent and starting to brown at the edges, about 5 minutes. Stir in the lemon juice, and set aside.

Add 2 inches of oil to a deep skillet on medium heat until a pinch of panko thrown into the oil fries rapidly, about 350°F. Add the cutlets, and fry for a few minutes on each side until golden. Do not overcrowd your pan, or the temperature of the oil will drop and you will end up with soggy cutlets. Adjust heat as needed to keep the temperature at about 350°F. Remove the cooked cutlets to drain on a cooling rack or paper towels, and sprinkle with salt.

Finish the mushroom sauce by adding the heavy cream and dill to the chanterelle mixture, and cook gently over medium-low heat until the mushrooms and cream are hot, a few minutes. Check the seasoning.

To serve, plate the cutlets and pour the mushroom sauce over them. For a very Baltic accompaniment, serve with simple boiled potatoes tossed in sour cream or butter and dill.

PORK WITH CHANTERELLES AND APRICOT JAM

BY KEVIN BONE, NEW YORK | YIELD: 4 SERVINGS

I got into mushroom hunting when my family and I started spending time in Colorado's North Fork Valley on the Western Slope of the Rocky Mountains. In the late summer, if there are monsoonal rains, the chanterelles proliferate, and we collect pounds of them. The apricots are in season about the same time. Colorado chanterelles have an intense apricot perfume, and because pork is a sweet meat, this pairing was a no-brainer.

1½ pounds pork tenderloin or pork spareribs

2 garlic cloves, peeled and smashed

Salt and freshly ground black pepper

1 tablespoon unsalted butter

6 ounces fresh chanterelles, whole buttons or large mushrooms cut in half pole to pole

⅓ cup dry white wine

⅓ cup apricot jam

⅔ cup chicken stock

Preheat the oven to 350°F.

Rub the pork with garlic cloves and salt and pepper to taste. Let the meat rest while you cook the mushrooms.

Heat butter in a medium pan over medium-high heat. When the butter is foamy, less than 1 minute, add the mushrooms and cook until they release their water and the water evaporates, 7 to 10 minutes. Add the wine and continue cooking until it is mostly evaporated, a few minutes. There should be a couple of tablespoons of liquid in the bottom of the pan.

Place the pork in a roasting pan and roast in the oven until golden, about 20 minutes. If using ribs, you will need to cook them longer, about 25 to 30 minutes.

In a small saucepan, add the apricot jam and chicken stock, and salt and pepper to taste. Bring to a gentle boil over a medium heat until the jam dissolves and the sauce is viscous and slightly reduced, about 5 minutes. Add the sauce to the mushrooms.

Remove the pork from the oven and pour the mushroom sauce over it, then return to the oven and cook for another 10 minutes, until a thermometer inserted in the meat reads 145°F. Baste the pork with the sauce a few times to keep it moist.

Remove the pork and let it rest for a few minutes, then place on a board and slice. Place slices on a platter and cover with the chanterelle sauce.

BEEF FILLET WITH CHANTERELLE MARSALA SAUCE

BY JUSTIN COURSON, MISSISSIPPI | YIELD: 4 SERVINGS

I got bit by the mushroom bug here in Mississippi, where I work at the Manship Wood Fired Kitchen. The more I learned about mushrooms, the deeper into mycology I fell. My daughter, Eva Claire, and I love foraging for, and dining on, chanterelles from old-growth mixed hardwood forests. I hope this will continue to be a family tradition for years to come. We love chanterelles best with a steak or pork chop. Keeping a recipe simple is the best practice, and Eva Claire and I created this one together!

Four 8-ounce beef fillets

Salt and freshly ground black pepper

1 to 2 tablespoons neutral oil (like corn or canola)

5 tablespoons unsalted butter, divided

1 teaspoon minced garlic

1 pound fresh chanterelle mushrooms

1 teaspoon chopped fresh thyme

½ cup dry marsala wine

1 cup heavy cream

Preheat the oven to 400°F.

Season the beef fillets with salt and pepper to taste. Heat a large skillet over high heat to the point of smoking and add the oil. Set the fillets in the skillet and sear them for 2 to 3 minutes, until the meat browns and releases easily from the pan. Flip the meat over and brown the other side for another couple of minutes.

Place the skillet and meat in the oven and cook for 6 minutes for medium-rare (or longer for desired level of doneness). Remove the skillet from the oven, add 4 tablespoons of butter, and baste the meat with the butter for about 1½ minutes. Transfer the meat to a platter and allow it to rest for 10 minutes.

While the meat rests, make the sauce. In the same skillet, melt the remaining 1 tablespoon of butter over medium heat and add the garlic. Cook until the garlic starts to sweat, 1 or 2 minutes, then add the chanterelles. Season the mushrooms with salt and pepper and add the thyme. Cook, stirring frequently, for 6 to 7 minutes, until the mushrooms release their liquid. Add the marsala and continue cooking until the liquid in the pan is reduced by half, a few minutes. Add the cream and reduce by about a quarter, about 4 minutes, until the sauce takes on a lovely caramel color.

Serve the fillets covered with the chanterelle sauce.

BRAISED SHORT RIBS WITH PORCINI

BY GRAHAM STEINRUCK, WASHINGTON | YIELD: 4 SERVINGS

Hunting porcini is one of my favorite things to do. Some people call me Steinpilz (German for porcini) because I am so good at finding them. I think maybe they like me. And I have spent a lot of time in the mountains in Colorado in the summer; it's beautiful at 10,000 feet, where we find the Boletus rubriceps. They are so meaty, they are like vegan beef. But like the late Gary Lincoff said, dried porcini may be even better than fresh porcini. The taste of porcini infuses this dish. These ribs are marinated overnight, though you can marinate them for as few as three hours and the dish is still good.

1 ounce dried porcini mushrooms

Salt and freshly ground black pepper

3 pounds beef short ribs, cut into 4-inch chunks

⅔ pound yellow onions, peeled and cut into 1-inch pieces, plus ⅓ pound yellow onions, thinly sliced, divided

8 ounces cremini or button mushrooms, quartered

8 ounces carrots, cut into 1-inch pieces (about 4 medium carrots)

4 stalks celery, cut into 1-inch pieces

1 whole head of garlic, peel on, plus 1 minced garlic clove

10 black peppercorns

2 bay leaves

½ ounce fresh thyme

1 bottle (25 fluid ounces) red wine

4 tablespoons duck fat or olive oil, divided

8 cups beef or veal stock

Place the porcini in a medium saucepan and add 4 cups of water. Add a pinch of salt and bring to a simmer over medium heat. Simmer for about 8 minutes to soften the mushrooms, then take off the heat and allow them to cool in the pan, about 20 minutes. Squeeze the excess moisture from the mushrooms, reserving the liquid. Strain the liquid and set both mushrooms and liquid aside.

Place the short ribs in a large bowl or nonreactive container. Add the 1-inch onion pieces, cremini mushrooms, carrots, and celery. Cut the head of garlic in half at the equator and add to the bowl. Add the black peppercorns, bay leaves, thyme, red wine, and reserved liquid from rehydrating the porcini. Add enough cold water to cover the meat, if necessary. Mix the ingredients, cover, and marinate in the refrigerator overnight.

Remove the short ribs from the marinade and pat them dry. Remove and discard the peppercorns and bay leaves. Strain the mushrooms and vegetables from the marinade and reserve both the solids and marinade separately. Season the short ribs generously with salt and pepper on all sides.

Heat 1 tablespoon of duck fat in a large pan over medium-high heat, 1 or 2 minutes. When the fat begins to smoke, sear the short ribs on all sides until brown, about 3 minutes per side. Remove the short ribs and set aside.

Preheat the oven to 375°F.

In a large Dutch oven or casserole dish with a fitted cover, add 1 tablespoon of duck fat and the reserved mushrooms and vegetables. Place in the oven uncovered and roast until the mushrooms and vegetables start to brown, about 15 minutes. Add the reserved marinade and continue to cook, uncovered, until the liquid has reduced to about half, about 30 minutes. Add the short ribs and the stock, cover, and continue to cook for about 2½ hours, or until the short ribs are very tender. Remove from the oven, but leave the oven on.

Gently remove the short ribs from the Dutch oven and set aside. Strain and reserve the braising liquid in a small saucepan; discard the mushrooms and vegetables. Bring the liquid to a boil over medium heat and reduce it by half, about 6 minutes. Set aside.

Heat the remaining 2 tablespoons of duck fat in a large skillet over medium-high heat and sauté the rehydrated porcini until the mushrooms start to brown, about 5 minutes. Add the sliced onions and sauté until translucent, a few minutes. Add the minced garlic and sauté for another minute.

Place the short ribs in a medium casserole dish. Add the onion-mushroom-and-garlic mixture around the short ribs and pour the reserved braising liquid on top. Place in the hot oven until heated through, about 5 minutes.

Serve this dish with creamy grits flavored with truffle butter or a sweet potato puree.

POT ROAST WITH PORCINI AND MASHED POTATOES

BY EUGENIA BONE, NEW YORK | YIELD: 4 SERVINGS

I make pot roasts flavored with dried porcini all winter long. This is my basic recipe. Sometimes I add carrots, cut about 2 inches long and added in the last half hour of cooking; sometimes I add a cup of dried white beans once the pot is set for the long boil; sometimes I throw in a handful of frozen peas during the last 15 minutes of cooking. Other times, I add warm spices, like nutmeg and cinnamon, or hot peppers. The recipe varies all the time, but I always like to include a mash.

Salt and freshly ground black pepper

1½ to 2 pounds beef pot roast meat, either one whole piece or cut into very large chunks

4 tablespoons unsalted butter, divided

2 cups sliced yellow or white onion

1½ tablespoons chopped garlic

6 fresh thyme sprigs

2 small bay leaves

½ cup dry red wine

2 teaspoons tomato paste

4 cups beef, mushroom, or chicken stock

½ ounce dried porcini

20 ounces russet potatoes, skin removed, cut into 1-inch chunks

½ cup heavy cream

Parsley for garnish (optional)

Salt and pepper the beef to taste. Heat 2 tablespoons of butter in a 4½-quart Dutch oven over medium-high heat. Add the meat and sear all over, about 5 minutes total. Remove the meat to a plate.

Add the onions to the Dutch oven and sauté for a few minutes, then add the garlic, thyme sprigs, and bay leaves. Cook for a few minutes more, until the onions begin to wilt. If the garlic begins to brown, turn the heat down to medium.

Add the red wine and let it boil until it has reduced by half or more, a few minutes, then stir in the tomato paste. Add the stock and the dried porcini. Increase the heat to medium-high, bring to a boil, then reduce the heat to medium-low and add the meat. Cover and cook the pot roast at a very gentle boil for about 3 hours. The meat should be very tender and the sauce reduced by about a third.

About 20 minutes before you are ready to eat, add potatoes to a large pot of cold water. Add salt and bring to a boil over high heat, then turn down to low. Cook about 10 minutes, until the potatoes are fork-tender. Drain, then return the potatoes to the pot and, over a low heat, allow them to dry out, 1 minute or so. Take the potatoes off the heat and mash them in the pot with a potato masher or fork. (Don't use an electric mixer, or the potatoes will become gummy.) Add 2 tablespoons butter and combine well. Check the seasoning and adjust to taste.

In a small pot, heat the cream over medium heat, a few minutes, and then add to the potatoes, a little at a time, as you stir them.

Serve the pot roast with a ladleful of sauce on top of the potatoes. Garnish with parsley, if you like.

WITHOUT YOU I'M NOTHING

HOW FUNGI SUPPORT, ENHANCE, AND PROTECT OUR FOOD SUPPLY

Fungi live in, on, and all over plants. So, why do plants tolerate them? Well, just as a human body without its microbial symbionts would have trouble doing everything from fighting off colds to making serotonin to digesting spinach, plants need fungi to provide nutrition that they need but don't make on their own and to help protect them against predators and environmental stressors. Without fungi, most plants would be vulnerable to disease and deprived of optimum nutrition. Without fungi, agricultural plants are less nutritious. So, you could say that without fungi, we are deprived, too.

The plant-fungal relationship is an ancient one. I'm talking about the primordial slime—the formative gunk that washed ashore and founded the terrestrial ecosystem. Life on Earth is 3.5 billion years old, and the first 3 billion years of it was spent in the water. Here's one conception of life in those faraway days: Early lineages of singled-celled organisms that did different chores, like nitrogen fixing or photosynthesis, hooked up to form little self-sufficient floating islands. As their numbers grew, these teams of aquatic microbes coalesced into sticky microbial mats that grew on the floors of shallow oceans, where light could penetrate, or they floated on top of the seas and freshwater springs.

In this scenario, microbial mats were complicated communities teeming with microbes that did different jobs: Some made food, and some lived off the by-products of other microbes. There were parasitic microbes and microbes that degraded the dead. A microbial mat was a complete ecosystem—really, the primordial terrestrial ecosystem.

Microbial mats made landfall about 475 million years ago, composed of bacteria, archaea, protists, fungi, viruses, and the scummy green forefathers of plants. Terrestrial existence represented opportunity: There was plenty of real estate to exploit, ample sun, and little competition, but the landscape of rock and sand was harsh. Maybe the fungi in microbial mats started the business of soil building by mining the rock for nutrients and decomposing the mat's dead organisms to capture their carbon. In the crowded company of the mats, fungi may have cooperated with plants, expanding their ability to acquire nutrients, and helping them deal with a hotter, dryer world.

Eventually, fungi took on antifeedant jobs as more types of critters, like insects and herbivores, evolved to threaten plants. The plant/fungus mutualism, a kind of beneficial symbiosis, may indeed date to the territorialization of plants and fungi. Some scientists will argue that they became landlubbers together— they helped each other make it on terra firma, and they still do.

Fungi help plants deal with their main problem: They can't move. Unable to run away, they must find other ways to deal with predators, and because they can't relocate, they must adjust to local environmental conditions. They can't forage beyond their immediate vicinity, so they need help getting nutrition beyond their root borders. A lot of the carbohydrates or sugary by-products made by plants trickles into the soil at the plant root tips, where it attracts bacteria and soil fungi, and the nutrients and security from foes and stress they bring.

The fungi involved in nutrition acquisition are the mycorrhizae, which attach to the plants' root tips, either topically or intercellularly. In exchange for the plant's yummy root sweat, mycorrhizal fungi help ensure a more dependable nutrient and water supply—micronutrients that plants need but don't make and that increase a plant's ability to withstand environmental pressures like drought. Dr. Suzanne Simard, from the University of British Columbia, and her colleagues have shown that mycorrhizae also provide nutrient highways between plants. Mature trees, for example, may share their photosynthates with seedlings whose nascent roots and scant foliage make it hard to thrive in the low-light conditions of the understory.

Mycorrhizal fungi, which can colonize the roots of multiple plants of different species at once, also have been shown to function as a communication system between plants. When pests and pathogens are afoot, plants can share chemical distress signals through the fungal network and shore up their chemical defenses in response. Most plants, including many crop plants, live in mutualistic relationships with arbuscular mycorrhizae, which penetrate the plant root cells. This kind of mycorrhizal fungus doesn't produce mushrooms—its spores are dispersed belowground—but it performs the same services as the types of mycorrhizal fungi that produce mushrooms. Plus, it makes glomalin (and glomalin-related products).

If you've never heard of glomalin, you're not alone. Glomalin, first identified in 1996—I have T-shirts older than the discovery of this very important fungal product—is a sugary protein that waterproofs the fungal hyphae like bark or skin. By doing so, it keeps nutrients in and water out of the fungal cells.

Glomalin-sheathed hyphae create a kind of sticky frame in which microorganisms, water, minerals, and nutrients collect into soil particles. These stick to other soil particles to form granola-like aggregates, which in turn stick to other aggregates, the whole stable enough to allow air and water to freely flow between them. These soil aggregates are rich in nutrients and resist erosion, and they are the fundamental building blocks of healthy soil.

Glomalin itself is carbon- and iron-rich, is resistant to microbial decay, and does not easily dissolve in water. Because it can last up to a half century before degrading, glomalin accounts for 20 percent of organic carbon sequestered in undisturbed soil. Arbuscular mycorrhizal fungi and the glomalin they produce—this stuff nobody knew about until twenty-five years ago—is beneficial to most crop plants, stabilizes soil, and sequesters massive amounts of carbon. It is part of the formula that makes for nutrient-rich soil, which feeds the plants that feed us.

Concurrently with the plant–mycorrhizal fungus mutualism is the plant–endophytic fungus mutualism. Researchers have suggested that all terrestrial plants house *endophytes* (from the Greek word meaning "inside plants"). These are microscopic filamentous fungi that live between the cells of stems and leaves, inside those aboveground tissues. Endophytic fungi perform a host of services for plants in exchange for food (carbohydrates) and a place to live. A plant may house many species, which may colonize the plant when it germinates, or even be passed from one plant generation to the next aboard seed; a first gift not unlike the way a mother passes her microbes to her child during delivery.

I learned about the many roles of endophytes from Dr. James White, a professor of plant pathology at Rutgers University whose lectures I was lucky enough to hear. Fungal (and bacterial) endophytes provide stress tolerance to plants by helping the plant deal with environmental pressures like heat and drought and salt inundation.

Plants are like us. When their cells get stressed from adverse conditions, they produce particles that can harm the cell. But unlike us, plants don't produce helpful chemicals to counter the effects of that stress. They shop that job out to the endophytic fungi. These improbably thin fungal threads emit an arsenal of compounds that calm the stress reaction of plants. As a result, the plant is better able to survive a drought or heat wave. They also participate in the chemistry that helps plants use water efficiently.

"These are ancient symbionts," says Dr. Rusty Rodriguez, whose company, Adaptive Symbiotic Technologies, studies the agricultural implications of plant-fungal symbiosis. "Every endophyte we've studied confers drought tolerance." And drought tolerance is perhaps one of the earliest challenges that plants faced when they made the move from sea to land in the first place.

But that's not all. Some endophytes suppress pathogenic fungi that may be coming after the plant, they modulate root developments—basically, they help plants grow bigger—and improve the plant's ability to absorb nutrients, and they can alter the chemical constituents of a plant. For example, endophytic fungi living in carrots help increase carotenes, some of which can be converted in our bodies into vitamin A.

Other endophytes defend plants from herbivores by means of a virtual armory of deterrent toxins, from bitter flavors to more lethal compounds like alkaloids, which can be poisonous. The mere presence of endophytic fungi provides an immune service to plants: They seem to irritate the plant just a little bit, and in the process, they activate the plant's own immune system, though not against the endophyte. The plant tolerates the endophyte, but with its primed immune system, it is better able to ward off real threats. That's like the rationale behind the hygiene hypothesis, which says that the rise in immune diseases like asthma may be the result of underexposure to the microbes that prime the human immune system. Taken in that context, a plant or seed exposed to fungicides that kill their endophytes could hypothetically develop an immune disorder.

There is growing recognition in the scientific community that these fungi benefit crops and may even help mitigate the impacts of a warming world by conferring stress tolerance. But we seem intent on the antifungal course we are on. Here's what's happening: Sometimes, tilling soil is a good thing. It can help warm or dry out or otherwise prepare a seedbed before planting. But tillage can also destroy the advantage crops receive from fungi. Tilling tears up fungal hyphae and chews up soil aggregates and the microbes that live within them.

At first, all that suddenly available nutrition—the stored water and carbon and micronutrients—creates a kind of boom economy in the soil and the plants grow like crazy. But when the soil food web is undermined year after year by tilling, the community of microbes never has a chance to develop beyond a certain degree of functionality. It's like letting a civilization get to the point of producing bronze and then bombing it back to the Stone Age again.

Tillage doesn't destroy microbial abundance; it destroys the complexity of the soil society. And when the complexity is reduced, so too are the number of services the soil and its microbial populations can provide plants. Here's a scenario: If an uncommon pest attacks a tilled field of corn, the right microbes may not be available to recruit and fight it off. And if there is a drought, the soil, no longer bound by fungi and its glomalin into particles and no longer capable of retaining water, may dry up. And as the Dust Bowl of the 1930s illustrated, it could just blow away. And if soil is gone, "the loss is irrevocable," said Wes Jackson, founder of the Land Institute. "And currently, U.S. soil erodes at a nonrenewable rate. Soil is as much a nonrenewable resource as oil."

Tilling is on its way out. But what industrial agricultural famers have done to maintain the high yields of tilling is replace the microbial roles in soil with synthetic inputs to, in the words of microbiologist Krista McGuire, "force-feed" the soil. Soil microbes provide nitrogen, phosphorus, sulfur, and other micronutrients to the plant in exchange for carbohydrates. But when synthetic fertilizers—typically, a cocktail heavy on nitrogen, potassium, and phosphorus—are introduced, root colonization by the fungi decreases, as do the ecosystem services they perform.

Likewise, the mycorrhizal fungi become parasitic when the net cost of the relationship disfavors the plant. In other words, if the plant is getting its phosphorus from the farmer, it doesn't need what the fungus has to offer. The fungus, however, has season tickets: It takes carbs from the plant anyway.

Synthetic fertilization may explain why there has been a decrease in minerals in American-grown fruits and vegetables over the last fifty to seventy years. A comparison of organic versus conventional farming methods shows that conventional agriculture alters microbial communities that move micronutrients like zinc, copper, magnesium, and iron from soil to plant, consequently affecting the nutrient load of the plants we eat. As the philosopher-farmer Wendell Berry wrote, "If eating is an act of agriculture, agriculture is an act of eating."

Broad-based fungicides are like broad-based antibiotics: They kill the good guys along with the bad. They are effective at killing pathogenic fungi, but they may also be effective at killing the fungi that are helpful to plants. Herbicides, which some farmers use as an alternative to tilling, can cause bacterial and fungal diversity to decrease, probably from a lack of varied food that is sweated out of different plant roots. What's more, glyphosate, a common herbicide, binds to minerals in soil, effectively competing with the microbes that would otherwise be delivering those minerals to plants.

Our system of synthetic inputs produces more food. That's a good thing. The downside is that by undermining fungal diversity, our food is less nutritious and our food supply less stable. But don't despair: Organic agriculture and the development of perennial crops are potential solutions to Big Ag's fungal problem.

Ultimately, the plant-fungus relationship is key to overall plant health. Plant health is, in turn, key to our health. Fungi facilitate so much activity in plants that I like to think of them as the verbs in a plant's life: Pathogenic fungi kill plants; saprobic fungi break down dead plants, releasing nutrients in the soil, where mycorrhizal fungi capture those nutrients and supply them to plants; and endophytic fungi protect plants as they grow until the plant succumbs to pathogenic fungi. And on it goes: Fungi kill, they degrade, they nurture, they protect; they kill, they degrade, they nurture, they protect; and on and on, as long as the sun shines and the rain falls.

SWEET MUSHROOMS, DRINKS AND CONDIMENTS

POACHED PEARS WITH CANDY CAP SYRUP

BY EUGENIA BONE, NEW YORK | YIELD: 4 SERVINGS

*This is an easy, flexible desert that you can also make with dried fairy clubs (*Clavariadelphus truncatus*).*
I sometimes add more sugar if the candy caps aren't as sweet as I'd like, so before reducing the sauce, give it
a taste and adjust the sweetness. Remember, the sugar will become more concentrated as the sauce reduces.

2 slightly underripe Bosc pears

1 cup apple cider

⅓ cup sweet white wine

½ cup granulated sugar

2 sprigs thyme

1 cinnamon stick

⅓ cup dried candy cap mushrooms

NOTE: I like to leave the stems on
for aesthetic reasons.

Peel and halve the pears. Core the pears (see note). Place the pears in a low pot with a fitted cover.

Combine the cider, wine, and sugar in a small pot and heat over medium heat until the sugar dissolves.

Add the sugar water to the pears, then add the thyme, cinnamon, and candy caps. Cover and poach over medium heat for 10 minutes, until the pears and mushrooms are tender. Remove the pears and set aside. Remove the cinnamon and thyme and discard. Reduce the liquid with the candy caps to a thick syrup.

Serve the pears garnished with the candy cap sauce.

STRAWBERRIES POACHED IN BIRCH POLYPORE SYRUP

BY DAVID BENNETT, WEST YORKSHIRE, UK | YIELD: 4 SERVINGS

I love birch polypore, and I'm always looking for a pleasant way to eat them. I've poached a few fruits in birch polypore syrups, but the strawberry–birch polypore combo is the best. The poached strawberries are lovely served with sorbet, ice cream, or panna cotta, and the syrup makes a refreshing drink on its own. The birch polypore fungus, however, doesn't taste too great, but it's nice for decoration.

2 cups ripe strawberries (about 10 ounces)

2 cups water

2 cups granulated sugar

⅓ ounce (a few slices) dried birch polypore

Wash and hull the strawberries.

In a medium pot, combine the water, sugar, and birch polypore slices. Bring to a boil over high heat, stirring occasionally. Turn the heat to low and simmer for 2 minutes, until the flavor and compounds of the mushrooms have infused the syrup. Turn off the heat and carefully add the strawberries so they do not bruise.

Cover the pan with its lid or with plastic wrap until the mixture has cooled to room temperature. The strawberries are now ready to eat, but they will taste better if refrigerated overnight. The syrup holds pretty much forever, but for safety's sake, keep for 7 days.

CANDY CAP SUGAR COOKIES

BY CINDY DAVIS, OREGON | YIELD: ABOUT TWO DOZEN 2- TO-3-INCH-COOKIES

I grew up in Idaho, where I picked mushrooms. Now my family and I live in Oregon's Willamette Valley and hunt mushrooms every season. We use a book called Mushrooms of Marys Peak and Vicinity *to learn about new mushrooms all the time. I created this recipe by combining various cookie recipes and simply adding candy cap powder for amazing maple flavor. This is a refrigerator cookie, so you can make the dough ahead of time; it holds well for up to two weeks. You will need a sheet of wax or parchment paper to roll the cookie dough. (After you eat all the cookies in the jar, take a sniff: The jar will smell like candy caps!)*

1½ sticks plus 3 tablespoons unsalted butter, softened and divided

1 tablespoon dried candy cap mushrooms, ground (see note)

2¼ cups all-purpose flour

½ teaspoon baking powder

¼ teaspoon salt

¾ cup granulated sugar

1 large egg, at room temperature

2 teaspoons vanilla extract

NOTE: I grind dried candy caps in my mortar and pestle, but you can grind them in a spice grinder or a coffee grinder as well, or you can chop them as finely as possible.

Melt 3 tablespoons of the butter in a small saucepan over low heat. Add the candy cap powder and stir. Cook for about 3 minutes, until the powder and butter are well integrated and the butter takes on a deeper brown color. Set aside to cool.

In a medium bowl, combine the flour, baking powder, and salt and set aside. In a separate bowl, either using an electric mixer or mixing by hand, combine the remaining 12 tablespoons (1½ sticks) of butter with the sugar and mix until smooth. Add the egg, vanilla, and candy cap mixture and blend another 3 to 4 minutes, until smooth and well combined. Slowly add in the dry ingredients, mixing on low with an electric mixer or by hand until thoroughly combined.

Lay out a 10-by-18-inch sheet of waxed or parchment paper and scoop the cookie dough onto it. Roll the paper around the dough to form a log about 2 to 3 inches in diameter. Refrigerate for at least 2 hours.

Preheat the oven to 350°F.

Remove the cookie dough from the refrigerator and discard the paper. Slice the dough into ¼-inch-thick rounds. Place the cookies on a parchment paper–lined cookie sheet, spaced about 1 inch apart. Bake for 12 minutes, until the cookies are golden. Let the cookies cool for about 5 minutes, then transfer them to a wire rack to cool completely.

The cookies will stay fresh in an airtight container for about four days.

CHAGA CHOCOLATE CHIP COOKIES

BY DAVID BENNETT, WEST YORKSHIRE, UK | YIELD: ABOUT 20 SANDWICH COOKIES

I've been a pastry chef for thirty years and a forager for three, and I decided to combine my love of desserts and foraging after hearing an interview with the mycologist Paul Stamets. The challenge is how to get the medicinal compounds found in fungi into desserts without compromising on the taste. I've often wondered about how to reuse chaga grinds, and so I experimented with this cookie recipe, which called for ground almonds. I simply substituted the almonds with the chaga grinds, and it worked like a charm. Soak the chaga grinds for about 72 hours before making this recipe.

FOR THE COOKIES

1 ounce finely ground chaga, soaked for 72 hours in 2 cups warm water

1 cup unsalted butter, softened

2½ cups packed light brown sugar

2 medium eggs

3¼ cups all-purpose flour

½ cup semisweet chocolate chips

¼ cup unsweetened cocoa

2½ teaspoons baking soda

½ teaspoon salt

FOR THE GANACHE

12 ounces semisweet chocolate, chopped

2 tablespoons unsalted butter

½ cup coconut cream

2 tablespoons espresso coffee or ½ teaspoon instant coffee diluted in 2 tablespoons hot water

TO MAKE THE COOKIES:

Strain and reserve the chaga soaking water. Reduce the reserved soaking water by simmering in a small pot over medium-low heat, uncovered, for about 1 hour, until it has reduced to 2 tablespoons. Set aside.

Preheat the oven to 325°F.

In a large bowl, cream together the butter and the brown sugar. Add the eggs and mix. Add the flour, chocolate chips, cocoa, baking soda, salt, and soaked chaga grinds. Mix together, making sure that all ingredients are distributed evenly throughout the batter. The dough should be quite stiff. Spoon dough onto a piece of plastic wrap; roll plastic wrap to form a log about 2 inches in diameter and tie the ends. You can refrigerate the wrapped dough for a few days, if you choose, or complete the recipe by removing the plastic wrap and cutting the dough into ½-inch discs. Place discs on a baking tray. Bake on the middle rack of the oven for 12 to 15 minutes.

TO MAKE THE GANACHE:

In a double boiler or a bowl set over a pot of boiling water, melt the chocolate and 2 tablespoons of butter over medium-low heat. Stir to combine, then remove from heat.

In a small pot, heat the coconut cream, espresso, and chaga water reduction over low heat until it is hot to the touch. Don't let it boil.

Slowly pour the coconut cream mixture over the chocolate and whisk gently until smooth and shiny. Pour into a medium mixing bowl and allow to cool.

Whisk the cool ganache until it is pale and thick, a few minutes, being careful not to overwhisk or it will turn grainy. Spoon the ganache into a piping bag and pipe rosettes onto half the cookies. Place the remaining cookies on top and press.

The cookies will hold in an airtight container for up to seven days.

CHANTERELLE SHORTBREAD

BY JANE B. MASON, COLORADO | YIELD: ABOUT 8 BARS

For me, chanterelles have always been the quintessential foraged mushroom, and I longed to hunt them for many years. Then, in the summer of 2020, I found myself in Minnesota at the same time as Trent and Kristen Blizzard of Modern-Forager.com, and we hunted these golden beauties in the grass along the St. Croix River. After filling our bags with multiple pounds, I jumped into the river for a swim. I had a hunch that chanterelles, with their apricot essence, would do well in shortbread. If you finely dice the chanterelles and sauté them until they are al dente, you get the added benefit of a chewy nuttiness. This recipe also works well with dried chanterelles.

4 to 6 ounces fresh chanterelle mushrooms, or ½ ounce dried chanterelles

1 cup (2 sticks) plus 1 to 2 teaspoons salted butter, divided

1⅔ cups all-purpose flour

⅓ cup cornmeal

¾ teaspoon salt

½ cup granulated sugar

⅓ cup toasted walnuts, finely chopped

1 to 2 tablespoons apricot jam (optional)

Preheat the oven to 325°F.

If using fresh mushrooms, wipe clean as necessary and finely chop. If using dried chanterelles, place them in a bowl, submerge in boiling water, and cover the bowl with a lid. Let rest 20 to 40 minutes until the chanterelles are tender, then drain and finely chop.

Heat a skillet over medium-low heat and add the chanterelles. Dry-cook them until they release their water and the water has evaporated, about 10 minutes, then add 1 to 2 tablespoons butter and continue to cook until browned, a few more minutes.

Place the flour, cornmeal, salt, and sugar in a mixing bowl and stir with a wooden spoon to blend. Dice the remaining 1 cup of butter and blend into the flour mixture with your fingers to a crumbly meal, 1 to 2 minutes. Stir in the sautéed chanterelles, walnuts, and apricot jam, if using.

Press the dough into an ungreased 8-by-8-inch pan and bake for 30 to 35 minutes, until the edges are golden brown. Cool on a wire rack or in the pan. Slice into bars when the shortbread is still a bit warm.

CANDY CAP ÉCLAIRS WITH REISHI CHOCOLATE GLAZE

BY GRAHAM STEINRUCK, WASHINGTON | YIELD: 12 ÉCLAIRS

I absolutely love éclairs, especially when they are filled with maple- or vanilla-flavored cream with a nice dark-chocolate glaze on top. I thought it would be fun to infuse this classic French pastry with fungi by adding candy cap mushrooms to the pastry cream and reishi to the glaze. This recipe has a few steps, but don't be daunted! Éclairs are really easy to make and a completely different experience when they are made fresh. This is the kind of desert I like to do at my mushroom-centric dinner events at the Telluride Mushroom Festival.

FOR THE PASTRY CREAM

½ ounce dried candy cap mushrooms, crushed

2 cups whole milk

1 large egg plus 3 large egg yolks

2½ tablespoons cornstarch

5 tablespoons granulated sugar

⅛ teaspoon salt

2 tablespoons unsalted butter, cut into ½-inch pieces

½ teaspoon bourbon vanilla extract (optional)

FOR THE PATE A CHOUX

4 tablespoons unsalted butter

¼ cup milk

¼ cup water

Salt

½ cup flour

2 large eggs

FOR THE GLAZE

¼ teaspoon red reishi-extract powder

4 ounces semisweet chocolate, broken into pieces

½ cup heavy whipping cream

TO MAKE THE PASTRY CREAM:

Combine the dried candy caps and milk in a small saucepan and bring to a simmer over medium-high heat, stirring occasionally. Remove from the heat and allow to steep, covered, for a minimum of 1 hour, or overnight in the refrigerator.

In a medium bowl, combine the whole egg, egg yolks, cornstarch, sugar, and salt. Whisk until just combined.

Reheat the mushrooms and milk in a medium saucepan over medium heat. Make sure the milk doesn't boil, or it will scorch. Strain the hot milk into a measuring cup. Pour about 1 tablespoon of hot milk into the egg mixture and whisk until combined. Continue to add the hot milk in small increments until two-thirds of the milk has been mixed in. Add the rest of the milk all at once and whisk until combined. Pour the mixture back into the saucepan and bring to a simmer over medium heat, whisking constantly until the mixture is the texture of a very thick pudding, 6 to 12 minutes. Lower the heat, continue to simmer, and whisk a few more minutes, until the mixture is thick and stiff. Again, stir constantly, and be careful not to burn the mixture. Turn off the heat and add the butter, one piece at a time, stirring all the while. Make sure each piece of butter is completely melted before adding the next. Whisk in the vanilla extract, if using. Pour the cream into a bowl and cover it with plastic wrap, making sure the wrap contacts the surface of the cream so it does not form a skin. Cool in the refrigerator for at least 1 hour, although it can hold in the refrigerator for up to a couple of days.

Continued on page 232...

TO MAKE THE PATE A CHOUX:
Preheat the oven to 425°F.

Combine the butter, milk, water, and salt to taste in a small saucepan and bring to a simmer over medium heat. When the butter has melted, add the flour all at once and stir vigorously with a wooden spoon. Once the flour has been incorporated, continue to cook, stirring, over medium heat, about 2 minutes, until the mixture forms a smooth ball and a thin film forms on the bottom of the pan. Transfer the mixture to a bowl and continue to beat with the wooden spoon for 1 minute to cool slightly.

Mix in the eggs one at a time, making sure that the first egg is fully incorporated before adding the second. The mixture should form a smooth dough. When the dough is pulled up away from the bowl, a thick ribbon should form. Place the dough into a pastry bag fitted with a ½-inch round or star tip. Pipe 12 strips of dough 4 to 5 inches long and about ¾ of an inch wide onto a baking sheet lined with a silicone mat or wax paper, making sure to leave 1½ inches between the pastries. Bake in the hot oven for 10 minutes, until the dough is set. Reduce the oven temperature to 325°F and bake for another 10 minutes, until the pastries are golden brown. Transfer to a wire rack and allow to cool completely before filling.

When the pastries are cool, fill a separate piping bag or pastry injection device (like a large syringe) with the pastry cream. Poke a hole at both ends of the éclairs and fill them with pastry cream.

TO MAKE THE GLAZE:
Combine reishi-extract powder and chocolate pieces in a bowl wide enough to dip an éclair. Bring the cream to a simmer in a small saucepan over medium heat. Pour the hot cream over the reishi-chocolate mixture and shake the bowl to make sure the chocolate is completely submerged in the cream. After a few minutes, gently whisk until the chocolate and cream are mixed and glossy. Allow to cool slightly before dipping the filled éclairs. Make sure to shake off any excess glaze, then place the pastries on a wire rack to allow the glaze to set.

The éclairs can be stored in an airtight container in the refrigerator for a few days or frozen for up to a month.

CANDIED WOOD EAR

BY DAVID BENNETT, LEEDS, UK | YIELD: 20 PIECES

There are lots of wood ears growing in the woods where I forage. I came up with the idea of preserving them in syrup so they can be enjoyed all year round. The key to candying is water evaporation during the simmering stage. Too much evaporation, and the syrup will become overly thick. Too little, and the syrup will not glacé the fruit. A 25 percent reduction of water is ideal. If you don't want to use brandy, you can candy the mushrooms with just 3 cups of water instead.

3 cups sugar

1½ cups water

1½ cups brandy

1 pound fresh wood ears or
   3 ounces dried and rehydrated

Place the sugar, water, and brandy into a medium pan and bring to a boil over medium heat, whisking occasionally to melt the sugar.

Turn the heat down very low and add the wood ears. Simmer, uncovered, for about 1 hour. The syrup will reduce over time, but do not let it reduce more than 25%. If it does, top it up with water and simmer again for 1 minute or so.

Turn off the heat and cool to room temperature.

Pack the wood ears and syrup into a sterilized pint-size jar. (To sterilize, boil the jar and lid in water for 10 minutes at sea level, adding 1 minute for every 1,000 feet above this.) Store in an airtight jar at room temperature, but keep in mind that over time, the mushrooms will lose their snap and become more jellified.

FLAN WITH BROWN SUGAR CANDY CAP SYRUP

BY PAM KRAUSS, NEW YORK | YIELD: TEN 3-OUNCE FLANS

When a friend gave me a jar of dried candy cap mushrooms, it took me a while to figure out what to do with them besides unscrewing the cap occasionally to marvel at their improbable maple-y aroma. When she suggested I use them to flavor a simple syrup, though, a whole world of possibilities opened up, including this easy dessert—the perfect sweet ending to a soup-to-nuts mushroom meal. I chose to use brown sugar for the syrup because its deeper, molasseslike tones complement the earthiness of the mushrooms. It's also a great way to use up small bits and pieces of candy caps; just strain them out before filling the molds or spoon some into the bottom of each cup and garnish with one or two perfect specimens.

FOR THE SYRUP

¾ cup light brown sugar, packed

¾ cup water

2 tablespoons candy cap mushrooms (broken shards and powder are fine), plus a few whole mushrooms for garnish (optional)

Pinch salt

FOR THE CUSTARD

One 14-ounce can sweetened condensed milk

One 10-ounce can evaporated milk

3 large eggs, lightly beaten

1 vanilla bean, split

Preheat the oven to 350F.

Set 10 small (3- to 4-ounce) ramekins or custard cups in a large roasting pan (or, alternatively, a silicon muffin tray).

TO MAKE THE SYRUP:
Combine the sugar and water in a saucepan and stir over medium heat until the sugar has completely dissolved. Add the mushrooms (pieces and whole mushrooms, if using), and continue to cook over medium heat until reduced to a syrupy consistency, 12 to 15 minutes, stirring occasionally. Strain the syrup into a small heatproof pitcher and set aside, reserving the whole mushrooms.

TO MAKE THE CUSTARD:
In a large measuring cup or a mixing bowl with a spout, gently whisk together the milks and eggs just until uniformly combined. Avoid beating the mixture vigorously to prevent adding any air. Using the back of a paring knife, scrape the seeds from the split vanilla bean and gently stir into the egg mixture.

Pour or spoon a generous tablespoon of syrup into the bottom of each ramekin, reserving any remaining syrup. Carefully pour the egg mixture onto the syrup, dividing it equally among the cups and trying not to disturb the syrup. Place the ramekins in a roasting pan and fill the pan with very hot tap water halfway up the sides of the ramekins. Carefully slide the pan onto the middle rack of your oven.

Cook until the flans are just set in the center, about 30 to 35 minutes, but starting to check after 25 minutes. Remove from the oven carefully, avoiding any of the hot water spilling onto the flans. Cool to room temperature then cover the flans and refrigerate until well-chilled and for up to 3 days.

To serve, run a small, sharp knife around the edge of each flan to release it. Cover the ramekin with a dessert plate and invert the flan and the syrup onto it. Decorate with the whole mushrooms, if using, and drizzle with some of the remaining syrup if you like.

CHANTERELLE FROZEN CUSTARD

BY MARISSA BISWABIC, WISCONSIN | YIELD: 1 TO 1½ PINTS

I spent the majority of my life thinking mushrooms were gross, but I opened up to fungi when a forager and grower sold me some oyster mushrooms at my local farmers market. I cooked them on a flatbread-style pizza and realized that mushrooms can be delicious! In my newfound enthusiasm for fungi, I joined my local mycological society, started foraging on my own, and began to experiment in the kitchen. I find a lot of chanterelles, which are so sweet and fruity. I thought they would be good in an ice cream, so I adapted a family recipe for vanilla frozen custard to make this.

1½ cups heavy cream

14 ounces sweetened condensed milk

½ cup milk

½ cup sugar

1 tablespoon cinnamon

Pinch of sea salt

1 pound fresh chanterelles (I like *Cantharellus phasmatis*, but other chanterelle mushrooms will do)

6 large egg yolks

In a large saucepan, heat the heavy cream, condensed milk, milk, and sugar to a simmer over medium heat for a few minutes. Add the cinnamon and salt and stir.

In a food processor or by hand, mince the chanterelles down to a near paste. The more you process the mushrooms, the smaller the bits will be in your ice cream. You can chop them bigger or smaller depending on your preference.

Add the minced chanterelles to the simmering milk mixture. Reduce the mixture, stirring frequently, until it becomes thick enough to coat the back of a spoon, 5 to 10 minutes, lowering the temperature to avoid scorching the custard, if necessary. Remove from heat.

In a large bowl, add the egg yolks and whisk them until they are smooth, then slowly pour the chanterelle custard over the egg yolks, whisking all the while. If you dump all the hot custard into the eggs at once, they will curdle, so be sure you add it very slowly, especially at first. Once it is combined, pour the custard into a container and refrigerate.

I use an electric ice cream maker to chill the custard to the right consistency, but a hand crank–style ice cream maker will do as well. Once your custard has chilled in the refrigerator, simply follow the instructions on your ice cream maker or use another DIY method to rapid-freeze.

For long-term storage (a couple of months) in the freezer, pack the custard into plastic or paper containers, cover with plastic wrap, making sure it touches the surface of the custard, cover, and freeze. This will prevent freezer burn and ensure that your custard stays soft.

CANDY CAP MILK PUNCH

BY JANE B. MASON, COLORADO | YIELD: 2 SERVINGS

After a day of putting words on the page—I write fiction for children and young adults—I usually stumble into the kitchen to make some kind of supper for the family. When dinner has been eaten and the dishes are done, I often find myself wanting a bit of soothing comfort. During fall and winter, in particular, this warm candy cap–infused bourbon (or brandy) drink fits the bill perfectly.

4 tablespoons (2 ounces) dried candy cap mushrooms, broken but not powdered

1¾ cups whole milk

¼ cup cream or half-and-half, or additional milk

1 ounce bourbon or brandy

2 teaspoons maple syrup

¼ teaspoon vanilla extract (optional)

Ground mace or nutmeg

Place the candy caps, milk, and cream into a saucepan and heat over low heat to a gentle simmer, stirring, for 2 minutes. Cover, turn off the heat, and let sit for 5 to 10 minutes. The longer the mushrooms sit, the stronger the candy cap flavor is in the punch.

Strain out the candy caps, reserving the milk, then return the milk to the saucepan and whisk to create a foam as you reheat. Remove from the heat and add the bourbon or brandy to taste, maple syrup, and vanilla extract, if using. Pour into two mugs or heatproof glasses and top with a bit of ground mace (my preference) or nutmeg.

LONGEVITY LASSI

BY ANNALIESE BISCHOFF, MASSACHUSETTS | YIELD: 1 SERVING

I have loved experimenting with ideas for this lassi. For over a decade, I taught an honors course on tea at the University of Massachusetts Amherst, where I explored the world of tea with my students. The idea for making a mushroom lassi was inspired by that class and our mushroom teas. I decided to make a strong brew of chaga and reishi, sweetened and spiced, and frozen in convenient ice cubes for easy lassi making. The lassi stiffens up as it rests or cools, so add a few plain ice cubes or water to keep it fluid if you make more than one drink at a time.

FOR THE POWER MUSHROOM ICE CUBES

¼ ounce chaga chunks

¼ ounce dried reishi mushrooms

1½ cups water

2 tablespoons honey (I like tupelo) or maple syrup

½ teaspoon turmeric

1 teaspoon finely grated ginger

½ teaspoon cinnamon

½ teaspoon ground black or green cardamom

½ cup oat milk, almond milk, or light cream

FOR THE LASSI

1 banana

1 cup plain Greek yogurt

1 teaspoon cacao powder

2 power mushroom ice cubes

1 teaspoon honey or maple syrup

Ground cacao nibs (optional)

TO MAKE THE POWER MUSHROOM ICE CUBES:
Place the chaga and reishi chunks into a saucepan. Pour the water over them and bring to a boil over medium heat. Lower the heat and simmer for half an hour, then remove from heat and allow the tea to sit for a few more minutes. The tea should be a deep brown color and be reduced to about ½ cup. Strain, stir in the honey or maple syrup, turmeric, ginger, cinnamon, cardamom, and oat milk, and let cool. Pour into an ice cube tray and freeze. (The spices will not thoroughly dissolve. That's OK.) This will be enough to make eight 1-ounce cubes, enough for 4 drinks.

TO MAKE THE LASSI:
Place the banana, yogurt, cacao powder, 2 power mushroom ice cubes, and additional honey or maple syrup to taste in a blender and blend. Serve garnished with ground cacao nibs, if you like.

SPICY CHAGA CHAI TEA

BY KRISTEN BLIZZARD, COLORADO | YIELD: 8 SERVINGS

One of my first dates with my husband, Trent, was on a mushroom foray. Our love of foraging developed at the same time as our love for each other. These adventures will always have special meaning for us. Later, we started Modern-Forager.com, which took off when we started to sell morel burn maps, and last year we published a cookbook with other foragers called Wild Mushrooms *(2020). When Trent and I found chaga at our family cabin in the Minnesota Northwoods, we were inspired to develop this recipe. It's now a cherished favorite! The tea calls for a multihour brewing process, so if you have a crockpot, that works best. You can reuse the chaga chunks four to five more times; simply air-dry and retain them for your next brewing.*

6 cups water

1 ounce chaga chunks

10 cardamom pods

¼ cup diced ginger

4 whole cloves

¼ teaspoon fennel seeds

2 cinnamon sticks

10 peppercorns

1 star anise

2 tablespoons loose black tea

1½ teaspoons ginger juice (see note)

Favorite milk product

Favorite sweetener

NOTE: To make ginger juice for this recipe, grate 2 tablespoons of peeled fresh ginger and pass the grated ginger through a cheesecloth. Give it a squeeze to produce the juice.

To brew the chaga tea, add the water and chaga chunks to a crockpot set on the warm setting, or place in a saucepan with a fitted lid over low heat. Using a thermometer, try to keep your tea below 160°F to retain the medicinal qualities of the chaga. Brew for 6 to 8 hours. Once your tea has taken on a rich, dark color, it's ready for the addition of chai spices.

To make the chai tea base, strain the tea to remove the chaga chunks. Add the cardamom pods, ginger, cloves, fennel seeds, cinnamon sticks, peppercorns, and star anise to the tea in the crockpot or saucepan. Brew for 1½ to 2 more hours, or until the tea is aromatic with the smell of cardamom and ginger. Add the black tea and brew for another 10 to 15 minutes. Taste your tea at regular intervals while it's brewing; use any black tea you like, but remember: Some teas steep faster than others. Add the ginger juice and stir to combine. This concoction can stay in an airtight jar in the refrigerator for up to 1 week.

To make a cup of chaga chai tea, add about 5 ounces of the tea base to a cup, fill the rest of the cup with your preferred warmed milk, and sweeten to taste.

CHANTERELLE SHRUB

BY JANE B. MASON, COLORADO | YIELD: 1 SCANT PINT

When I was a child, I dumped vinegar over spinach and ate entire jars of pickles. I still prefer sour tastes over sweet, and I often mix a shrub with sparkling water to sip before dinner or guzzle in the garden on a hot summer day. Shrub is generally known as a sweet-and-sour syrup made from vinegar, sugar, and fruit (or, in this case, mushrooms!), served mixed with sparkling water and sometimes alcohol. The vinegar in a shrub will mellow with age, so patience is always a virtue. Feel free to adjust the ratios according to your taste!

4 to 5 ounces fresh chanterelle
   mushrooms, sliced, or ½ ounce dried
   chanterelles

⅔ cup white wine vinegar

⅓ cup apple cider vinegar

1 cup sugar

Place the chanterelles, either fresh or dried, white wine vinegar, and apple cider vinegar in a saucepan. The vinegar should cover the mushrooms. Bring to a low simmer over medium-low heat, stirring occasionally, and cook for 5 minutes, being careful not to let the mixture come to a boil. Cover, turn off the stove, and let cool, about 20 minutes.

When the shrub is cool, pour it into a pint-sized jar with a lid and leave it at room temperature for 2 to 4 days, shaking once a day or so.

Place the mixture back in a saucepan, and bring to a bare simmer over medium-low heat. Add the sugar, and cook just until the sugar has dissolved, 1 to 2 minutes. Cool, strain out the mushrooms (the chanterelles are edible, like sweet pickles), and place the shrub back in the pint jar or a bottle, if you like. It will be slightly viscous and will hold in the refrigerator for several months.

To serve, pour sparkling water into a glass with ice and add the shrub to taste. Add a slice of lemon, if you like.

GOLDEN VODKA

BY KELLY DEMARTINI, CALIFORNIA | YIELD: 2 PINTS

Thanks to an abundance of juicy golden chanterelles, as well as a desire to capture their elusive and distinctive fragrance and gorgeous apricot color, I decided to try my hand at infusing them into vodka. This is great to make during the chanterelle season, because there are two 6-week resting periods, each demanding 4 ounces of fresh chanterelles. Don't drink the vodka early; it needs time for the flavor to deepen. I have used the resulting liquid in my Chanterelle Risotto recipe (page 138) in place of half of the wine. It creates an extremely concentrated chanterelle flavor in the risotto.

8 ounces fresh, chopped golden chanterelles, divided

3½ cups vodka

Place 4 ounces of chopped golden chanterelle mushrooms in a clean, quart-sized glass mason jar with a new lid. Add the vodka and put on the lid. Gently shake a few times, then store in a cool, dark place for six weeks.

After the resting period, strain the vodka and mushrooms through a fine metal sieve and discard the mushrooms. (I don't use cheesecloth, because it produces a cloudy product). Add the second 4 ounces of chopped mushrooms to the jar and pour the vodka back in. Gently shake a few times, then store once again in a cool, dark place for an additional six weeks, shaking the jar every week or so.

Strain the vodka through a fine sieve (again, do not use cheesecloth) and discard the mushrooms. Store in the freezer.

Serve 1 to 2 ounces of the chilled vodka straight up in a chilled glass.

BLACK TRUMPET BUTTER

BY CHARLES LUCE, NEW JERSEY | YIELD: ABOUT 2½ CUPS

This recipe was a solution to a delicious problem: abundance. My wife, Leslie, and I had just picked two backpacks full of foraged black trumpets, and I needed some way to preserve them other than dehydration. I never imagined how popular this aromatic paste would become. Swiped across steamed sweet corn, smeared onto cornbread, dolloped onto pizza crust, or piled atop sizzling scallops, black trumpet butter is mind-blowing. Best of all, it's incredibly simple to make: Two ingredients, a big skillet, and a food processor will get you a year's worth in under half an hour, foraging time and grit removal excluded. It freezes wonderfully, keeps under refrigeration for a week or so, and is endlessly useful.

8 cups black trumpet mushrooms, cleaned of grit and forest debris (see note)

1½ cups unsalted butter, softened to room temperature, divided

NOTE: You can make this butter with fewer trumpets, as pictured here, but it won't be as dark.

Chop the black trumpets coarsely. Place a large, well-seasoned skillet over high heat. Add 4 tablespoons of the butter and melt. When butter stops sizzling and begins to shimmer, add the mushrooms all at once.

Sauté the mushrooms on high heat for about 2 minutes, turning occasionally. As they begin to release water and shrink, reduce the heat to medium. Continue to cook, turning the mushrooms over every minute or so, for another 6 to 8 minutes, or until all are reduced in size and the water has evaporated. Remove from heat. Caution: If using a black skillet, it might be very difficult to know if you are burning the mushrooms!

When the mushrooms are cooled, add them and the remaining butter to a food processor fitted with the standard blade. Pulse to break down the butter, and then run for 1 to 2 minutes, until a dark-gray paste forms. Continued processing will smooth the paste.

Place into a butter form or freezer-safe container and refrigerate or freeze.

PICKLED GRAYLING MUSHROOMS

BY CHARLES LUCE, NEW JERSEY | YIELD: 1 HALF-PINT JAR

I spend a lot of my free time picking mushrooms, and of all the mushrooms I collect and eat, graylings are the most unusual: They are tiny, the caps are rarely bigger than a dime, they grow only in haircap moss, and they emerge just days before autumn's first frost. I find them beautiful, tasty, and emotionally stirring. Cropping up in groups against the moss's vivid green, their blue-gray, nippled caps are distinctive. Their very long stems stain red when handled, and their gill symmetry is striking. It takes hours to harvest enough for a batch of the condiment described here, hours that can be spent in the clear, sloping light of a crisp October afternoon or in a driving sleet storm or under the puzzled gaze of deer hunters. The pickles hold well in the refrigerator for at least ten days. I use them in salads, on avocado toast, scattered across grilled steak, and atop hamburgers.

1 teaspoon virgin coconut oil

2 cups fresh grayling mushrooms

⅔ cup extra-virgin olive oil

2 tablespoons white wine vinegar

1½ teaspoons minced garlic

1 teaspoon dried thyme

1-inch piece of fresh rosemary

1 small bay leaf

1-inch piece lemon peel

Salt and freshly ground black pepper

Melt the coconut oil in a large, heavy skillet over high heat. When the oil is shimmering, add the mushrooms and cook for about 1 minute, then reduce the heat to medium-low. Continue to sauté until the mushrooms are limp and partially browned, 5 to 10 minutes, then remove from heat and transfer to a medium bowl.

Add the olive oil, white wine vinegar, garlic, thyme, rosemary, bay leaf, lemon peel, salt, and pepper and toss well, until thoroughly mixed. Cover with plastic wrap and refrigerate overnight.

Sterilize a half-pint glass jar and its lid (a larger jar is fine— you just won't be filling it up) by boiling the jar and lid in water for 10 minutes at sea level, adding 1 minute for every 1,000 feet above sea level. Pour the mushroom mixture into the sterilized jar. Add additional olive oil if needed to cover mushrooms; this is important because the olive oil acts as a prophylactic against spoilers that may linger in your fridge.

SOY-PRESERVED SHIITAKE MUSHROOMS

BY DON PINTABONA, NEW YORK | YIELD: ABOUT 2 CUPS

I discovered my passion for mushrooms in the markets of Osaka, Japan, and learned from my fellow chefs the Japanese way to cook them. When I opened the Tribeca Grill in New York City with actor Robert De Niro in 1990, my most popular appetizer was rare seared tuna with somen noodles, served with these soy-preserved mushrooms.

1 pound shiitake mushrooms, brushed
    clean and stems removed

½ cup rice wine vinegar

½ cup sake

½ cup mirin

¼ cup soy sauce

1 tablespoon granulated sugar

½ teaspoon *hon dashi*

Coarse salt and freshly ground pepper

NOTE: The mushrooms can be cut into thicker slices if you wish, as pictured here.

Cut the mushrooms into a fine julienne and place them in a large nonreactive saucepan (see note).

Stir in the vinegar, sake, mirin, and soy sauce. Add the sugar, *hon dashi*, and enough water to cover the mushrooms.

Place the pan over medium-high heat and bring to a boil. Lower the heat and simmer for about 30 to 60 minutes, until the liquid has evaporated.

Remove from the heat and season to taste with salt and pepper. Store in an airtight container in the refrigerator for up to 2 weeks.

Serve with grilled fish or meat, in a rice bowl, in addition to ramen or udon noodles, in salads, or even on sandwiches!

SRIRACHA PICKLED CHANTERELLES

BY SEBASTIAN CAROSI, OREGON | YIELD: 3 PINTS

Of all the mushrooms in the world, the Pacific golden chanterelle is my favorite. In season, it makes up probably 80 percent of my diet! Nothing ever comes close to the fruity taste; I can still visualize the first chanterelle I ever found. You can make this recipe with any kind of chanterelle, but I make it with what I find locally: Pacific golden chanterelles, Cascade chanterelles, or white chanterelles. Although it's made with sriracha, the heat is in no way overbearing, and it is especially good on an artisan meat-and-cheese board, on a sourdough grilled cheese sandwich, in a favorite ramen, or in a composed seasonal salad.

1½ pounds chanterelle mushrooms, cleaned and cut to about the size of a quarter

1½ cups seasoned rice wine vinegar

1 tablespoon tamari or soy sauce

½ cup apple cider vinegar

½ cup granulated sugar

¼ cup roughly chopped fresh cilantro stems

¼ teaspoon turmeric

2 tablespoons sriracha, or more, as desired

1½ teaspoons sea salt

1 teaspoon whole black peppercorns

1 tablespoon fresh green coriander seeds (optional)

1 bay leaf or kaffir lime leaf

1 tablespoon dried garlic bits

1½ tablespoons dried onion bits

1 tablespoon dried coriander seeds

½ teaspoon red pepper flakes, or more, as desired

FOR THE JARS

3 to 4 fresh cilantro sprigs

3 to 4 bay leaves or kaffir lime leaves

3 to 4 clusters fresh green coriander seeds (optional)

1½ teaspoons dried coriander seeds

In a deep, wide skillet over medium-high heat, dry-sauté the mushrooms until they give up their liquid and it evaporates, about 10 minutes. Do not overcrowd the pan, or the mushrooms will steam; cook in batches if necessary. Add the rice wine vinegar, tamari, apple cider vinegar, 1 cup of water, sugar, cilantro, turmeric, sriracha, sea salt, peppercorns, fresh green coriander, if using, bay leaf, garlic bits, onion bits, coriander seeds, and red pepper flakes and bring to a boil.

Reduce the heat to low and simmer for 15 minutes, then turn off the heat and let the mushrooms rest for about 15 minutes to soak up the pickling liquid.

Sterilize three 1-pint jars by boiling the jars and lids in a pot for 10 minutes at sea level, adding 1 minute for every 1,000 feet above sea level.

In each jar, place a sprig of cilantro, a bay leaf, a cluster of green coriander seeds if you have them, and ½ teaspoon of dried coriander seeds. Remove the mushrooms from the skillet with a slotted spoon and pack them firmly into each jar, leaving about 1 inch of space at the top. Ladle the pickling liquid into each jar, making sure it covers the mushrooms. Wipe the jar rims, twist on the lids, and refrigerate. The pickles are ready to eat but will hold in the refrigerator for weeks.

TRUFFLE OIL

BY ROSARIO SAFINA, NEW YORK | YIELD: 8 OUNCES

I have been in the truffle business for almost four decades, and I'm a longtime leader in the US truffle industry, selling fresh and preserved truffles. For the last fifteen years, I've produced 100 percent organic truffle products that I sell through my website Darosario.com. This is my homemade recipe for fresh truffle oil. I prefer to use Perigord or Italian white truffles, but this method works just as well for other truffles, like Oregon black and white truffles, and Tuber aestivum, *pictured here. Just keep in mind that the intensity and tastes of these different truffles vary. You can also use a botanical extractor to infuse olive oil with a truffle's aromatic molecules.*

½ cup mild-flavored extra-virgin olive oil
(see note)

½ ounce fresh truffles (such as the
Perigord truffles, Italian white truffles,
or Oregon white or black truffles),
sliced paper thin

NOTE: Avoid a highly flavored, spicy oil,
which can overpower the delicate truffle
aroma.

In a deep, 1-quart pot (a Dansk Kobenstyle saucepan is perfect), add the olive oil and heat over very low heat to 120°F. Immerse the truffle slices in the oil, cover the pot, turn off the heat, and wait 60 seconds. Then pour the ingredients into a clean 1-pint jar and seal it tightly. Place the pint jar in a large, clean pot and slowly cover it with cold water. Allow the oil to rest in the cold-water bath for 1 hour.

The truffle oil holds for a few days at room temperature and up to a week in the refrigerator. If refrigerated, allow the oil to come to room temperature, then give it a good shake before using.

MUSHROOM ESCABECHE

BY ALAN MACGREGOR, PAISLEY, CANADA | YIELD: 1 PINT

Being a lazy city dweller, I've never really gone mushroom foraging. Through my work as a chef, however, I get to eat them and let someone else do all the hard work. I am mostly vegan when I am at home, so mushrooms regularly take center stage in my home cooking. I find them the perfect substitute for meat, and I now prefer chicken of the woods to real chicken. I make this escabeche with mixed wild mushrooms, like porcini, maitake, and chanterelles. It can be stored in a sterilized jar in the fridge for about 10 days.

10 ounces mixed wild mushrooms

2 large shallots (I like banana shallots)

2 tablespoons olive oil, divided

¼ cup white wine

¼ cup sherry vinegar

1 tablespoon light brown sugar

1 teaspoon salt (I like Maldon), divided

½ cup chopped flat-leafed parsley

3 tablespoons garlic, thickly sliced

1 sprig fresh rosemary

1 sprig fresh thyme

1 pinch dried chili flakes

1 pinch ancho chili flakes

Tear mushrooms into bite-sized pieces (rustic suits this dish best).

Cut the root tips off the shallots, slice in half lengthwise, and remove the brown skins. Separate the shallot halves into petals. Keep the smaller ones from the center whole, and slice the remaining outer ones lengthwise.

Heat a large, heavy skillet over medium heat and add 1 tablespoon of oil. Add the mushrooms to the pan in one layer, being careful not to overcrowd. If necessary, cook the mushrooms in batches. Avoid stirring to prevent them from stewing, and allow them to become crispy. Cook the mushrooms until they release their liquid, the liquid evaporates, and the mushrooms begin to burnish gold, about 10 minutes, gently tossing them in the pan so that all sides are evenly browned. Remove them with a slotted spoon, and drain in a colander or sieve set over a bowl. Reserve the drained cooking liquid.

Turn the heat up on the pan slightly and return the reserved liquid and add the white wine. Boil for a few minutes, until the wine has reduced by half and the alcohol has burned off, all the while scraping the bottom with a wooden spoon to remove any crispy bits. Add the vinegar and sugar and return to boiling for 1 minute or so to temper the acidity. Pour the mushroom-and-vinegar mixture into a bowl along with any pan scrapings. Add half a teaspoon of salt and stir to combine, then stir in the parsley.

Rinse the pan, add the remaining olive oil, and heat over medium heat. Add the garlic and cook gently until fragrant, taking care not to burn it, 1 minute or so. Add the rosemary and thyme sprigs, the shallot petals, and the chili flakes and continue to cook until the shallots begin to wilt, 3 to 4 minutes. Once everything has softened, remove from the pan, add the remaining salt, and mix with the mushrooms.

Have ready a sterilized pint jar. To sterilize, boil a glass canning jar, lid, and ring for 10 minutes at sea level, adjusting for your altitude by adding 1 minute of boiling time for every 1,000 feet above sea level.

Pack the mushroom mixture and all its liquid into the jar. Store in the fridge and allow the escabeche to rest for a few days while the flavors mature.

Serve with roasted meats, firm-fleshed white fish like halibut and cod, or oven-roasted squash. The mushrooms themselves are also excellent when strained of the juices and eaten on hot buttered toast.

PORCINI POWDER, BUTTER, AND SALT

BY EUGENIA BONE, NEW YORK | YIELD: ½ CUP

I use Boletus rubriceps, *for this recipe, but* B. edulis, B. aereus, B. pinophilus, *or* B. reticulatus *or any combination of these will do. Porcini powder is a great condiment to have on hand, and I use it in lots of ways. One of my favorites is as a rub on meat. Beef rubbed with the powder, seared, and cooked in a pot roast is fabulous. You can also make Porcini Butter using this recipe, which Daniel Winkler—an expert on* Ophiocordyceps sinensis—*taught me. Use the butter to spread on toast, steaks, or fish, to melt on top of an omelet or potatoes, or as a dressing for a simple spaghetti with garlic and oil. I first published these recipes in my book,* The Kitchen Ecosystem.

FOR THE POWDER

1½ cups loosely packed dried porcini

FOR THE PORCINI BUTTER

8 ounces high-quality lightly salted or
    unsalted butter

3 tablespoons porcini powder, or more if
    you like

FOR THE PORCINI SALT

2 tablespoons very coarse salt (see note)

1 tablespoon porcini powder

NOTE: I like to use a coarse sea salt, but you can make this with regular kosher salt as well. I use the salt as a finisher, sprinkled on beef, eggs, and pasta with mushrooms. It also makes a great gift.

TO MAKE THE POWDER:

Grind the dried porcini in a spice grinder. You will notice a lot of porcini dust when you open the top of the grinder. Don't worry; it's mostly dried spores. You can keep the powder in a clean jar in your pantry. The flavor will hold for about a year.

TO MAKE THE PORCINI BUTTER:

Bring the butter to room temperature. In a small bowl, combine the butter and porcini powder. If you use unsalted butter, add salt to taste. Spoon the butter into a glass tub with a plastic top and refrigerate until firm. You can freeze the butter for up to 8 months or store in the refrigerator for a couple of weeks.

TO MAKE PORCINI SALT:

In a spice grinder, combine the salt with the porcini powder. Grind until well combined. Place in a small, airtight container and store in the pantry for up to a year.

INDEX OF RECIPES
BY MUSHROOM TYPE

Birch polypore: 222

Black trumpet: 48, 56, 75, 124, 159, 164, 248

Bunashimeji (beech mushrooms): 54

Caesar's mushrooms: 26

Candy caps: 18, 33, 221, 225, 230, 234, 239

Cauliflower mushrooms: 185

Chaga: 226, 240, 243

Chanterelle: 56, 91, 116, 121, 139, 148, 187, 205–206, 209, 229, 236, 244, 247, 254

Chicken of the woods: 32, 38, 87

Cordyceps: 113

Cremini: 34, 60, 80, 84, 117, 156, 198, 205, 210

Dryad's Saddle: 103

Enoki: 54, 99, 173

Graylings: 251

Hericium (lion's mane): 131

Honey mushrooms: 137, 155, 205

Huitlacoche: 46, 51, 109

Leccinum (red-capped scaber stalk): 188

Lobster mushrooms: 65, 106

Maitake (hen of the woods): 21, 54, 84, 87, 117, 128, 134, 182, 195, 203, 256

Matsutake: 56, 110, 140, 182

Mixed (mixed cultivated; mixed wild; mixed cultivated and/or wild): 53, 56, 59, 65, 80, 83, 84, 87, 117, 133, 152, 256

Morels: 22, 25, 56, 89, 100, 132, 155, 162, 178, 201

Mushroom stock: 106, 191, 213

Oyster mushrooms: 24, 31, 37, 41, 51, 60, 80, 163, 236

Porcini (boletes): 18, 26, 29, 53, 56, 65, 76, 78, 114, 117, 118, 127, 137, 151, 175, 181, 188, 210, 213, 259

Portobello: 67, 118

Reishi: 230, 240

Saffron milk caps: 65, 152

Shimeji: 173

Shiitake: 37, 45, 80, 84, 117, 173, 191, 252

Truffle butter: 28, 211

Truffle oil: 28, 31

Truffles: 28, 160, 255

White buttons: 26, 34, 42, 53, 60, 117, 195, 203, 210

Wood ear mushrooms: 190, 233

ACKNOWLEDGMENTS

Every book is ultimately the product of a community, of editors and copy editors, art directors and photographers, stylists and cooks, experts and enthusiasts. So here, I'd like to thank the community *within* this community cookbook.

First, thanks to Louie Schwartzberg, who is the heart of the project. It was Louie's notion that mycelium is a metaphor for collective action, a notion that gave rise to the idea of a community cookbook. Thanks to Raoul Goff from Insight Editions. He understood this idea perfectly from the very beginning and was constantly relaxed and supportive. Many thanks to Vanessa Lopez, who edited this book with speed and grace, and Chrissy Kwasnik and Leah Lauer, who designed it beautifully. Thanks to Anna Wostenberg and Jennifer Sims for their editorial support, and Jennifer Bentham, Rachel Anderson, and Mark Nichol for keeping our text clean and consistent, and to our press agent, James Faccinto, who is uniquely creative and open to trying radical ideas. They were all great, easygoing collaborators. I don't know; maybe it's a California thing.

We didn't know we had the making of a book until after the recipe-sharing platform was around for a while. Many thanks to Magical Threads, which built the platform, especially Jason Boog, Bethany Gillan, Alyssa Chertcoff, and Paul Ko. Special thanks to David Campbell of Mycoventures and Ryan Bouchard and Emily Schmidt of the Mushroom Hunting Foundation for their knowledge about edible mushrooms. They are all experts at answering the question "Well, how poisonous?" Thanks to Charles Luce and Paul Sadowski: I foraged for many of the wild mushrooms used in testing the recipes, and I did that with my brothers in the woods.

I also want to thank a few purveyors that really came through for us. Far West Fungi sent us the most beautiful wild mushrooms I ever saw. They even came up with a gigantic, dried cauliflower mushroom so I could test Jane Mason's Cornish Game Hens with Cauliflower Mushroom recipe. The Hokto Kinoko Company grows exquisite specimens, which made their way into many photos. Simple Man Mushrooms on Etsy and Oregon Mushrooms Co. supplied us with some of the more exotic specimens. I am grateful to these wonderful vendors and encourage you to check them out.

Once we knew we had enough recipes for a book, we started photography. Many thanks to Evan Sung, a man of great talent and an incredibly even keel, a quality most appreciated, especially when we were trying to photograph ten dishes a day. Thank you to my beautiful models, Carson Bone, Mo Bone, Hak Dixon, Martin Lewis, and Jeff Sorel. Deserving more than thanks, Pam Krauss, a cookbook writer herself, who edited my books *Well-Preserved* and *Mycophilia*, and Neni Panourgia, anthropologist and splendid home cook, helped make the dishes for photography. Kitchen goddesses that they are, they deserve worship. And when it was over, all they asked for was a bourbon.

In order to style these diverse dishes, we needed props, and while no thrift store in my area was left unexplored, the best stuff was borrowed from Nathalie Smith, whose store Global Table is the most fabulous tabletop store in New York City, and from the collection of a fellow New York Mycological Society (NYMS) member, prop stylist Sara Wacksman. When Liza Jernow, also a member of the NYMS and a food stylist, came aboard for a day of shooting, she elevated every set she touched. Thank you all for your taste and generosity.

Insight Editions wanted five essays in the book on mycology. I did my best, with lots of help from Dr. Tom Volk of the University of Wisconsin–LaCrosse; Dr. Nicholas Money of Miami University in Ohio, ethnomycologist Elinoar Shavit; microbiologist Tradd

Cotter of Mushroom Mountain; Dr. Timothy Crews of the Land Institute; Dr. Kenji Ouchi of the Hokto Kinoko Company; forager chefs Alan Bergo and Chad Hyatt; and author Langdon Cook. But most of all, thanks to Britt Bunyard, editor of *Fungi* magazine and executive director of the Telluride Mushroom Festival, for reviewing the science in these essays. He allowed me to keep my dignity when he pointed out my mistakes with a modest "Yikes!" instead of a "WTF?"

I'd also like to thank my family, who ate nothing but mushrooms for dinner for a year and never complained about it. I especially want to thank my husband, Kevin, for triggering the community-book idea in the first place when he said, while we were stuck in traffic on the Long Island Expressway, "Why don't you just do a book with all your mushroom friends?"

And indeed, most of all, I'd like to thank all my mushroom friends—the new ones I've made through making this book and the old ones who have helped along the way. It is one of my greatest joys to be in your company.

See you in the woods.

INSIGHT
EDITIONS

PO Box 3088
San Rafael, CA 94912
www.insighteditions.com

Find us on Facebook: www.facebook.com/InsightEditions
Follow us on Twitter: @insighteditions

Library of Congress Cataloging-in-Publication
Data available.

ISBN: 978-1-64722-295-6

Publisher: Raoul Goff
VP of Licensing and Partnerships: Vanessa Lopez
VP of Creative: Chrissy Kwasnik
VP of Manufacturing: Alix Nicholaeff
Editorial Director: Vicki Jaeger
Designer: Leah Lauer
Associate Editor: Anna Wostenberg
Production Editor: Jennifer Bentham and Jan Neal
Senior Production Manager: Greg Steffen
Production Manager: Sam Taylor
Senior Production Manager, Subsidiary Rights:
Lina s Palma

Photographer: Evan Sung

Photographs on pages 12 and 47 by Eugenia Bone;
photograph on page 105 by Elinoar Shavit.

Insight Editions would like to thank
Louie Schwartzberg for his support of this project.

Although the authors, editors, and publishers have made
every effort to ensure that the information in this book
was correct at press time, the author and publisher do
not assume and hereby disclaim any liability to any party
for any loss, damage, or disruption caused by errors or
omissions, whether such errors or omissions result from
negligence, accident, or any other cause. This book is
not intended as a substitute for the medical advice of
physicians.

The reader should consult a physician in matters relating
to his/her/their health.

Further, this book is not intended to provide recommendations about the safety of eating certain mushrooms.
Never consume a mushroom that has not been properly
identified and determined to be safe and edible by a
trained professional.

ROOTS of PEACE   REPLANTED PAPER

Insight Editions, in association with Roots of Peace,
will plant two trees for each tree used in the manufacturing of this book. Roots of Peace is an internationally
renowned humanitarian organization dedicated to
eradicating land mines worldwide and converting war-
torn lands into productive farms and wildlife habitats.
Roots of Peace will plant two million fruit and nut trees
in Afghanistan and provide farmers there with the skills
and support necessary for sustainable land use.

Manufactured in China by Insight Editions

10 9 8 7 6 5 4 3 2